Ready for Any Good Work

History of the Sisters of Saint Joseph, Chestnut Hill, Philadelphia 1944–1999

Mary Helen Beirne

University Press of America,® Inc.
Lanham • Boulder • New York • Toronto • Plymouth, UK

Copyright © 2015 by University Press of America,® Inc.
4501 Forbes Boulevard, Suite 200, Lanham, Maryland 20706
UPA Acquisitions Department (301) 459-3366

Unit A, Whitacre Mews, 26-34 Stannary Street,
London SE11 4AB, United Kingdom

All rights reserved
Printed in the United States of America
British Library Cataloguing in Publication Information Available

Library of Congress Control Number: 2015933807
ISBN: 978-0-7618-6584-1 (cloth : alk. paper)—ISBN: 978-0-7618-6585-8 (electronic)

∞™ The paper used in this publication meets the minimum requirements of American National Standard for Information Sciences Permanence of Paper for Printed Library Materials, ANSI/NISO Z39.48-1992.

Contents

Preface v

Acknowledgments vii

1 Forging Our Identity: 1650–1944   1
2 Embracing Our Identity: 1944–1965   31
3 Rediscovering Our Mission: 1965–1969   65
4 Renewing Our Mission: 1969–1979   81
5 Expanding Our Vision: 1980–1989   129
6 Deepening Our Vision: 1989–1999   161

Timeline: 1944–1999   191

General Councils: 1944–1999   193

Index   197

Preface

This new history of the Sisters of Saint Joseph of Philadelphia studies the sisters' reshaping as women religious in the eastern United States during 55 years spanning from 1944 to 1999. Concentrating on these years, this history portrays the Congregation's evolution in spirituality, ministry, and government. It begins with a synopsis of the Congregation's development from 1650 through 1944 and provides an insight into the Congregation's first history, *Sisters of Saint Joseph of Philadelphia: A Century of Growth and Development 1847–1947,* by Sister Maria Kostka Logue SSJ, published in 1950. While the first history was primarily narrative in style, this one attempts to look not at the Congregation as an institution but at the *sisters* as individual women and as a whole community grappling in faith with enormous change. With analysis and anecdote, the intent is to present the experiences of the sisters in response to Vatican II and American social developments in the second half of the twentieth century.

In order to accomplish this goal, the input of the sisters themselves, who experienced the often tumultuous changes of the decades after World War II leading up to the new millennium, has been solicited and incorporated. Nearly 200 sisters participated in 37 focus groups, while others communicated their personal stories and reflections through interviews, e-mails, and conversations. Research encompassed congregational documents, artifacts, videos, audiotapes, reports, archival records, surveys, and records, both formal and informal, from the proceedings of Chapters (a general governance meeting of elected representatives). Oral interviews connected to the Congregation's Living History Project and the Oral History Project conducted by the CSSJ Federation were also utilized.

This publication is taken from the original extensive history document located in the SSJ archives, which has full scholarly references and bibliography. The contents of the original document were presented to the sisters in a live presentation by the author on November 8, 2008, and through a DVD distributed to the Congregation afterward.

While it is hoped that all readers will gain new understanding of the sisters, this history offers more than simply a retelling of their past. For the Sisters of Saint Joseph, this reflection upon their past—both distant and near—has empowered them to reclaim with new vigor and purpose their mission and vision and to track its continuity through the centuries up to this present day. Rooted in a contemplative life stance, the Sisters of Saint Joseph have embraced, even more dynamically, their mission of unity and reconciliation as they enter a new millennium fraught with singular challenges, but abounding in even greater opportunities for service to the "dear neighbor."

The "Little Design" envisioned by Father Médaille SJ, and espoused by the founding women has endured for over three centuries. As the Sisters of Saint Joseph continue their journey in the twenty-first century, they pray that they will be ready for any good work.

Acknowledgments

Writing any history book demands a great deal of work and determination. But writing a congregational history about a particular group of women religious requires a deep understanding of the unique nature of the specific Congregation as well. Great appreciation is due to Dr. Mary Helen Beirne SSJ, primary author and general researcher, who in writing this history carefully researched the facts and captured the heart of the Congregation's development and change from 1944 through 1999. Thank you to Mary Helen Kashuba SSJ, who began writing a "bridge" between the early congregational history and the post-World War II years that eventually became the first chapter of the book.

We are most grateful to the numerous contributors who shared so many gifts and so much time to bring this volume to publication. The goal was to complete the congregational history up to the beginning of the twenty-first century, building on the work of Marie Kostka Logue SSJ, *Sisters of Saint Joseph of Philadelphia: A Century of Growth and Development 1847–1947*, published in 1950.

We would like to thank those who contributed in any way by researching the material, writing parts of the story, reading the manuscript, refining the material, asking questions, editing the chapters, participating in focus groups, offering suggestions, providing technical assistance, and offering support and encouragement during the entire process of bringing this volume to life.

Movement toward the publication of a second volume of the history of the Sisters of Saint Joseph, Chestnut Hill, Philadelphia, began in the fall of 2000, when Patricia Kelly SSJ, Superior General, gathered a group of sisters to begin a congregational history project. The group who went to work initially included Sisters Mary Helen Beirne, Suzanne Bellenoit, Harriet Corrigan, Margaret Fleming, Eugenie Madeleine Gaddi, Agnes Marie Gunn,

Dorothea Newell, Catherine Looker, Mary Helen Kashuba, and Margaret Mary Smith. We thank them for getting this project off the ground.

We are grateful to Rose Andrea Loughery SSJ, who with the assistance of Colleen Dauerbach SSJ shepherded the progression of the manuscript toward publication. In particular, we acknowledge Marianna Fieo SSJ, for her dedication to skilled editing throughout the process. A special thanks to Mrs. Cecilia Rupell, congregational Director of Communication, for her assistance with digital artwork. Appreciation is also extended to Patricia Annas SSJ, congregational archivist, who honored all requests for information and photographs. We are indebted to Mary Barrar SSJ, Elizabeth Ferguson SSJ, Mary Veasy SSJ, Rita Woehlcke SSJ, Dr. Margaret M. McGuinness, Ms. Mary McKenna, and Karen Kennelly CSJ, each of whom carefully read and commented on varying aspects of the text. To Dolores Liptak RSM, Patricia Byrne CSJ, Dr. David Contosta, Dr. Christopher Kauffman, Mrs. Elizabeth McGahan, Dr. Tracy Schier, and Dr. Marie Conn, we offer thanks for their advice and suggestions.

Many whose names are not included above contributed to this publication in ways large and small. To each and every one . . . Thank You!

General Councils
1999–2014

Chapter One

Forging Our Identity

1650–1944

1650–1700

Seventeenth-century France, known as the Great Century, was a time of stark contrasts. While powerful monarchs and writers of genius helped create a strong national identity, about 80 percent of France's 20 million people lived in rural areas and small villages. Approximately one-fourth of this number owned some land, whereas the other three-fourths worked as hired hands and day laborers, earning little and living miserably. On the other hand, this era was a time of greater social mobility and growth of the middle class, which emerged from the third estate, the common people, which comprised about 95 percent of the population. In larger towns and cities, artisans and civil servants also climbed the social ladder. Toward the end of the seventeenth century, with the growth of literacy, both women and men had opportunities for advancement.

At a time of violent religious disputes, France remained a Catholic country. The Council of Trent (1563) had instituted reforms; however, it had also frozen religious life into a model that recognized only cloistered orders of women with solemn vows, requiring any new foundation to adopt an already existing rule. Given these restrictions on new orders, a new model of community emerged, communities that did not have solemn vows or a cloister and that were oriented to active service. They remained relatively untouched by civil or religious powers, since they were not considered religious. The Sisters of Saint Joseph was one of these new communities that focused on apostolic activity.

Foundation of the Sisters of Saint Joseph

In 1650, six women who had been leading a life of charity and prayer at the Hospice of Montferrand in Le Puy met Jean-Pierre Médaille SJ, who encouraged them in their vocation. On October 15, 1650, Bishop Henry de Maupas of Le Puy received them into what was to become the Congregation of the Sisters of Saint Joseph. He gave his formal approval in the *Letters Patent* of March 10, 1651. In order to guide these six women, Father Médaille wrote a Constitution. In the Jesuit tradition, he used the *Rule* of St. Ignatius Loyola as a base. He delineated the spirituality of the Sisters of Saint Joseph in simple and straightforward terms: union with God, one another, and the dear neighbor. In the spirit of the Trinity, he emphasized relationships: relationship with God, with one another, and with all God's people. The balance between the active and the contemplative modes of religious life has remained crucial to the spirit of the Sisters of Saint Joseph.

Another important document written by Father Médaille, known as *The Eucharistic Letter,* came to light only in 1870 and again in 1878. Marius Nepper, writing in 1969, believed that it predated the official founding of the Congregation in 1650 and that it probably was addressed to a secret group in Saint-Flour in 1646. Marguerite Vacher, writing in 1991, dates it at 1660 and believes it was sent to an individual, probably Mother Jeanne (Marguerite) Burdier, one of the original sisters. The letter emphasizes the hidden character of the Congregation, modeled on the Eucharist, and contains reflections on the vows not found elsewhere.

Ministry

The original documents indicate that the sisters addressed the needs of their locality, focusing in particular on works not performed by other women religious, especially care of the sick and poor. The first Sisters of Saint Joseph wore the dress of the day, notably the attire of respectable widows, in order to facilitate their ministry without drawing undue attention to themselves. Their manner of service, with great love of God and neighbor, distinguished them.

Contrary to communities of cloistered religious, who lived in monasteries and often owned extensive property, the early Sisters of Saint Joseph lived simply. The first sisters who cared for orphans at the Hospice of Montferrand in Le Puy lived in the orphanage. Sisters in other towns often followed this model, sharing part of the house with the people they served. Others lived in small separate houses. These living arrangements were adequate since each group had only a few sisters, especially in the villages. In order to support themselves, the sisters and the orphans engaged in lace and ribbon making, an important business of that time. By 1693, the Sisters of Saint Joseph also taught in schools in nine dioceses. They gave training in basic literacy and provided religious instruction to children. The sisters enjoyed the respect of the local population, and their rapid growth attested to their loving response to the needs of the day.

Governance

In an area noted for its rugged terrain and harsh climate, each establishment of the Sisters of Saint Joseph remained autonomous, with no central motherhouse. The sisters in each house elected their superior, who was sometimes also responsible for other smaller groups. When the first sisters assembled in Le Puy, all assumed the duties of the house without any distinction among them. By 1694, the *Constitutions* and the records of the Sisters of Saint Joseph mention lay sisters without indicating when and how this distinction occurred. From this time on, both groups, choir and lay, lived together in various independent communities.

The early sisters lived a collaborative life within their local communities. The *Primitive Constitutions* called for regular meetings to discuss the practice of virtue and to confer on the order of the house. The rules for the superior directed her to treat the sisters as peers, asking them for a favor rather than commanding them. As an aid to ministry, the sisters were invited to share the state of their hearts with humility and candor. By the end of the seventeenth century, Father Médaille's "Little Design" numbered no fewer than sixty houses.

1700–1799

Spirituality

Most groups of Sisters of Saint Joseph retained the apostolic spirituality that the original documents mandated. By 1728, some characteristics of the monastic life began to appear, such as the chanting of the Divine Office and changes in the religious habit to include a long veil and a guimpe. The spirituality of the Sisters of Saint Joseph also changed its focus at this time, due to the influence of non-Jesuit clergy who directed the sisters according to their own interpretations of the *Rule*. This led to a more contemplative mode of life. The sisters continued many of the earlier practices, such as providing spiritual direction to one another and to those they served. Documents praising the Sisters of Saint Joseph applauded their lives of zeal and edification.

Governance

While some Sisters of Saint Joseph continued to live in hospitals, orphanages, and houses of refuge, others acquired or rented dwellings in the town or village. Each house remained independent, although exchanges occurred. While most continued the collaborative mode of governance, some experienced interference from civil and religious authorities, who attempted to influence the choice of superiors. The lives of the sisters revolved around the parish or the institution in which they worked.

Ministry

With the dramatic increase in literacy in the eighteenth century, the sisters assumed various forms of education. They gave religious instruction in the cities and in the villages. They also provided vocational training as they had done with lace and ribbon making in the original foundation. They participated in the education and rehabilitation of wayward women, or penitents, in houses of refuge. The sisters also opened boarding schools for young girls from wealthy families, which helped provide funds for free schools for the poor. In addition to these new endeavors, the Sisters of Saint Joseph continued the corporal and spiritual works of mercy, such as caring for the sick in their homes and in hospitals and visiting the poor and prisoners. As the Congregation grew in numbers, the Sisters of Saint Joseph constituted a significant presence in southcentral France at the beginning of the French Revolution, in 1789.

French Revolution (1789–1794)

More fortunate than some other groups of religious, the Sisters of Saint Joseph survived the French Revolution, although they felt its impact. Many communities of sisters were disbanded, and some sisters were executed. Two sisters were guillotined at Le Puy, at the Place Matouret, on June 16, 1794. Three others were guillotined at Privas, on August 5, 1794. Among the sisters imprisoned by the revolutionary leaders was Jeanne Fontbonne, who would later refound the Sisters of Saint Joseph. According to tradition, she and her companions were to die on July 27, 1794. That day, however, Robespierre fell, and they escaped the death sentence. Disappointed that they were not found worthy of martyrdom, they returned to the Fontbonne home in Bas-en-Basset where they continued the life and works of their small community.

1800–1899

Refoundation: Lyon (1808–1836)

Little by little, the Sisters of Saint Joseph who survived the Terror returned to their former lives. Lyon led the refoundation in 1808. M. Cholleton, vicar-general of Lyon, invited Mother Saint John Fontbonne to reunite her sisters along with another congregation known as the Sisters of a Happy Death, or Black Daughters, into one group, according to the *Rule* of the Sisters of Saint Joseph. They received the habit in Saint-Étienne, on July 14, 1808. This was not the widow's dress worn by the first sisters in 1650 but rather one that had evolved during the eighteenth century. After a generation in which religious dress had been prohibited, the sisters now welcomed the habit and wore it with pride.

Restoration meant a return to the original sources of the Congregation, but it required the forging of a different identity. The new group included young women and widows who had never known the Congregation, former cloistered nuns unfamiliar with active apostolic work, and some Sisters of Saint Joseph who had survived the Revolution but knew little of community life. This diverse group who came together in 1808 possessed a deep spirituality and a willingness to undertake any endeavor to which they were called. They no doubt saw a reflection of their call in Mother Saint John, whose reputation of courage and leadership had spread throughout the area.

When refounded, the Sisters of Saint Joseph accepted whatever work they were asked to do. Education had become an important focus in post-revolutionary France. A tremendous surge in literacy resulted, mainly due to the re-Christianization efforts of the Church. The Sisters of Saint Joseph participated in this renewal. They attended state-run teacher training schools and conformed their teaching to state standards. They later established a normal school in Lyon to train teachers and in 1832 published a book on methods of instruction. The sisters also resumed educating the deaf, a work begun in the seventeenth century.

Because of Napoleon's insistence on centralization, local house autonomy gave way to a central diocesan motherhouse, a model followed in other Congregations of Sisters of Saint Joseph. Mother Saint John Fontbonne thus became superior general of all the houses in the diocese of Lyon. The Congregation grew rapidly, and at the time of Mother St. John's death in 1843, it comprised 244 houses with a total membership of 3,000 sisters.

Due to the conservative spirit of the post-revolutionary Church, the *Constitutions* of 1824 were far more prescriptive than the original documents. Nevertheless, the newly restored Sisters of Saint Joseph, like other religious congregations, rejoiced in their freedom to lead a structured community life in public. Their mandate to "undertake all the spiritual and corporal works of mercy of which women were capable" would provide a valuable measure of freedom as they embarked on a new venture.

American Pioneers: St. Louis (1836–1847)

The newest post-revolutionary call of the Sisters of Saint Joseph became a missionary venture to America. Because of the tremendous size of his diocese, which included Missouri, Kansas, Iowa, Arkansas, the western part of Illinois, and the Native American peoples living in the territory that stretched from Missouri to the Rocky Mountains, Bishop Joseph Rosati of St. Louis, Missouri, advertised for sisters from France. Mme de la Rochejacquelin, a wealthy countess of Lyon and friend of Mother Saint John Fontbonne, read the notice and immediately offered to pay all the expenses involved to send six Sisters of Saint Joseph to America. The bishop asked for two additional sisters to work with the deaf. Soon they negotiated the move, and the first six sisters departed from France on January 4, 1836.

The young volunteers included Sisters Delphine and Fébronie Fontbonne, nieces of Mother Saint John, and Sisters St. Protais Deboille, Fébronie Chapellon, Marguerite-Félicité Bouté, and Philomène Vilaine. Father Jacques Fontbonne, nephew of Mother Saint John, accompanied them. After an eventful trip on the *Natchez*, they arrived in New Orleans, Louisiana, on March 5 and reached St. Louis, Missouri, on March 25. In 1837, Sisters Celestine Pommerel and Saint-Jean (Saint John) Fournier arrived after completing their training in the education of the deaf at Saint-Étienne since the school directed by the Sisters of Saint Joseph in Lyon had not yet reopened. Sister Celestine was 23 years of age; Sister Saint John was 21 years old and a novice. Six of these eight were never to see France again.

Life in the new world was a challenge to these women. Born well after the French Revolution, into a society which now expected religious dress, they were shocked at having to wear secular clothes upon arrival in the Protestant, sometimes anti-Catholic society of the United States. The sisters had received a good education and had come from relatively comfortable middle-class families; thus the austerity of frontier life surprised them. Not only did they face a harsh climate, repeated floods, and frugal living conditions, they also had to earn their own living without receiving any financial aid from church or state, as had been customary in France. Internal struggles also threatened the small community, including interference from Father Fontbonne and Mother Delphine Fontbonne's literal interpretation of the *Rule*. Life in the United States demanded adaptations under such unusual circumstances.

Upon arriving in St. Louis, the sisters opened schools, amid many difficulties. Nearby Cahokia had a colony of French Canadians. The sisters opened a school there and gave their instruction in French, although some records mention Latin. They had no language problem, but floods beset the site of the school, eroding the health of some of the group and almost destroying the buildings in 1844. They established another school in Carondelet, which had a better climate but fewer resources. Local residents called it *Vide-poche* (empty pocket) because of its poverty. The sisters served orphans, tuition-paying boarders, and nonpaying day students. This arrangement followed the eighteenth-century precedent of maintaining a tuition school and a free school side by side. The Sisters of Saint Joseph learned English with the Religious of the Sacred Heart at their Academy in St. Charles, where they met their first postulant, Eliza Dillon. They opened other schools as resources permitted. In 1839, the school board voted to pay a salary of $375 annually for the services of the sisters to the deaf-mutes, a welcome addition to their meager finances.

In 1845, the sisters opened a school for black children at Third and Poplar Streets in St. Louis, under the direction of Sister Saint John Fournier. They intended it for daughters of freed slaves, but some owners sent their slaves to the school as well, which enrolled about 100 girls. The sisters taught elementary subjects, French, and needlework. Although not yet prohibited by the state, such a school did not meet with the approval of local white citizens who feared that blacks might read abolitionist literature and revolt. After several assaults by their neighbors, the sisters were forced to close the school, although they continued to teach catechism to the young girls privately.

While adapting their ministry to the needs of the frontier, the sisters faced yet another issue of identity. Mother Saint John Fontbonne had sent eight sisters to America, but after her death in 1843, demands in France prevented her successor, Mother Sacré Coeur Tazenas, from sending more. In order to survive, they needed to recruit American women who, the sisters in France believed, could adapt better to the climate and frontier life. Candidates did come, both local women of diverse ethnic origins and others from Moutiers, France. Mother Celestine Pommerel, chosen as the superior, welcomed them all. She wanted English to be the common language and had the *Rule* translated into English in 1847. By 1850, the community had 44 members, 36 percent of them born in the United States. After Mother Celestine's death in 1857, the American sisters rebelled openly against the appointment of a French superior, Mother Saint John Facemaz, fearing she would interpret the *Rule* too rigidly. In 1860 St. Louis and several other American Motherhouses of Saint Joseph separated their governance from Lyon, thus alleviating the situation. Meanwhile, the sisters spread from St. Louis to other parts of the vast new world. The first of these movements brought them to Philadelphia in 1847.

Sisters of Saint Joseph: Philadelphia (1847–1900)

By the mid-nineteenth century, the original Quaker character of Philadelphia had evolved as immigrants from Ireland and Germany arrived in the city. When Mother Saint John Fournier and Sisters Magdalen Weber, Elizabeth Kincaid, and Mary Joseph Clark arrived in Philadelphia on May 4, 1847, they found a city in transition. Sister Magdalen came from Conewago, Pennsylvania; the other two sisters were originally from the vicinity of St. Louis, Missouri. Mother Saint John was the only French-born woman among them; Mother Delphine Fontbonne later joined them briefly (1850–1851) but left to found the Toronto Congregation of Sisters of Saint Joseph in Canada.

The early candidates to the Congregation in Philadelphia were primarily first-generation Irish Americans. A list of 54 professed sisters dating from 1857 shows 35 born in Ireland, three in Germany, and the remainder in America, with most of these from Philadelphia. Virtually all of the American-born sisters had Irish surnames. The Profession Book of the 1860s records similar percentages. These were the pioneers who would help create an American identity for the Sisters of Saint Joseph of Philadelphia, fusing it with their Irish roots and the Congregation's French heritage, staunch Catholics in a predominately non-Catholic country.

Ministry

The first four Sisters of Saint Joseph took up residence in St. John the Evangelist parish on Thirteenth Street, one of the best areas of the city. Because of the unrest in the city caused by Nativists they went out rarely; when they did, they wore secular clothing. They assumed responsibility for St. John's Orphanage, which the Sisters of Charity had been forced to abandon in 1846 at the insistence of their father superior, Rev. Louis Deluol, who did not wish them to care for boys. Bishop Francis Patrick Kenrick (1842–1851) welcomed the newly arrived sisters. He had met the Sisters of Saint Joseph in St. Louis when visiting his brother, Bishop Peter Kenrick. In 1847 he wrote to his brother, "The arrival of the Sisters of Saint Joseph has given us all great joy. They have indeed a generous spirit ready for any good work."

In response to the call for "any good work" in the vast diocese, the sisters quickly established other Motherhouses. Three sisters opened a school in 1848 in St. Patrick parish, Pottsville, about 80 miles north of Philadelphia. By this time, three postulants had joined the community in the improvised novitiate housed in St. John's Orphanage. In 1849, five sisters took over the administration of St. Joseph Hospital in Philadelphia from the Sisters of Charity. Even though they had neither prior experience nor a natural inclination toward this work, they grew to love it; and when asked to leave in 1859, they were clearly disappointed. They also opened St. Ann's Widows' Asylum in 1850 and the Catholic Home for Destitute Children in 1863, which was intended for Civil War orphans.

The novitiate in St. John's Orphanage briefly moved to St. Joseph Hospital, but this arrangement proved unsuitable. In 1854, the sisters took over a school in McSherrystown, Pennsylvania, formerly directed by the Ladies of the Sacred Heart. Here they established an academy and a novitiate. Although its rural setting seemed suitable for training postulants and novices, it was too far removed (120 miles) from the other missions where the sisters lived and worked. In August 1858, upon the recommendation of Bishop (Saint) John Neumann (1851–1860), the Sisters of Saint Joseph chose the Middleton Mansion, Monticello, in the Chestnut Hill section of Philadelphia for their novitiate. On October 4, 1858, they opened a boarding school, Mount Saint Joseph Academy, which rapidly grew and prospered.

Education soon became the focus of the small congregation. Bishop Kenrick had made the establishment of schools a priority in his diocese and had started a system of free parochial schools, first run by lay people. As sisters became available, they eventually replaced the lay women who taught side by side with them. Thus, the Sisters of Saint Joseph moved quickly into education, establishing parish tuition schools, known as academies, as well as free schools in their early missions. Parish academies such as St. Joseph, St. Philip, and St. Patrick, in Philadelphia, helped to educate nonpaying children as well as support the sisters, whose income was often uncertain.

The Sisters of Saint Joseph worked mainly in an urban ministry to immigrant Catholics. As might be expected, the Philadelphia schools they staffed in the nineteenth century appeared largely in areas that were heavily Irish: Moyamensing, Southwark, Gray's Ferry, Kensington, and Port Richmond. In addition, sisters ministered in St. Joseph, Brandywine (1853) and St. Mary (1867), both in Delaware, until recalled by Archbishop James F. Wood, when Pope Pius IX created the Diocese of Wilmington in 1868. The sisters also worked in the city of Baltimore and rural Westernport, Maryland (1875). In 1853, Pius IX created the Diocese of Newark, New Jersey, separating it from the New York Diocese. Sisters staffed schools in Newark (1872), Bayonne (1879), and Orange (1882). In 1881, Pope Leo XIII established the Trenton Diocese to serve Catholics in southern New Jersey, who had formerly been part of the Diocese of Philadelphia. From 1874 to 1885, the Sisters of Saint Joseph also ministered in Immaculate Conception parish in Camden, New Jersey, which was then part of the Trenton Diocese. By the end of the nineteenth century, the sisters staffed 32 schools in four dioceses.

In the spirit of their original foundation, the Sisters of Saint Joseph remained ready for "any good work." In parishes where they had schools, they also visited the poor and the sick, provided religious instruction to children not enrolled in the parish school, and held evening classes for working women. In addition, the sisters also gave catechetical instruction to the deaf in Philadelphia and to the blind at McSherrystown, as well as attending to the domestic duties of St. Charles Seminary in Philadelphia (1870–1934). Especially attentive to young immigrant women, more than one sister went to the Delaware River docks to guide these newly arrived women in the right direction, away from houses of prostitution.

During the Civil War, 14 Sisters of Saint Joseph joined the corps of nurses who cared for the wounded of both armies. At the request of Dr. Henry Hollingsworth Smith, who had served on the staff of St. Joseph Hospital and knew the sisters well, six volunteers went to Camp Curtin in Harrisburg, Pennsylvania, in January 1862. Among them was Mother Mary John Kieran, future superior general of the Congregation. Others joined them and later sailed on the *Commodore* and other small boats down the James River in Virginia to care for the wounded of both the Union and the Confederacy. Their service lasted until June 1862. Many testimonials from Governor Andrew G. Curtin of Pennsylvania, Dr. Smith, and Dr. Charles K. Mills attest to the generous service of these sisters.

The end of the Civil War saw a growth in the number of women teachers, both in public and parish schools. Thus, it is not surprising that the work of the sisters continued predominantly in education, especially after the Third Plenary Council of Baltimore (1884) insisted on Catholic schools to counteract what were then believed to be negative forces in the expanding public school system. By 1899, the Sisters of Saint Joseph staffed 25 schools in the Archdiocese of Philadelphia and nine outside it. They maintained two private boarding academies, Mount Saint Joseph, Philadelphia, and St. Joseph Academy, McSherrystown.

As early as 1859, the year after the establishment of Mount Saint Joseph Academy, Chestnut Hill, sisters were attending classes in academic subjects in the novitiate. These courses were rather haphazard at first. Sister Assisium McEvoy, future Prefect of Studies, records:

> Class, as class, was but sporadic, owing to building operations; there was no place to have class, even had it not been as was the case, that the students were engaged in avocations far from literacy, such as weeding, attending to dairy-farm work, and so on.

Despite these obstacles, the sisters' education continued. Among the novitiate teachers, Sister Saint Ephrem Sneeringer garnered high praise from Sister Assisium:

> As early as 1873, Sister Saint Ephrem, music teacher at the Mount, devoted all her time and energies to the younger sisters preparing to teach music. They were few, and very backward in the work. But from after her supper until 9 o'clock, Sister Saint Ephrem would devote to them every moment of her time.

In fact, the attitude toward study was less than positive, according to Sister Assisium:

> To tell the truth, there seemed something of a fear of allowing a Sister to devote much time to study, lest religious humility and simplicity be injured. Time and experience, however, proved that lack of wider knowledge was no safeguard of humility, and that the modern requirements called for more strenuous preparation.

After 1875, following the construction of a new building for Mount Saint Joseph Academy, the situation regarding the sisters' education improved. There were classrooms available for their use, especially in the summer when the Academy students left and sisters could return from the local convents. The young sisters had classes in Latin, French or German, English, mathematics, science, music, and art. While they did not have specific courses in methodology, younger sisters learned from experienced teachers in the school as they began their careers. Sister Assisium McEvoy, who had been among the novitiate teachers from 1868, assumed the role of prefect of studies, as well as mistress of novices, in 1887. In the 1890s, she devised a rating system for each teacher, which included such items as personality (self-control, posture, voice, judgment, and fair-mindedness), courtesy, health, attention to study, class preparation, treatment of children, and classroom management.

Many factors contributed to the high quality of education in the schools. In 1885, the Sisters of Saint Joseph appointed Mother Saint Gervase Morton, Sister Assisium McEvoy, and Sister Mary Clement Lannen to arrange a common course of studies for the schools. In 1889, Sister Sacred Heart Stewart was appointed congregational supervisor of schools, a significant step. In 1886, Sister Assisium composed a course of study in religion, which the sisters piloted in their schools before its official printing in 1904. She intended it to "broaden the sisters' view of education, even while conforming to the canonical regulations as to study." With such encouragement, the Sisters of Saint Joseph became part of a corps of teachers who helped the immigrant population to rise quickly from unskilled laborers to property owners and some to business proprietors.

Governance

Life in most local houses of Sisters of Saint Joseph in the second half of the nineteenth century centered around the parish and its school. The sisters lived in a house provided by the pastor, who was responsible for its upkeep and for the $50 annual salary for each sister, as determined by Bishop John Neumann (1873). A superior governed each house, aided by an assistant (the house's second-in-command), both of whom were named by the superior general and her council. The superior often taught in the school, gave instructions to the young sisters, and supervised the spiritual exercises of the house.

School commitments left little time for leisure, even on weekends. In her letter to Lyon, Mother Saint John records how the sisters spent Sundays:

> In each parish the sisters take their children to Mass . . . from Mass to the school and dismissed them. In the afternoon they give their children an hour's instruction and take them to Vespers. . . . So with our own exercises and the children, our sisters can scarcely call Sundays and Feast Days "days of rest."

Since all the sisters in a house were engaged in the same work, they could easily assemble at regular times for meals, devotions, and recreation. On Sundays the superior presided over the conference, and all the sisters were expected to contribute. On Fridays they held the Chapter of Faults, where each sister accused herself of minor failings committed during the previous week. In addition, the houses held local chapter meetings, for example, to vote on the admission of novices to vows or on the temporary professed "junior" sisters to final profession.

The teaching sisters helped to take care of the house, while the lay sisters did the cooking and other major housekeeping charges. The latter embodied the spirit of the Congregation in their informal dealings with students, especially in the academies. Mother Saint John referred to the custom of sending a lay sister to each convent when it opened to expedite the work involved. The first recorded indication of dissatisfaction with the division into choir sisters and lay sisters occurred in 1875, at the election of Mother Mary John Kieran, who wrote in her diary that the lay sisters (who did not have the right to vote) "were in a very bad humor all day." Still, in 1894, one-fifth of the 397 members of the Congregation were lay sisters.

In 1868, Harrisburg, Pennsylvania, became an independent diocese under Bishop Jeremiah Shanahan. The McSherrystown Academy, administered by the Sisters of Saint Joseph since 1854, was located here. The bishop did not wish to keep sisters from another diocese, but he found it impossible to replace them. In an agreement with Archbishop James Wood of Philadelphia, McSherrystown became an independent motherhouse of the Sisters of Saint Joseph in 1869. Mother Magdalen Weber, a native of neighboring Conewago and one of the founders of the Buffalo, New York, Congregation, became the first superior. No Chapter seems to have sanctioned this move, and archival material points only to documents of the two bishops. The names of fourteen sisters appear on a list signed by Bishop Wood.

The McSherrystown community at first grew and established other foundations. They continued the Academy, opened a school for the blind, and opened a small orphanage on the same property. They branched out into St. Joseph, Hanover (1873), and Corpus Christi, Chambersburg (1888). From

1891 to 1893, three sisters taught in local public schools, for which they received $25 a month, far better than the $50 a year that was the standard salary at that time.

By 1897, the number of students in the Academy and the number of sisters in the community had declined so sharply that Mother Ignatius Ryan asked Mother Mary Clement Lannen, then superior of Chestnut Hill, for permission to rejoin the Philadelphia Congregation. At first unwilling, Mother Clement accepted the group at the urging of Bishop John Shanahan, the brother of the former Harrisburg bishop, who indicated that the quality of education in the Academy had declined as sharply as the numbers. In 1899, Chapters were held in both Congregations to approve the merger.

The General Chapter, the highest legislative body in a religious congregation, was a late nineteenth-century development for the Sisters of Saint Joseph. In fact, there seemed to be no involvement of the sisters in the appointment of Mother Saint John Fournier or in the nomination of her assistant. In 1859, at a community gathering, when all were present in the chapel, Mother Saint John asked Bishop Neumann to be relieved of her office as superior general, which she had held since 1847. Sister Assisium McEvoy relates that, "instead of granting her request, he then and there confirmed her for life. Mother Mary John Kieran was named assistant." In obedience to ecclesiastical authority, Mother Saint John faithfully discharged this office for the rest of her life.

The first meeting that might be called a Chapter took place in 1875, upon the death of Mother Saint John Fournier. Her successor and former assistant, Mother Mary John Kieran, recorded the election thus in her diary:

> I felt that I would faint when I heard my name called out so often and found that I was the unworthy one the Lord had chosen to govern so large a community. All the professed and novices voted, but I had no control of the election, but should I ever live to see another, I would only allow the professed to vote.

Mother Mary John Kieran likewise tried to be released from her office after each term, in 1878 and 1881, but the archbishop reappointed her each time. There is no evidence that the sisters re-elected her on either of these occasions. In 1884, a Chapter of Election took place, at which it seems all professed choir sisters participated. Mother Mary John recorded the details carefully:

> December 26th: "Thank God I am free! All the Sisters are crying; I feel sorry for them." December 28th: "Free as a bird but working pretty hard." December 30th: "All the voting sisters went to meditation. . . . The Archbishop came. . . . I was re-elected; only 16 against me in 170 votes; God's holy will be done. . . . I asked to be dispensed with the Sisters kissing the hand as they had before. He allowed it to be dispensed with. That was a relief."

By the time of Mother Saint John Fournier's death in 1875, Mount Saint Joseph Convent had become not only a home but also a motherhouse and an administrative center. Growth in numbers signaled growth in complexity. Yet Mother Saint John Fournier (1847–1875), Mother Mary John Kieran (1875–1888), and Mother Mary Clement Lannen (1888–1910) knew each sister well. They were also shrewd businesswomen who bought and sold property, erected buildings, and established the Corporation of Sisters of Saint Joseph as early as 1863. In addition, they negotiated the opening and closing of schools and other institutions and appointed the sisters best able to staff them. They appointed superiors to be leaders, not autocrats. The minutes of the superiors' meeting in 1896 stated that superiors should not make completely unilateral decisions but should involve the sisters as much as possible. Though now more complex, the governance structure nevertheless maintained the concept of relationship in the spirit of Father Médaille's ideal of love of God and the "dear neighbor."

Spirituality

The French traditions of spirituality going back to 1650 gradually fused with American adaptations. In addition, a strong influence on the spiritual lives of the Philadelphia sisters came from Saint John Neumann. Noted for his devotion to the Eucharist, Neumann introduced the diocese-wide Devotion of the Forty Hours into the diocese of Philadelphia. It first took place at St. Philip Neri Church, where the Sisters of Saint Joseph served, in 1853. Bishop Neumann often visited Mount Saint Joseph after the sisters moved there in 1858, and he frequently gave them spiritual counseling.

Sister Assisium McEvoy seems to embody most clearly the sisters' spirituality in the second half of the nineteenth century. Her instructions reveal deep piety, strong roots in the Ignatian spirituality of Father Médaille, a visionary sense of liturgy, and an appreciation for the spiritual devotions that characterized the Irish American Catholic immigrant Church. Her instructions to the novices often centered on the Gospel for the day and contained positive messages. In speaking of the practice of admonition, weekly meetings for spiritual encouragement and correction, she emphasized the importance of virtue. Although daily Communion was not permitted at the time, she encouraged the reception of the sacrament as often as possible but insisted that no one should question a sister's decision. She emphasized moderation and common sense in penances, noting, "Better what God sends than asking [for penances] or any of our own choice."

In the spirit of the times, popular devotions occupied an important place in the spiritual lives of the sisters. Sister Assisium often based her conference on the saint of the day and the virtues he or she practiced. The Blessed Virgin, under many titles, and St. Joseph were the most popular. In addition she frequently cited St. Francis de Sales, St. Aloysius, St. Stanislaus, St. Anthony, St. Bernard, and the special patron, which the sister drew each month. She recommended devotions such as the Stations of the Cross, spiritual bouquets, the rosary, spiritual communions, and indulgenced prayers.

Sister Assisium encouraged the young sisters to read and follow the *Rule* and to observe its spirit in every way. She put particular emphasis on poverty and respect for material goods, at a time when luxuries were uncommon. For her, spirituality included good manners and decorum, especially at table, courtesy to others, and thank you letters. In all things, consideration of others and common sense predominated.

On a more administrative level, Sister Assisium was instrumental in preparing for the papal approbation, or approval of the *Rule*, a process begun in 1882. She noted that the Sisters of Saint Joseph in St. Louis had their *Rule* approved by Rome in 1877. She used this as a model as she assisted Father A. Sabetti SJ, in the final editing of the Philadelphia *Rule* prior to its submission to Rome in 1892. When she wrote to the French Congregations, asking for their *Constitutions* and *Directories*, she received friendly and informative letters in return. She also collaborated with Mother Clement Lannen in her efforts to convince the local hierarchy, still intent on controlling the sisters in their own dioceses, to accept the papal approbation of the *Rule*. In 1882, Father Pacificus Neno, Superior of the Augustinian community at Villanova College (University) and later their superior general, a strong advocate of the Philadelphia Congregation, wrote to Mother Mary John Kieran that the greater obstacle to the papal approbation of the *Rule* (more than the Vatican bureaucracy) is "in the Bishops themselves, who want to have you under their control exclusively." All these difficulties notwithstanding, the *Rule* was approved in 1896.

Although the approved *Rule* prescribed the times and circumstances for prayers, the school schedule did not always permit strict adherence to it. Sisters made adaptations rather frequently, as indicated by the numerous regulations forbidding schoolwork during lecture (spiritual reading), eliminating the Office on Sundays, saying missed prayers in the evening, and reciting afternoon prayers in the morning. As a compromise for these adaptations, the clause "may be done only with the Superior's permission" appears frequently in Chapter enactments. Fortunately, flexibility characterized the spirit of the Congregation.

While the annual retreat remained a high priority in the spiritual life of the Congregation, not all the sisters could make it. In 1885 Sister Assisium noted, "This is the first time *all* the sisters made the Annual Retreat." The *Rule* stipulated a 30-day retreat before final profession, but it likewise could not always be implemented. A property in Sea Isle City, New Jersey, used by the sisters from 1890 to 1909, helped alleviate the situation. It served as a vacation home and occasionally for retreats. All the sisters took turns spending some time there. During vacations, rules of silence were relaxed somewhat and the times of spiritual exercises were modified. Prior to the days at Sea Isle City and throughout the years, the sisters came to Mount Saint Joseph, popularly called "home," for vacation and retreat.

As the nineteenth century drew to a close, the Sisters of Saint Joseph affirmed the spiritual values in their documents and in their lives. They instilled into the children under their care the spiritual practices they had learned from Sister Assisium McEvoy. The sisters participated in the life of the parish, attending not only Mass but also Vespers and Benediction. They sacrificed for the construction of a chapel at Chestnut Hill, finally dedicated in 1891. They resolved to end the century by having exposition of the Most Blessed Sacrament in this chapel with the pronouncement of vows by the novices at midnight. The combination of prayer and action inspired by Father Médaille remained as vibrant in 1899 as in 1650, thus preparing the Sisters of Saint Joseph to face another century of challenges.

1900–1944

At the beginning of the twentieth century, Philadelphia was still the second largest Catholic diocese in the United States. Many US Catholics had formed strong ethnic neighborhood communities, and their parish had become the center of their social and spiritual lives. Prior to World War I, the immigrant population consisted largely of lower- to middle-income families, but by the 1920s this same group exhibited greater confidence and optimism and a tendency toward Americanization. These social changes also affected the candidates who entered the Congregation of the Sisters of Saint Joseph.

While tradition remained firm in the Catholic Church in Philadelphia, which had only one spiritual leader, Dennis Cardinal Dougherty, from 1918 to 1951, outside factors affected the membership of the Congregation. Inventions like the telephone, radio, automobile, and the airplane led to greater mobility and increased communication. In 1920 women gained the right to vote, and many entered the previously male-only political sphere. While the primary roles of women had been restricted to the home, the newly gained freedoms of the era broadened this scope considerably.

The Sisters of Saint Joseph were part of this society, although conservative forces often pulled them in the opposite direction. Thus, the tension between a rigid interpretation of religious life and the possibilities of new mobility, easier communication, and a more significant role for women grew more acute as the century progressed. As the tension between the contemplative and active sides of their lives increased, it became more difficult to identify the original spirit of Father Médaille in the Sisters of Saint Joseph of Philadelphia.

Ministry

The pull toward modernization notwithstanding, large numbers of young women came to the Congregation to further its ministry. From a little over 600 in 1900, the Sisters of Saint Joseph numbered almost 1,000 in 1916. The 1920s saw the greatest surge in candidates, with close to 400 received from 1922 to 1928. While there was a slight decrease during the Depression years of the 1930s, the numbers remained healthy. By 1944, there were 1,900 members in the Congregation.

Despite the enticements of modern culture, young women still entered in such steady numbers because of several factors. The Sisters of Saint Joseph were highly visible, especially in the Philadelphia area, with growing numbers in New Jersey, Delaware, Harrisburg, and the Baltimore-Washington area. They worked almost exclusively in education and, for the most part, staffed parish schools valued for their quality. Many sisters came from low- to middle-income immigrant roots themselves, and they understood the needs of the children. Very often they did more than just teach a class; they saw to the personal needs of children who lacked food and clothing and discreetly provided them with these necessities. People respected the sisters, and as a result, young women wanted to model their lives after their teachers.

One of the great milestones in the ministry of the Sisters of Saint Joseph in the early twentieth century was the establishment of post-elementary school education for girls, called senior centres. It began in St. Joseph Senior Centre in the Cathedral of Saints Peter and Paul School in Philadelphia on September 8, 1900, under the leadership of Sister Stanislaus Quigley. Three such schools began around the same time, the second staffed by the Sisters, Servants of the Immaculate Heart of Mary, and the third by the Sisters of the Holy Child. Shortly thereafter, the Sisters of St. Francis and the Sisters of Notre-Dame de Namur opened similar schools. Girls came to the senior centres from the parishes where the specific congregation taught. The senior centres offered a two-year curriculum, incorporating such academic subjects as Latin and geometry along with stenography, bookkeeping, and typing. The schools were free and open to all who passed the eighth-grade examinations. Among the graduates of the first class in Saint Joseph Centre was Sister Clare Joseph O'Halloran, first Registrar and Director of Sisters' Education at Chestnut Hill College (1926–1968).

In 1912, the Catholic Girls' High School, renamed John W. Hallahan in 1925, replaced the senior centres. The school offered a four-year program with two options: general and commercial. In addition to providing free secondary education to girls, deemed unnecessary by many critics, the great original experiment of this school consisted in a faculty comprised of women religious from various congregations, including the Sisters of Saint Joseph. While many predicted its failure, this model became a standard adopted in other Philadelphia high schools, and it later extended beyond the Archdiocese. In addition to mixing the sisters, the new Catholic high schools also mixed the girls who came from various parish schools and ethnic groups or from public schools. Since a number of these young women entered religious life, membership in the various congregations also became diversified and surnames of various nationalities other than Irish began to appear on the lists of those entering the Sisters of Saint Joseph.

In addition to secondary schools, the Sisters of Saint Joseph also established their own private academies to serve various populations. Mount Saint Joseph Academy, Philadelphia (1858) and St. Joseph Academy, McSherrystown (1854) already existed. New endeavors included St. Mary's Academy (1912); The Cecilian Conservatory, dedicated to the arts and languages (1917); Norwood Academy for Boys (1920); and Fontbonne Academy for Girls (1924), all in Philadelphia. Beyond the Philadelphia area the sisters opened St. Mildred's Academy in Laurel, Maryland (1921–1934) and Holy Family Academy in Bayonne, New Jersey, (1925), founded originally for commercial studies. All of the academies established after Mount Saint Joseph were intended to serve a broader range of students from less affluent families. This resonated with the spirit of the early sisters, who had been called upon to address the needs of their times and minister to all social classes.

The twentieth century was also a time of unprecedented growth in Catholic higher education for women. In the 1920s three Catholic colleges for women were founded in the Philadelphia area, including Mount Saint Joseph College, founded by the Sisters of Saint Joseph in 1924. In 1938, the name was changed to Chestnut Hill College. With the support of many Sisters of Saint Joseph in secondary education in Pennsylvania, New Jersey, and Maryland, the new college prospered, even during the Depression. As the sisters drew many young women to the Congregation by their personal interaction, support, and friendship, so also they attracted them to higher education at Mount Saint Joseph (Chestnut Hill) College. The close relationship of the college sisters to their students provided a nucleus of dedicated alumnae who exemplified religious and moral values in society.

Sisters' Education

Greater numbers of schools and higher levels of instruction necessitated better-educated teachers. From 1900 to 1910, only a few sisters engaged in formal study on Saturdays or in the summer in order to complete either of their high school diplomas or teacher certificates of proficiency. Beginning in 1910, many more sisters enrolled in formal Saturday and summer classes under Mother Saint Gervase Morton and Mother Saint Pierre Byrne, much to the relief of Sister Assisium McEvoy, who noted that the Sisters of Saint

Joseph "were falling behind, while other congregations were out in front." In 1911 Sister Assisium, along with Mother Saint Gervase, directed the program, which was divided between the "elementary" and the "academics," the latter being those who taught in the upper grades and were required by the Congregation to have a high school diploma.

Higher education also became an option for the Sisters of Saint Joseph at this time. In 1910, The Catholic University of America opened its doors to women religious, and the first three Sisters of Saint Joseph attended summer classes in 1911. In 1915 and in 1916, two sisters remained for the entire year to complete their undergraduate degree. Sisters of Saint Joseph also studied for degrees at the University of Pennsylvania.

The great emphasis on study, particularly under Mother Bonaventure Stinson (1911–1915), proved to be a gigantic step forward. The approximately 50 sisters who went to The Catholic University and other institutions of higher learning met people from outside their own congregation. They studied under well-educated professors, gained insights into the academic life, saw the world from another viewpoint, and became more articulate themselves.

Not every sister had the opportunity of a university experience. While Sister Assisium McEvoy wanted it for everyone, financial strains and commitments to schools made this difficult. Consequently, only a few could pursue advanced study. The choice of some and elimination of others sometimes created the impression of preferential treatment that colored many sisters' memories. Although the Sisters of Saint Joseph prepared a highly educated cadre of teachers, general education remained more basic, compatible with the criteria of the times and the level at which the sisters taught or would be teaching. Many sisters' studies, especially before 1920, consisted of completing their high school work. Among those who entered from 1909 to 1916, 78 percent had completed only the eighth grade or below. This figure was comparable to the educational level in the general population of women at the time.

As predicted by Sister Assisium, higher education for sisters first came about through state requirements, which insisted on a minimum of normal school training for all teachers. Thus, Mount Saint Joseph Normal School was founded in 1920. It certified 1,000 Sisters of Saint Joseph from 1922 to 1928, under the direction of Sister Rosalia McGlone. The school consisted of a four-semester curriculum based on state regulations, which included courses in the liberal arts, science, and teaching methodology. The sisters received a state teacher's certificate, and the school was accredited by the University of Pennsylvania, The Catholic University of America, and the Department of Labor. Any sister who wished, "from the oldest to the youngest," was given the opportunity to receive this certificate. The school closed in 1931 when state normal schools required four years leading to a Bachelor of Science degree. By this time, many sisters took courses at Mount Saint Joseph (Chestnut Hill) College. About 160 sisters studied part time on Saturdays, and in the summer about 300 attended classes.

Sister Assisium McEvoy explicitly referred to the need for sisters' higher education in her application for permission to open Mount Saint Joseph College in 1924:

> There are about 1,300 Sisters of Saint Joseph, more than one thousand actively engaged in teaching or preparing for teaching in elementary and secondary schools. There are about two hundred sisters attending college or extension courses at the University of Pennsylvania, Catholic University, Villanova and Fordham. The expense is very great and calls for many sacrifices on the part of the Community. And had we college facilities here, some of the Sisters could pursue at least some of their courses on the premises.

By the end of the 1930s, sisters teaching in elementary school began to receive a BS in elementary education through the extension courses offered by Villanova College (now University) from 1937 to 1952. They attended these classes on a part-time basis, on Saturdays at Hallahan High School, and in the summer at Villanova or at Mount Saint Joseph (Chestnut Hill) College. Sisters destined to teach in high schools and college received an AB, almost always from Mount Saint Joseph (Chestnut Hill) College, usually on a part-time basis. Some earned an MA from Villanova and other universities.

Although this distinction between types of degree prompted a measure of discontent in some, most sisters enjoyed one another's company when they met for study. Superiors may have viewed the exuberant greetings as indecorous, but reunions with friends provided a source of mutual support. Perhaps the perceived mixing of "business with pleasure" is what prompted numerous regulations in Chapters and letters regarding sisters' behavior at Saturday classes and summer school!

While education remained the primary ministry for the majority of sisters, other specialized works continued. The foundation of the Archbishop Ryan Memorial School for the Deaf (1912) built on the sisters' earlier catechetical work in Philadelphia and continued the tradition of the Sisters of Saint Joseph in France. Other ministries already existed, such as care for orphans at St. John's Home (1847) and at the Catholic Home for Girls (1865) and for widows at St. Ann's Widows' Asylum (1850). The sisters also expanded into St. Margaret's Vocational School (1923). All of these institutions were located in Philadelphia. In 1915, the sisters opened Paradise School for orphan boys in Abbottstown, Pennsylvania. In 1909, they began to staff a fully equipped infirmary, including an operating room, at Mount Saint Joseph Convent, for the sick and elderly of the Congregation.

Among the significant nonteaching members of the Congregation were the lay sisters. In the early part of the twentieth century, they numbered about one-fifth of the Congregation. The lay sisters tended to the domestic chores of the houses and, until 1909, dressed very differently from the choir sisters. They took rank, or seniority, after the choir sisters and sat with the novices and juniors (temporary professed) at the end of the table for meals and recreation. As the level of formal education for women increased, the number of applicants to be lay sisters decreased. In 1928, 31 percent of all applicants had only an eighth-grade education or below, whereas in 1940, that percentage dropped to 6.1 percent. From 1936–1940, only four women applied to become lay sisters. In 1940, long after most other congregations of Sisters of Saint Joseph had abolished the distinction between choir and lay sisters, the Chapter unanimously agreed to grant rank (seniority according to profession) to lay sisters. However, Cardinal Dougherty opposed such a move, noting that the *Rule* had just been sent to Rome, and the sisters should not ask for further amendments. In 1940, there were 120 lay sisters, about 6 percent of the total membership. They often endeared themselves to the young people under the care of the sisters, especially in orphanages and residential schools, and became the queens of their kitchens in others.

Impact of Educational Ministry on the Lives of the Sisters

An increasing number of sisters and a better-trained corps of teachers meant that the number of schools grew and expanded rapidly in the first half of the twentieth century. Enrollment grew, but the number of sisters remained insufficient to fill the needs. As early as 1903, Mother Mary Clement Lannen reminded the sisters that they must accept lay teachers. The exception rather than the rule, lay teachers had served in the early days of Catholic education, only to be replaced by the sisters.

Many schools staffed by the sisters had excellent reputations. By 1940, there were approximately 1,900 sisters serving in 106 parish elementary schools, seven academies, 12 high schools, three diocesan high schools with annexes, one college, and nine other institutions. The decree of the Third Plenary Council of Baltimore had stated that every Catholic child should be in a Catholic school, and many parents considered it their obligation to send their children to the parish school, which at that time was staffed predominantly by sisters, who for the most part were deeply committed to their mission.

Governance

In the first half of the twentieth century, governance in congregations of women religious became much more formalized. The increase in numbers necessitated greater structure in the Congregation, and the approval of the *Rule* (1896) gave a different focus to authority. Papal approbation afforded the Congregation a certain independence from local jurisdiction, allowed the sisters to move more freely into other dioceses, gave the sisters confidence in their mission, and brought the Congregation into the ecclesial structure of the Church in a definitive way.

The papal approbation of the *Rule*, however, proved to be a two-edged sword. Congregational Chapters now focused on the letter of the law and spent many hours interpreting the exact wording of their *Decrees*. The expression "Rome said, the Holy See decided," appeared frequently. "The *Rule* says" was also cited on almost every page of these *Decrees*. Dispensations from the *Rule* could be obtained only from Rome, and the Congregation hesitated to ask. The model sister kept the *Rule* perfectly, which meant obeying the letter of the law. The *Decrees* read: "Fidelity in asking permissions is a gauge of religious fervor."

In this religious climate, the role of the superior grew in scope and importance. The 1903 Chapter decreed that all superiors would be addressed as "Mother." The superior general would be known as reverend mother. Although these titles had been used previously, this enactment formalized the practice. The title introduced a distinction in the local house between the sisters and the superior. In her letters to local houses, the superior general used the salutation "Dear Mother and Sisters." Some of these letters addressed to "Dear Mother" were intended for the superior alone. In certain cases, superiors were told not to inform sisters that letters had come from the Motherhouse. In 1932, the practice of voting to admit novices and temporary professed sisters to profession, formerly the responsibility of all the sisters of a local house, was restricted to superiors only. Beginning on September 25, 1915, quarterly meetings of superiors replaced the annual meeting begun in 1894. The practice of a special retreat for superiors, begun in 1898, continued to convey the image of a privileged class, especially when these sisters received special considerations not given to the other members of the Congregation.

The 1897 Chapter mistakenly named only superiors as delegates, a radical departure from previous practice. However, canon law required that all professed sisters be eligible to serve as delegates. Therefore, it was decided to allow all superiors to attend the retreat exercises that coincided with the Chapter sessions but permit only the delegates to vote. In the Chapters held between 1903 and 1928, only eight to 10 delegates were not superiors. In 1934 there was only one, in 1940 three, and in 1944 none. Sisters who entered the Congregation during in the 1930s and 1940s recalled that it was common practice to vote for the superior as a delegate, although according to the *Rule*, any professed sister was eligible.

Once named a superior, a sister kept this office for the rest of her life. While the Code of Canon Law (1917) required superiors to leave office after two terms, the members of the General Council interpreted this to mean that the canon did not specify a particular interval of time between the end of the term and reappointment. Thus, the superior could move to another house and begin anew in office, since technically she was not the superior of any house while she traveled between the two. Only under extraordinary circumstances did a sister relinquish this office, and she kept the title of Mother even if illness forced her retirement.

Communications from the superior general urged the local superior to relate to the sisters with maternal affection. Mother Mary Clement Lannen wrote that superiors must respect the sisters and not reject them if they came for a penance or asked a question. They should make the yoke of obedience light for others and show sympathy when a sister had troubles or family concerns. However, regulations often made the superior's office much more demanding. Sisters could do very little without the superior's permission, which they needed for visits outside the house, even phone calls and letters, lest the wall of separation from the world break down. Travel outside "the city" (Philadelphia) necessitated permission from the superior general. A change in the time of prayers required a Chapter enactment.

General Chapters occurred every six years, unless the death of a superior general necessitated an extraordinary Chapter of Election (as it did in 1910 and 1944). All Chapter business remained completely confidential; only those present knew what transpired. The secretary, elected by the delegates, kept accurate records. During the Chapter, the various officers, such as the superior general, the mistress of novices, and the inspectresses of schools, gave reports. The superior general usually used her report to remind the sisters of important practices, such as uniformity in dress, permissions the sisters should obtain, and times and places for prayers. Delegates voted not only in the elections but on other important items as well. The system of black (negative) and white (affirmative) balls determined the number for or against a measure. Some votes were taken by standing and sitting. While the early twentieth-century Chapters appeared to have handled matters of greater importance, those held from 1922 to 1944 seemed to have had little or no effect on the ordinary sister, who was hardly aware that they had happened except for the election.

The *Decrees,* a book containing Chapter enactments and customs, was codified after the 1916 Chapter and sent to all houses. The contents of this document were to be read in all the houses during every Ember Week, special days of prayer, fasting, and abstinence. The updated *Decrees* were first sent to Rome in 1920 and received the proper approbation. While one General Chapter could abrogate the decisions of a previous one, customs often remained in the *Decrees* long after they could reasonably be practiced. For instance, sisters who were teachers could not attend parent-teacher meetings in the evenings. No sister could travel to visit friends who were sisters. Visiting sick family members and attending their funerals was strictly regulated, with distinctions for those "in the city" (Philadelphia) and those "outside the city."

Despite the rigorous nature of these customs and practices, they were often qualified by the statement, "of course, exceptions may arise." Sisters were not to visit their families on Christmas, but there might be exceptions. There was to be no traveling on Sunday, but business might make it necessary. Only small watches costing one dollar (in 1909) were to be worn, but if a sister already had a larger or more costly one, she might keep it. It was this common-sense attitude toward law that often prevented the Sisters of Saint Joseph from developing too legalistic an interpretation of rules and practices. While the superior held all the authority in a local house, she knew that there were exceptions to every rule, particularly in internal matters. In fact, the repeated warnings from superiors general in Chapter reports and in letters indicate that not every practice received the same respect. Sisters found ways to circumvent certain minute regulations, such as those prohibiting change in dress, letter writing, and interaction with people of the parish.

The revision of the *Code of Canon Law* (1917) affected all congregations. Much of this legislation reflected in the documents of the Sisters of Saint Joseph concerned elections and officers. Previously, the superior general chose the assistant from the four elected councillors. This was no longer allowed after 1917. The superior general could not function as superior of the motherhouse (actually decreed in 1909), nor was the mistress of novices to have juniors (temporary professed) under her care. Local houses of more than six sisters were to have councillors. All constitutions and formularies (books of congregational prayers) were to be sent to Rome with the appropriate changes made. While the officers of the Congregation attended to all these matters in a timely fashion, the 1917 *Code of Canon Law* had little impact on the ordinary sister, whose life was already regulated by minute Chapter decrees and customs. The revised *Constitutions* were approved on December 7, 1924, and were distributed to each sister on the feast of the Sacred Heart 1925, accompanied by a spiritual message from Mother Mary James Rogers (1916–1934). A subsequent printing in 1939 contained an updated version of the historical preface.

While the Congregation as a Papal Institute was technically not subject to the regulations of the local ordinary, the bishops often imposed restrictions on the sisters. In 1902, Bishop John W. Shanahan of Harrisburg asked the sisters not to attend evening Benediction in parishes. In 1909, Archbishop Ryan of Philadelphia forbade the sisters to go to confession in the parish churches. Cardinal Dougherty of Philadelphia promulgated many regulations. For instance, he would not allow sisters to eat in restaurants in the city. In 1932, he forbade all religious in the Archdiocese of Philadelphia from participating in any political election. Mother Mary James Rogers commented that, "As we have not been voting, it makes no change for us." In 1940, he disapproved of the Chapter decision to give rank to the lay sisters. His decision not to submit to Rome the paragraph in the *Rule* regarding smaller houses' election of delegates to the General Chapter met with some opposition from the 1940 Chapter body. While bishops in dioceses outside Philadelphia interfered less, the fact that the Motherhouse was located within this archdiocese meant that Cardinal Dougherty's regulations took on special importance. In light of obedience and a sense of solidarity with the Church, the Congregation usually acquiesced.

Superiors general took a stronger stand with pastors, especially in insisting on fair compensation as much as possible for the sisters who worked in their schools. If the pastor did not make an attempt to do this, the Congregation withdrew the sisters. In 1912, the annual stipend in Philadelphia was fixed at $250 per teacher, superior, or directress. Lay sisters received $100. In 1915, Bishop John W. Shanahan of Harrisburg said he could pay no more than $120 per sister, and this was acceptable. The amount agreed upon in 1912 remained about the same for many years, with sisters teaching in high school receiving $400 when possible. In 1936, the stipend per sister was fixed at $300, except in Harrisburg where it was $260. The profit from teaching music accrued to the house, although the houses sent $125 of this money annually to the motherhouse, along with $50 for each sister. Additional funds sometimes came from selling candy, pretzels, and other small items. Pastors usually paid for the upkeep of the local convent, but the sisters were responsible for food, clothing, and medical bills. Many doctors and dentists donated their services to the sisters, thus helping the budget enormously. It is no wonder that the *Rule* and the *Decrees* emphasized poverty, care of clothing, and saving food, given the meager income of many houses. In houses of the Congregation, although no one lacked the necessities of life, a simple lifestyle was imperative. Superiors had to stretch the income as far as possible, particularly during the Depression.

The highly structured system of governance among the Sisters of Saint Joseph provided security to some members and also served as a model for potential leaders. Although rigorous, the system was seldom inflexible. World War II, however, threatened the stability of this very secure but rigid structure. In the 1940s, those entering the Congregation were better educated; some even held college degrees and often came from more financially secure or upwardly mobile families. These changes in educational levels and social economic status, evident in both society and in candidates who applied to the Congregation, signaled a new era that would encourage personal freedom rather than unconditional obedience or conformity.

Spirituality and Formation

American Catholic spirituality in the early part of the twentieth century tended to follow the traditional patterns of sin, authority, ritual, and the miraculous. These trends also influenced the Sisters of Saint Joseph. Their unquestioning acceptance of religious and papal authority appeared in the rigid legalism of their governance. Their consciousness of sin followed a somewhat Jansenistic heritage and was a part of the Irish immigrant mentality. Sisters were told not to "count" Mass with the children as their Sunday obligation because of the obvious distractions. If they did so, they might be guilty of mortal sin. Ritual followed the same scrupulous details.

In the spirit of fidelity to tradition, the sisters modified the content of their daily communal prayers very little. They recited the same litanies and prayers, used the Ignatian method of meditation and *examen* (examination of conscience), and practiced other devotions that could be traced back to their foundation in the seventeenth century. However, the 1909 Chapter made a major adjustment by allowing all community prayers in English. Previously, the sisters had recited the litanies and the *Office of the Holy Ghost* in Latin. The *Office of the Blessed Virgin*, required in all houses with more than six sisters, remained in Latin, but exceptions to its recitation became more and more frequent, with other prayers offered instead.

Other substitutions became more numerous. High Mass on Sunday could take the place of the 1:00 p.m. prayers and *examen*; the sermon could serve for Lecture (Spiritual Reading). At Vespers celebrated in the parish, sisters could say their afternoon prayers and "make Meditation." Despite the numerous Chapter decrees on the horarium, circumstances forced local houses to adjust the time schedule. 4:00 p.m. prayers could actually be recited in the morning before school!

Triduums were three days of prayer before St. Joseph's Day (March 19), the Visitation (July 2), and the Immaculate Conception (December 8). They presented singular problems. Since everyone had to make an additional half-hour of meditation, almost impossible to incorporate into an already heavy school schedule, sisters repeatedly asked for exceptions. The only one granted was for St. Patrick's Day (March 17).

The sisters' annual retreats adopted a formalized structure with specific times allocated for conferences, reflection, Mass, and vocal prayers. Most followed an adaptation of the *Spiritual Exercises* of St. Ignatius. Retreats continued at Mount Saint Joseph, with a few at Sea Isle City, New Jersey. Needing more space, the sisters sold the Sea Isle property to the Sisters of Mercy in 1909. In the same year, with the help of Father Daniel I. McDermott, the Congregation purchased the former Shoreham Hotel in Cape May Point, New Jersey. At his suggestion, it was called St. Mary by-the-Sea. The sisters could now enjoy both spiritual and physical refreshment at the Jersey shore. The retreats lasted a week, with some followed by a few days of vacation. The selection of a particular retreat time depended on the sisters' study and work schedules, and since all retreats followed the same pattern, there was little need for options.

Personal prayer, like all other exercises, was regulated by the *Rule* and practices of the Congregation. It consisted of two half-hour daily meditation periods, visits to the Blessed Sacrament, and at times the Stations of the Cross. The Congregation prescribed specific books for meditation, from which a designated sister read aloud. The format followed the Ignatian tradition, evoking a composition of place and a personal response.

Three long-term mistresses of novices from 1887 to 1966 brought great stability to the formation experience of the sisters and influenced their later lives. Sister Assisium McEvoy (1887–1911), Mother Maria Concepta Flaherty (1911–1927), also mistress of juniors (1927–1940), and Mother Marie Estelle Duggan (1932–1966) filled this role. Women of deep spirituality, they emphasized the primacy of prayer and relationships with God and neighbor. These women embodied the directive in the *Rule* that admonished the mistress of novices to "attentively study in each, the special attraction of the Holy Ghost and the way in which He desires to lead the soul, so that she may cultivate those movements of grace, and not train the Sisters according to her own inclinations or practices of virtue, at the risk of impeding, by such conduct, the action of the Holy Spirit in them." Sisters recalled that Mother Concepta "was not enamored with the letter of the law that kills, rather she was animated by its spirit which gives life." Sisters who entered in the 1930s and beyond remembered Mother Marie Estelle's instructions in prayer, noting especially how she modeled meditation for them. Her prayer evinced an intensely personal relationship with God and Jesus, and these sisters felt that they too were able to enter a similar prayer experience by following her example.

At this time, the Church and the Congregation considered "separation from the world" as a virtue intended to protect the interior life. As a result, the sisters were often not permitted to attend functions in the parishes where they lived and ministered. They could not attend Benediction or Vespers in the churches in the evening or go to other parishes for Forty Hours devotions. In addition, they were unable to participate in the reception of the sacraments by members of their families or former students. Exceptions might be allowed for the ordination of a young man in a sister's immediate family. Although sisters could attend funeral Masses for close relatives, they could not accompany their families to the cemetery. Families were aware of these regulations and accepted them, often with regret. Sisters, too, felt the pain of separation from family and friends at times of great rejoicing and deep sorrow.

Another source of separation was the religious habit. Originally intended to foster ease of communication with the people the sisters served while maintaining the decorum of religious modesty, it became anchored in tradition. After World War I fashions changed dramatically, while the habit remained basically the same as it had been since postrevolutionary France. In fact, the 1922 Chapter used the occasion to insist on uniformity, since materials not available because of the war could again be procured. Minute regulations governed its appearance. The *Decrees* stated:

> Sisters may not change in any way the form of the religious habit. If not conformed to custom, it is not the habit of the Sisters of Saint Joseph. The same is true of the head-dress. Uniformity of appearance is required by obedience.

A major development in the habit occurred in 1909. In contrast to the veil and cornet worn by the choir sisters, lay sisters wore a bonnet with white ruching, similar to the postulant dress adopted in the early twentieth century. In 1908, the Vatican decreed that all sisters in the same congregation, choir or lay, should wear approximately the same type of dress. The Sisters of Saint Joseph of Philadelphia adopted an identical habit for both groups, with the exception of the cincture (waist belt), which would be braided for the choir sisters, and made of cord for the lay sisters.

In general, the Catholic population respected the habit, and the sisters wore it with dignity and pride; but they made subtle changes. They often removed the plastic guimpe in the house, since it was too warm and cumbersome for work and even dangerous in the kitchen. The band (worn in the middle of the forehead) was widened to appear more "stylish," and narrowed the pleats in the skirt. They replaced some parts with more comfortable material, lengthened some, and shortened others. Repeated warnings from superiors general and junior mistresses had little effect.

The evolution of the Sisters of Saint Joseph in the twentieth century reflects the changing spirit of American Catholicism. A heightened consciousness of unjust labor practices followed the publication of the encyclical *Rerum Novarum* by Pope Leo XIII (1891), though not always understood or appreciated. While the congregational documents make no official mention of this encyclical, or even of fair labor practices, the teaching of the social gospel resonated with the original spirit of the Sisters of Saint Joseph encouraging them to address the ills of their time. Sister Assisium McEvoy, in her *Course of Christian Doctrine* (1904), insisted on practical applications of the life of Christ, the saints, and prominent secular models. She included in her instructions for seventh-grade children just relationships between employers and employees. Many sisters responded to the social needs among the children they taught, in the newly arrived immigrants, and in the various types of schools they established.

After World War I, the liturgical movement gained great momentum in the United States. In 1905, following the lead of European Benedictines, Pius X urged frequent reception of Holy Communion and encouraged the participation of the laity in the Mass. The Sisters of Saint Joseph had always encouraged frequent Communion and required that superiors not question any sister's decision in this matter. They also respected a sister's freedom in choosing a confessor, although the actual decree forbade their going to Confession in the parish church.

The *Rule* prescribed that sisters attend Mass daily unless prevented by illness or necessity. Through Sister Assisium's influence, the sisters learned to participate more fully in the Mass. In her 1904 publication, she urged them to instruct children in liturgical participation in the Mass, Vespers, and Forty Hours. In 1915, she addressed the sisters on the value of the Mass for grades 1–3. In the 1930s, when she herself was approaching 90 years of age, she continued to instruct the sisters on the use of the missal. She kept them attuned to the liturgical renewal that stressed the "spiritual nature of Catholicism" and its focus on Christ, with the Mass as its "chief prayer."

As the sisters responded to these newer directions in spirituality, they found many resources, including their own visionary leaders and formation mistresses. Further inspiration came from outside the Congregation, especially when selected sisters began to study in universities. Although the sisters did not earn degrees in religious studies at this time, they met professors and colleagues who shared new trends with them. Finally, the importance of the media cannot be underestimated. Bishop Fulton J. Sheen's popular radio program, *The Catholic Hour,* aired in 1930, and the circulation of Catholic newspapers and magazines increased. While tensions existed between established forms of prayer and newer insights, sisters adapted to this reality by calling on their inner resources of a solid relationship with God and a spirit of closeness to one another in community living.

Conclusion

By 1944, the Sisters of Saint Joseph had become a large Congregation (over 1,900), highly Americanized in its religious identity. Father Médaille's "Little Design" had been transformed into a complex, centralized ecclesial institution. Although no longer "hidden," the Sisters of Saint Joseph retained the spirit of their founder and of their early documents, which urged them to move among the people with gentleness and joy and to be ready for any good work. At this point "good work" signified primarily education. Experience and training prepared the sisters to engage in that ministry better than at any previous time in their history. The post-World War II period held unknown challenges as the Sisters of Saint Joseph elected Mother Thecla Brennan as Superior General in 1944 and faced a new era.

PUBLISHED SOURCES

Byrne, Patricia, CSJ. Sisters of Saint Joseph: The Americanization of a French Tradition. *U.S. Catholic Historian,* 5, no. 314 (1986): 244.
Coburn, Carol K., and Martha Smith. *Spirited Lives: How Nuns Shaped Catholic Culture and American Life, 1836–1920.* Chapel Hill: University of North Carolina Press, 1999.
Connelly, James F. *The History of the Archdiocese of Philadelphia.* Wynnewood, PA: Unigraphics, 1976.
Dolan, Jay P. *The American Catholic Experience.* Garden City, NY: Doubleday and Company, 1985.
Kashuba, Mary Helen, SSJ. *Tradition and Risk* Virginia Beach, VA: The Donning Company, 1999.
Kennedy, Emmet. *A Cultural History of the French Revolution.* New Haven, CT: Yale University Press, 1989, 39–41.
Logue, Maria Kostka, SSJ. *The Sisters of St. Joseph of Philadelphia.* Westminster, MD: The Newman Press, 1950. Although Sister Maria Kostka Logue edited the text, she relied largely on the contributions of Sisters Consuelo Maria Aherne, Margaret Rose Brown, Bernard Francis Loughery, and Juanita Morgan. While Logue, *Sisters of St. Joseph of Philadelphia,* was published in 1950, it addressed material only up to 1944.
Nepper, Marius, SJ. *Origins.* Buffalo, NY: Villa Maria College, 1975.
Savage, Mary Lucida, CSJ. *The Congregation of Saint Joseph of Carondelet.* St. Louis, MO: B. Herder Book Co., 1923, 31.
Sisters of Saint Joseph of Brentwood. *Mother Saint John Fontbonne.* Westminster, MD: Newman Press, 1936, 25.
Vacher, Marguerite. *Nuns without Cloister.* Trans. Patricia Byrne and the United States Federation of the Sisters of St. Joseph. New York: University Press of America, 2010.

ARCHIVAL SOURCES

Mount Saint Joseph Convent, Philadelphia, Pennsylvania
Primitive documents, records of General Chapters, personal papers, focus groups, and other records.

Chapter Two

Embracing Our Identity

1944–1965

From 1945 until the 1960s, the Sisters of Saint Joseph of Philadelphia, like other American Catholics, experienced significant challenges and shifts. This era circumscribed by the presidencies of Truman, Eisenhower, and Kennedy was characterized by the tensions of the Cold War, the spread of communism, and the violent conflicts in Korea, the Middle East, and Vietnam. Still, an economy of abundance grew amid exploding consumer demands for new technologies for home and industry. Cars, televisions, and home appliances became regular features of the middle-class lifestyle as many US Catholics moved to the suburbs. Simultaneously African Americans and, to a lesser degree, Mexicans and Puerto Ricans migrated to the North. Although educational levels for women had risen, creating possibilities for advancement in careers outside the home, the primacy of home and family went basically unchallenged. The creation of the GI Bill of 1944 enhanced the opportunity for higher education for returning servicemen but did not guarantee the same privilege for women in society. For those outside the middle class, especially minorities, segregation and poverty rendered the "American Dream" virtually unattainable.

In this milieu, the American Catholic Church also entered into a period of growth and expansion. In the 1950s, the so-called Builder Bishops and bricks-and-mortar pastors constructed new churches and schools in practically every diocese in the United States. At the same time, organizations like the Christian Family Movement were producing an emerging lay leadership. Even though many Catholics still embraced the devotional Catholicism of preceding generations, the media highlighted developments like the nationally acclaimed TV show *Life Is Worth Living*, hosted by Bishop Fulton J.

Sheen, which attempted to relate Catholic thought to the larger American culture.

With the election of Mother Thecla Brennan in March 1944 and the end of World War II in 1945, the Sisters of Saint Joseph of Philadelphia joined this emerging postwar era as a Congregation of women religious imbued with the traditional values of the American Catholic Church. From 1944 through the mid-1960s, the Sisters of Saint Joseph expended a great deal of energy on the expansion of their educational ministry and membership while maintaining the uniformity of lifestyle typical of congregations of women religious who followed traditional monastic horarium (schedule of prayer and practices), even though engaged in apostolic works.

MINISTRY

During this period, education was clearly the primary ministry of the Sisters of Saint Joseph. In the decades after World War II, the Congregation responded to the burgeoning Catholic population by increasing the number of elementary and secondary schools in which they served. Many of these schools were located in suburban areas of Philadelphia, Newark, Baltimore, Washington, DC, and Wilmington, but the sisters continued to retain a strong presence in the schools in the urban centers as well. By the time of the 1968 Chapter, the number of elementary schools staffed by the Congregation had increased by 60 percent and secondary schools by 100 percent. Unfortunately, the number of applicants to the Congregation during this time did not match the expanding number of staffing commitments; the total number of sisters had risen from 1,929 to 2,669 by the 1968 Chapter, only a 38 percent increase. Despite this discrepancy, by the end of the 1960s, the Sisters of Saint Joseph served in parish schools and secondary schools, in a broad range of socioeconomic areas in 12 dioceses in five states (New Jersey, Pennsylvania, Delaware, Maryland, Virginia, and North Carolina) and the District of Columbia.

The personal lives of the sisters were often impacted by the continual expansion into new schools, sometimes in unfamiliar places. As the yearly personnel list or *change list*, as it was called by the sisters, was read aloud in the community room or chapel, sisters would hear their own names or those of friends assigned to a new mission. Where, they wondered, was Miller Heights or Royersford? Had anyone heard of Falls Church or Oxon Hill? How about Oakland, Manasquan, or Bangor?

For some sisters, opening a new school and convent became a familiar experience. Sister Margaret Isabel Baney was a veteran of three "new foundations." She recalled how privileged she felt to be the first superior/principal of these missions. Whether Saint Anne, Bethlehem, Epiphany of Our

Lord, Norristown, or Our Lady of Mercy, Jersey City, Sister Margaret pronounced the experiences to be "a blessing to the community and to us."

As ever-increasing enrollments exceeded the capacities of buildings and the size of the faculties, concerns about overcrowding arose. The congregational school supervisors regularly noted this overcrowding in their reports to the General Chapters. Sister Salvator Doyle, a school supervisor in charge of five dioceses, clearly articulated the unsatisfactory situation. She opposed the large classes because of the instructional difficulties these imposed. Sister Salvator advocated reaching the individual soul, not merely engaging in mass instruction. Sister Rita Gervase Morton, a supervisor in New Jersey, spoke passionately about the negative impact of overcrowding on the sisters. She cited one school where three grades were divided into part-time groups with the same sister teaching one group for three full hours in the morning, and a second group for three more hours in the afternoon. "Many sisters are teaching eighty, ninety, or even a hundred children. It is a killing grind . . ."

The Congregation responded to the demand for personnel in two ways. First, when Reverend Mother Thecla and her successor Mother Divine Shepherd Flaherty decided to accept the request to staff new schools, they continued the example of their predecessors and made a corporate commitment to fully staff the school. This meant that the Congregation agreed to provide a principal and all the teachers for the school. When previous superior generals did not have enough sisters to meet the demand, they instructed the principal to combine grades. In May 1948, Mother Thecla alluded to this practice when she asked the principals if they could provide additional sisters by combining grades in their own schools.

By the early 1950s, the second solution was initiated: the hiring of lay teachers. Historically, some parish schools had had a lay teacher. In these instances, the principal employed a woman usually known to the sisters personally and respected for her background as a parishioner and as a teacher. The diocesan high schools and the congregational academies also recruited lay teachers for particular departments or courses. Chestnut Hill College had hired lay professors since its founding.

A more extensive use of lay teachers in the 1950s in American Catholic schools constituted a major change in staffing procedures. By 1954, all superiors were requested to consider the number of sisters needing to be replaced with lay teachers. From 1955 onward, the Congregation's leadership began to use the ratio of one lay teacher to five sisters per school, in all these schools. This ratio was originally initiated by Cardinal John O'Hara (1951–1960) for the Archdiocese of Philadelphia. In March 1956, Mother Divine Shepherd's letter to the superiors expressed the exigencies of the situation:

> IT IS IMPERATIVE THAT I CALL UPON YOU FOR ASSISTANCE. WE ARE DESPERATELY IN NEED OF SISTERS FOR SEPTEMBER, 1956. . . . If you can in anyway give me a sister, please do so. Make any combination you can. Do keep these needs in your prayers. [Capitals in the original]

Increasing the number of lay faculty in the schools presented some challenges, especially to sisters who were used to working only with other members of the community. Gradually, though, sisters began to view the lay teachers as an integral part of the faculty, not merely secondary participants. School discussions, planning, announcements, and decision making that might ordinarily have occurred in the convent over a meal or during the evening recreation time were now conducted in the school, with all faculty participating. In her letters to the principals during the late 1950s, school supervisor Sister Francis Loretto Conlin advised this total inclusion of the lay members of the faculty in all school matters, and not to have information pertinent to school operation be relayed by a sister to the lay teacher. In 1962, Sister Mary Thomas Murphy, supervisor for the Archdiocese of Newark, concurred that "For the future, we must include lay teachers in all our planning. . . . It is important that we accept lay teachers graciously and help to develop them in the best traditions of Catholic education."

During the 1950s and 1960s, the civil rights movement and concomitant northern migration of African Americans dramatically changed the demographics of urban centers in the Northeastern United States. The Sisters of Saint Joseph serving in the now inner-city parishes of cities like Philadelphia, Newark, and Washington, DC, faced a unique set of challenges. The students of these parish schools had previously been white and predominantly Catholic. The newly arrived African American students were more frequently non-Catholic. While the previous population had been basically Caucasian working class, the African Americans were dealing with poverty and discrimination on a larger scale. Naturally, there were mixed feelings regarding the losses suffered by the parish as former members exited the city and began to populate the newly established suburban areas. The number of students in the schools also decreased, compounding the financial burdens of both parish and school. In the midst of the changing landscape, the Sisters of Saint Joseph maintained their commitment to no fewer than fifteen inner-city schools.

In her report to the 1956 Chapter, Sister Bernard Francis Loughery, school supervisor, chronicled the experience of the sisters in Washington, DC, after Archbishop Patrick A. O'Boyle announced the integration of Catholic schools in 1951. In her matter-of-fact way, she explained that only those directly involved in the process could fully understand the many problems encountered in the process of successful integration. She cited the excellent leadership of the principals of the Sister of Saint Joseph schools in the Washington area as an important factor in the ongoing development of the new apostolate to African American youth. She also noted that the sisters were advised by their superiors to be prudent in their responses to parishioners who sought the sisters' reactions to the integration process. Sister Bernard Francis seemed fully cognizant of the potentially divisive atmosphere in some of the parishes underlying this transition, but she recognized the efforts of the sisters to transcend even their own biases in order to promote the unity and reconciliation characteristics of the Sisters of Saint Joseph.

At Our Lady of Mercy School on Broad Street in Philadelphia, for example, the sisters joined with the newly appointed pastor in 1962 to try to create a new spirit in the parish and school. The formerly "Irish parish" school was now composed of about 99 percent African American children. In the parish, the Legion of Mary was established along with religion classes for those desiring to become Catholics. In the spring of 1963, the school participated in the North City Festival, which included banners, a parade with Mayor James Tate (1962–1972) of Philadelphia, Catholic devotions, and Benediction. Despite the attempt to create unity and neighborhood pride, in August 1964 North Philadelphia erupted in rioting. The sisters did not flee but chose to stay with their neighbors even though conditions on nearby Columbia Avenue were dangerous. The house annals of Our Lady of Mercy convent briefly noted their two-week experience: "Riot on Columbia Avenue, August 28 [1964] under heavy police guard until September 8."

Ministry to Latinos

Latinos, specifically from Puerto Rico, had been coming to the Philadelphia area in growing numbers since the 1940s. By the early 1960s, four schools staffed by the Sisters of Saint Joseph served this growing population: Holy Infancy in Bethlehem, Pennsylvania; Holy Name in Camden, New Jersey; and the Cathedral School and Saint Michael School, both in Philadelphia. One sister stationed at the Cathedral School at the time recalled that since the poverty of the people was so great, the sisters served the people in many ways, even washing the children's clothes in the convent basement. The sisters also took Spanish classes three times a week in order to improve their ability to communicate with those whose English language skills were minimal.

School Supervisors

Since 1889, the Sisters of Saint Joseph had appointed supervisors to monitor and shape the quality of education in the schools in which they served. During the post-World War II era, four Sisters of Saint Joseph supervisors figured significantly in their role in education. Sisters Francis Loretto

(1932–1960), Rita Gervase (1937–1968), Felicitas Martin (1941–1970), and Bernard Francis (1951–1971) were the four supervisors responsible for overseeing the Congregation's educational ministry in 11 dioceses in six states. During the 1960s and early 1970s, their leadership was augmented by several additional personnel.

The supervisors worked with the mistress of novices to train new sisters for the classroom and provide ongoing educational opportunities. In 1955, when renovations at Chestnut Hill College caused the cancelation of the summer classes, supervisors organized two workshops of 14 days each for the sisters teaching in elementary schools. The supervisors visited every school, met with each pastor, inspected every school building, and evaluated each sister's performance in the classroom.

Because the school supervisors often stayed for a few days in a particular school, they also gained valuable insights into the dynamics of community living in the local community. Given the breadth of their work, the supervisors had played a major role in personnel placement, which also impacted local convent life. The annual reports from the school supervisors provided much data that could be utilized in determining personnel placement, or "changes" as they were unofficially called. The supervisors' "black books" listed every sister by school, and the superior general paid attention to the information provided by these sisters.

In addition to their official duties, these sisters were instrumental in the development of curriculum and the pioneering of new programs and educational trends. By the mid-1960s, Sisters of Saint Joseph were members of diocesan elementary and secondary curriculum committees in practically every subject area. In 1958, the Sisters of Saint Joseph revised their spelling book, *Words in Action,* published by Sadlier, and in the mid-1960s they updated their text *Poems for the Grades.*

The Sisters of Saint Joseph also inaugurated several new educational programs. In 1951, the sisters at All Saints, Baltimore, piloted the Detroit Method of Reading, developed in response to the book *Why Johnny Can't Read.* In 1958, at the request of the Archdiocese of Philadelphia, the sisters at Saint Andrew School, Drexel Hill, pioneered a televised French-language program for students in grades four through eight. Sisters teaching in the primary grades at Resurrection, Saint Charles, and Cathedral School in Philadelphia and Saint Isadore in Quakertown introduced *Initial Teaching Alphabet (ITA),* an innovative technique designed to facilitate the teaching of reading in the mid-1960s.

Sisters of Saint Joseph often found themselves in the vanguard of new trends in education. In 1939, Mother Marguerite Friel and Sister Florine Donovan opened the first kindergarten at Saint Vincent School in Germantown. Soon after, Mother Victorine Riehl and Sister Saint Mary Magdalen McKay followed suit at Saint Leo School in Tacony. In 1943, Sisters Florine

Donovan and Saint Mary Magdalen began instructing other teachers in kindergarten methods. In North Jersey (1962–63), Sisters Trinita Reilly and Mechtilda Kimple trained many sisters in the "New Math," a trend which gained prominence in the early 1960s.

Other sisters created activities, authored textbooks, and wrote educational articles. In 1949, Sister Margaret Rose Brown created and published articles on a new Advent activity she called The Jesse Tree. Another innovator, Sister Mary Thomas, PhD, authored science texts for use in grades seven and eight in Catholic schools: *Thinking about God's World* and *Knowing about God's World* (Mentzer, Bush and Company). Sister Agnes Marie Gunn (Agnes David) authored a text, *Modern American Drama,* part of a secondary English series called Pageant Of Literature (Macmillan). The February edition 1966 of *Catholic Educators Magazine* carried Sister San Jose Shield's article entitled "An Approach to Graphing," and the Winter 1966 *University of Notre Dame English Journal* published Sister Elizabeth De Sales Dee's article on the teaching of poetry.

Expanding Educational Ministries

Given the sisters previous service to children who were blind and deaf, they responded to new trends in Catholic education. In 1953, the Sisters of Saint Joseph opened Our Lady of Confidence School in Philadelphia and, in 1955, Saint Joseph Day School in Pottsville, Pennsylvania. By 1962, Our Lady of Confidence served over 200 students ages seven to 17, while Saint Joseph Day School, a companion school to the parish school in Pottsville, worked with 30 students from nine parishes. In both institutions, the sisters provided a Catholic special education program, including sacramental preparation.

The sisters engaged in this new work often found it very challenging. Sister Leona Tucker (Elizabeth Leona), who had handled large first-grade classes for many years, found her beginning years in special education difficult:

> Each day with God's grace, I'd try again. My cry was that I couldn't get these children to do what my little first graders could do. Then I realized that if I could, there would be no need for the school [Our Lady of Confidence] nor of my being there. . . . This was what God was asking of me.

Sister Leona Tucker remained at Our Lady of Confidence School for 10 years, completed her masters in special education, and, in 1965, became director of Saint Joseph Day School in Pottsville.

High Schools

In response to the increased demand for secondary education in the post-World War II years, the Sisters of Saint Joseph became more fully immersed in high school work, doubling the number of secondary schools where they served. Some sisters continued in parish high schools such as Saint Rose High School (1926) in Belmar, New Jersey. Others taught in the many brand-new schools such as Wildwood Catholic High School (1947) in Wildwood, New Jersey, Cardinal Dougherty High School (1956) in Philadelphia, and John Carroll School (1964) in Bel Air, Maryland.

Commercial Schools

In addition to staffing secondary schools, the Sisters of Saint Joseph taught in commercial schools attached to some local parish schools. Commercial schools focused on teaching practical skills needed for the work forces. Four of these sites were in Philadelphia and one in Newark, New Jersey. The students enrolled in these typical two-year programs needed to work but were required by child labor laws to be in school. At the four Philadelphia sites of Saint Anne, Saint Michael, Nativity, and Our Lady of the Holy Souls and the Newark site of Blessed Sacrament, sisters prepared students to find good jobs. Often, one or two sisters taught the entire business program, with additional courses in literature, grammar, composition, religion, and church history, to students holding part-time jobs. Sister Mary Alacoque Fitzmaurice was the sole teacher at the Blessed Sacrament Business School for over 30 years where she successfully trained many students for business careers in the Newark and New York areas.

In their ministry as educators during the post-World War II years, Sisters of Saint Joseph were characterized by their dedication and creativity. One supervisor summed up the scope of their contribution to education when she claimed that

> practically every innovation that has been suggested or recommended in our professional reading, workshops . . . has been introduced in our schools: ungraded primary, homogeneous grouping, educational television programs, teachers' aides, library guilds, science fairs.

The Sisters of Saint Joseph embodied the words of Bishop Kendrick who observed that the sisters were "ready for any good work." At this time in their history the good work was still clearly education.

Sisters of Saint Joseph Schools

From 1945 until the 1960s, the Sisters of Saint Joseph invested their resources into the expansion of facilities and development of new programs of their congregationally owned and administered academies and college. For example, Cecilian Academy acquired two neighboring houses and reconfigured them to create more classroom space, an assembly room, and a multipurpose space. In 1951, Saint Mary's Academy added a gym, auditorium, science labs, and home economics facilities in its new building. In Bayonne, New Jersey, Holy Family Academy erected a completely new building in 1954, considered "the finest building in Bayonne." The rebuilding was prompted by increased enrollment, and it provided space for an art studio, music rooms, science labs, chapel, library, and administrative offices. In 1967, Norwood Academy undertook plans for a new building and gymnasium. The Principal, Mother Mary Scanlon (James Anthony), directed the project, which was aimed at implementing a challenging educational curriculum.

In McSherrystown, Pennsylvania, major renovations were made possible by a miracle—literally! In 1958, the Sisters of Saint Joseph were notified that Saint Joseph Academy needed to completely fireproof the school, in accordance with updated codes. The owner of the nearby Hanover Horse Farm, when informed of the sisters' dire need, asked how much money would be needed to fund the project. Although no outright donation was forthcoming, the owner did promise to talk with the sisters later. Meanwhile, the sisters at the Academy placed a small plastic horse at the foot of the statue of Saint Joseph. Attached to the little horse was a note that might have echoed the silent prayers of the sisters to make "our horse worth $50,000!" Evidently the sisters' benefactor decided to assist them by providing the revenue from one of Hanover Farm's money-making trotters, Star Pride, because one week later, the owner's secretary delivered a check for $50,000. Later, that summer, a second $50,000 check arrived. It seems that Star Pride really saved the day for Saint Joseph Academy, McSherrystown.

In 1961, the Sisters of Saint Joseph undertook a major building project: the erection of a new, state-of-the-art Mount Saint Joseph Academy located on the 78 acres of the Rex Farm property (previously purchased by the Congregation), in Flourtown, Pennsylvania. The new facility, just a mile and a half from the original Motherhouse site, was a fully equipped, modern school with specifically designed art studios, science and language labs, home economics facilities, chapel, and auditorium.

At the same time, Chestnut Hill College completed construction of the Logue Library (1962) and the Fontbonne Residence Hall (1961), with a capacity for 70 students. In addition to these major projects, Saint Joseph Hall was renovated, and state-of-the-art science labs were installed. Renovations also included two new faculty offices, and an automated elevator. The former site of Mount Saint Joseph Academy was fully incorporated into the campus of Chestnut Hill College.

Although a great deal of expansion and construction took place during this time, other congregational schools faced closure. Fontbonne Academy had opened in 1924, serving elementary grade girls, but in 1959 closed its doors due to declining enrollment. In 1968, Saint Mary's Academy (Philadelphia) closed due to both enrollment decline and structural problems. Since Albert Einstein Hospital on Broad Street was seeking to expand, the Sisters of Saint Joseph were able to sell the property, which was adjacent to the hospital, in December 1967.

Another change in the educational format of three of the existing congregational academies was the elimination of the boarding school. This occurred at Mount Saint Joseph Academy (1960); Saint Joseph Academy (McSherrystown) closed the boarding school for boys (1962) but continued a boarding school for girls from grades five to 12 until 1968. Finally, Norwood Academy ended its boarding school program in 1969.

The remaining congregational schools continued to expand and enhance their respective curricula. Cecilian Academy (Philadelphia) and Holy Family Academy (Bayonne) focused on the development of excellent music programs. In the 1950s, Cecilian was known for its operettas, and Holy Family boasted of an orchestra of 103 members in 1962. By 1963, Chestnut Hill College and all congregational secondary academies had earned Middle States Accreditation, a solid endorsement of the high quality of education and professionalism of the faculty.

Care of Widows and Orphans

During the 1950s and 1960s, about 2 percent of the Congregation worked at special diocesan institutions with the elderly and the young, including ministry to widows. Though the sisters had faithfully cared for the residents at Saint Ann's Widows' Home in Philadelphia since 1850, the institution did not comply with the health and safety laws governing a nursing care facility in the postwar years. This inability to meet state requirements, along with redevelopment due to the Philadelphia Independence Mall project, resulted in the relocation of Saint Ann and subsequent removal of the residents to a new location. In April 1964, five sisters and 20 residents moved to the new Germantown location, called Saint Ann's Widows' Home/Villa Laboure, because the site was owned by the Miraculous Medal Association of the Congregation of Vincentian Priests and Brothers. Those residents who required skilled care were transferred to a nursing care facility. The sisters continued their ministry at Saint Ann's Widows' Home/Villa Laboure until it closed in 1976.

When the Sisters of Saint Joseph first arrived in Philadelphia, they assumed administration of Saint John's Orphanage for Boys. In the post-World War II years, care of orphans evolved from placement in institutions to either adoption or placement of children in foster care. Those children placed in institutions, even temporarily, more often were troubled and in need of specialized services. At four institutions the sisters' roles shifted during this time as the numbers of children decreased. At Saint John's, for example, in the mid-1950s, 10 sisters taught nearly 300 boys in grades K through eight, and an additional 13 sisters helped provide for the boys' needs. By the late 1960s, the "nearly 300" had become approximately 35 boys who attended Our Mother of Sorrows School and came home to 12 sisters who served as "group mothers," caring for their needs in a home-like atmosphere.

In addition to Saint John's Orphanage, the Sisters of Saint Joseph ministered at Catholic Home for Girls (Philadelphia), Saint Margaret Vocational School (Philadelphia), and Paradise School for boys (Abbottstown, Pennsylvania). Sister Mary Edwin Freed taught at the Catholic Home for Girls (1943–1968) and eventually became a group mother. Sister Gertrude Cecilia Flynn, missioned at Paradise School for Boys for 11 nonconsecutive years, recalled with great glee that one of her pleasant duties had been teaching one of the teenagers to dance so that he could develop skill in "tripping the light fantastic" and enjoy his prom. In this ministry, as in traditional educational venues, the sisters, once again, demonstrated that they were "ready for any good work."

Health Care

The primary ministry of the Sisters of Saint Joseph was clearly education, but the Congregation wisely intuited the need for training some sisters in the medical field so that the sisters could care for their own elderly and infirmed members.

During the 1940s and 1950s, the Congregation educated a group of nurses, dieticians, and even some medical technologists to tend to the needs of the sisters who lived in the infirmary at the Motherhouse and at Saint Joseph Villa, Cheltenham. In the 1950s, the Motherhouse Infirmary boasted of its own operating room, supervised by Sister Bernard Marie Strocko, head nurse. The dietary needs of the sisters were served by Sister Tolentine Mellon, a feisty little Irish sister, beloved (maybe a little feared!) by novices who carried breakfast, lunch, and dinner trays to the sisters well into the late 1960s. While the infirmary could only accommodate about 30 persons, the Cheltenham facility could hold more than twice this number. In 1968, Saint Joseph Villa, Cheltenham, was classified as a nursing care facility, and 70 Sisters of Saint Joseph called it home.

At the beginning of the 1960s, there were 40 retired sisters living at the Motherhouse and another 70 at Cheltenham. Community leaders recognized that more sisters would be retiring from full-time ministry, but neither existing facility would be able to handle this overflow. The plan called for enlarging the Cheltenham facility, but zoning problems with the township nullified this option. The sisters then decided on a more dramatic measure: building a brand new facility. Since the Congregation still had 25 acres remaining of the Rex Farm property, the new facility was erected there, adjacent to Mount Saint Joseph Academy, with several acres of field between the buildings themselves. A short time later, those fields became the new cemetery for the sisters, since the one at the Motherhouse was near capacity.

The new Saint Joseph Villa was a nine-story, $5.3 million dollar, state-of-the-art nursing care and retirement facility that could accommodate 300 persons. The architect, Paul Getz, won an award for his bold, innovative cruciform design; the nursing station on each floor was centralized, and the corridors branched out from it, like spokes on a wheel. Saint Joseph Villa, Flourtown, opened its doors to receive its first residents on June 21, 1968.

Sisters' Education

As Catholic schools expanded in the 1950s and 1960s, so did the need for sister's professional education. From 1925 through 1970, Sister Clare Joseph O'Halloran, the registrar and prefect of studies at Chestnut Hill College, directed each sister's major, with the exception of the music majors who were under the jurisdiction of Sister Regina Dolores Devanney, chair of the music department. As a result of Sister Clare Joseph's approach to education, sisters accumulated many more credits than the ordinary college student. In describing this approach, Sister Mary Kieran McElroy, who had a doctorate in chemistry from the University of Pennsylvania and taught at Chestnut Hill College, summarized the experience of most Sisters of Saint Joseph:

> Choice of classes was not something Sister Clare Joseph gave out freely. At my first interview with her she asked what I would like my major and minor to be. My reply was English and French. Guess what I ended up majoring in . . . mathematics and science! Of course Sister Clare Joseph was planning ahead and thinking of the good of the Congregation. All of us who graduated from Chestnut Hill College and went on to graduate studies, did well . . . because Sister Clare Joseph had us so "well rounded" in all the humanities, especially English.

While being "well-rounded" had its benefits, the practice extended the college experience for most sisters to 10 or more years.

Although sisters progressively worked on their formal education, they still had to handle the challenge of being professionally prepared for ministry. When Sister Gertrude Bernadette Smith was sent to Notre Dame High School in Easton, Pennsylvania, in its opening year (1957), she taught English, physics, and chemistry and moderated the school newspaper. Although Sister Gertrude preferred teaching English, she "never got out of science," she explained, because "Sputnik went up" during her first year there.

By the mid-1950s, more than 30 sisters were faculty members of the College, and in the succeeding years an additional 12 sisters taught classes on Saturdays and in the summers. These sisters, many of whom had earned their masters and/or doctorates through part-time educational programs, held the students to high academic standards and empowered them to grow professionally and personally. One sister fondly declared, "Sister Ann Edward [Bennis], who taught me English on Saturdays, knew so much. . . . she gave me confidence in myself. . . . she opened me to another world." Another sister recalled an incident that occurred in Sister Consuelo Maria Aherne's history class in 1962, the year Vatican II began: "In the background bells were ringing steadily. Sister held up her hand. 'Everyone, please listen.' Sister said, 'The bells mark the opening of Vatican Council II. Your lives will never be the same.'" Experiences like these heightened the awareness of the students, sparking enthusiasm and dedication for both life and ministry.

In 1967, nearly one-third of the Congregation's members (2,600) were engaged in academic pursuits at the graduate or undergraduate level. Twenty-eight sisters took advantage of National Science Foundation and National Defense Educational Association grants for in-depth work in the humanities and sciences, computers, international studies, theatre, and music. For graduate studies and grant workshops, the Sisters of Saint Joseph continued the pattern of studying at both Catholic and secular universities. Living and learning in these diverse settings continued to enhance the sister's personal and educational development.

Personnel Assignments and Relocations: Changes

In order to facilitate the mission of education, multiple factors needed to be considered in the process of personnel assignments and relocations: superiors' terms of office, initial placement of new sisters, commitments to staff new schools, and sisters' personal situations. In general, every six years, a number of superiors completed their terms in a local convent and were rotated to leadership in another. Novices usually received their first placement in the Philadelphia area; creating vacancies for them necessitated moving other sisters out of city schools. Openings, created due to new staffing needs or death or illness of a sister or family member, also needed to be filled.

Each August became a time of great migration. About 20 percent (over 500) of the sisters were reassigned annually. There were actually three "change lists" containing the details of this large movement of personnel.

The superiors received their changes on August 10 and moved to their new houses several days later. The sisters who taught in high schools also received their assignments on August 10 but moved on August 18. The third list, for sisters who taught in the elementary schools, was announced on August 24, and these sisters were required to move to their new locations the very next day, August 25. Each year, sisters prepared for the possibility of being "changed" and made sure that everything was in order in both convent and school, so that they would always be ready.

This process obviously engendered both anxiety and curiosity, and the rumor mill was in full gear at the beginning of August. When the change lists were mailed at 30th Street Station, the word spread like wildfire. Telephones rang in every convent and sisters checked the mail every day. Even the postal workers seemed to sense the urgency of the event and tried to give top priority to the delivery of the lists.

Being changed from one mission to another had a significant impact on the lives of sisters. It meant living with a new group of sisters, often being assigned to teach a new subject or even a new grade level, and adjusting to the rhythms of a new parish and neighborhood, even a new state or diocese. Although some relocations might have seemed like going to a foreign mission, this complicated, sometimes heart-wrenching procedure caused many sisters to view changes as a part of their lives as Sisters of Saint Joseph. While their obedience in these years brought them to situations not of their choosing, sisters often found fulfillment, challenges, and opportunities for spiritual, professional, and personal growth in these new missions.

School and Convent Living

During the decades of the 1940s, 1950s and 1960s, the communal life of the sisters revolved around the school. The daily horarium of the convent was set to accommodate the time of morning Mass in the parish. Since many schools sent children home for an hour lunch period, the sisters had enough time to eat their main meal in the middle of the day. In some cases, the integration of school and convent extended even further. The principal of the school was usually the superior of the convent. The eighth-grade sister was often the assistant in the house and advised the superior on school and convent issues. She was perceived by the other sisters as a leader in both the school and convent. Since seniority in grade level often matched seniority in the house hierarchy, moving up the grades was viewed as a promotion and a recognition of both experience and expertise.

Another sister who occupied a unique but integral position was the music sister. She shaped the school's music program, taught piano lessons, and was a major contributor to the financial status of the convent. In addition to teaching classroom music and giving private piano lessons, the music sister had a highly visible role in the local parish and civic community because of the Christmas shows and musical productions she directed.

In the local convent, however, the music sister often led a separate life, because her rigorous schedule prevented her from joining the others at prayer or recreation. On Sunday she took her cooking turn while the other sisters prepared their school work. The income generated by the private lessons she offered constituted a major source of revenues for the local convent.

Conclusion

As the decade of the 1960s was drawing to a close, education was still the primary ministry of the Congregation. In addition to this formal apostolic work, sisters also reached out to the local community, visiting the sick, consoling the grieving, and working with immigrants. They also taught CCD classes and provided food and clothing to the needy. In other words, the Sisters of Saint Joseph continued their heritage of being "ready for any good work," the phrase Bishop Kenrick used to describe them.

SPIRITUALITY

The spirituality of the Sisters of Saint Joseph, like other apostolic religious congregations, reflected the impact of the 1917 codification of canon law in the areas of prayer life, vows, communal life, and the habit. Young women who entered the Congregation in these years were trained in a spirituality that reflected a monastic tradition more consonant with contemplative orders than with those engaged in the active apostolate.

Prior to the opening of Vatican II, the institutional nature of the church was reflected in the communal life and spirituality of the Sisters of Saint Joseph and other congregations of men and women religious. Coupled with a definition of holiness that tended to separate the secular from the sacred, this uniformity led to an institutionalism that solidified a spirituality of devotional Catholicism focused on rituals, private prayers, and other devotional practices. The Rosary, Marian feasts, special novenas, Forty Hours celebration, Adoration, Benediction, and First Fridays were characteristic practices. Parish organizations like the Holy Name Society, Altar and Rosary Society, Legion of Decency, and Sodalities were established and prospered, and they created a common framework to support the beliefs of devotional Catholicism.

Concepts and Types of Prayer

During the late 1940s through the 1960s, communal and personal prayers were formalized, uniform, and inclusive of many devotional prayers of the

Church. The sisters continued to spend two half-hour periods each day in meditation, to practice examen, and to pray the Rosary daily; these religious devotions were historically part of the spirituality of the Sisters of Saint Joseph.

For common prayer, the sisters used a *Formulary,* a small book that contained all required daily prayers. These included the Office of the Holy Ghost, litanies to the Holy Name of Jesus, the Blessed Virgin, Saint Joseph, and the saints, prayer before and after meditation, morning, afternoon, and night prayers, particular examen, grace for meals, Mysteries of the Rosary, prayer before the tabernacle, and Stations of the Cross. The *Formulary* also included the Office of Blessed Virgin, recited on Saturdays, consecration to the Sacred Heart, prayed on Fridays, and other seasonal, devotional prayers.

The periods of meditation took place communally in the convent chapel. The materials for these times of contemplation were taken from a prescribed book that followed the Ignatian method of meditation. This included a three-point focus on some aspect of the life of Christ and was scripturally based. One sister read aloud the content, or points, for meditation. After the 1962 Chapter, the sisters were given the freedom to choose their own content for meditation from an approved list. However, on major feast days, all used the same book, *Meditations for Special Occasions.*

In addition to the daily horarium, the sisters participated in the spiritual life of the parish. Always present at daily Mass, sisters went to two Masses on most Sundays: their own and the children's Mass. The music sisters usually conducted the choir for Sunday Masses and for other parish devotions. Sisters attended parish missions and other devotions such as Lenten services, Benediction, Vespers, Forty Hours, First Friday, and feast day celebrations.

Adaptions to the Horarium

Following the exact times assigned for particular prayers became increasingly more difficult as their ministry demands increased. The designation of particular times for each period of prayer reflected the monastic style of living and was often ill-suited to the life of a sister engaged in the active apostolate. The recollections of some sisters concerning the shouting of anticipated afternoon prayers over the din of doing breakfast dishes before rushing to school underscores the tension between the active and contemplative lifestyles.

To ease the struggle, sisters requested adaptations, which sometimes were granted. Primarily, the adaptations were permitted for vocal prayer or spiritual reading, but a good deal of caution was shown with regard to substitution for meditation, which was considered the most important. For example, a request made at the 1950 Chapter for the sisters who taught catechetical classes to offer that teaching for meditation and spiritual reading received an affirmative response for the spiritual reading but a negative one for meditation. The *Decrees* clarified that meditation might be made at a second Mass or Benediction, stations or other devotional exercises, if the regular horarium was not being followed, as on a Sunday; however, "the full half-hour [for meditation] must be completed."

Annual Retreats

The annual retreat was another spiritual experience characterized by common prayer and instruction from a retreat master, often a Jesuit priest. Many of these retreats were conducted at Saint Mary by-the-Sea, Cape May Point, New Jersey. Once the Shoreham Hotel, the retreat house boasted a magnificent ocean view but had few modern amenities. Lighting fixtures were in the corridors but not the bedrooms, and the word "rustic" best describes furniture and other appointments of the small rooms, which numbered 150 and usually hosted two occupants.

The daily schedule for the retreat replicated a type of monastic schedule, integrating the sisters' communal prayer with conferences. The rising bell was rung at 7:00 a.m., morning prayers and communal meditation at 7:30 a.m., followed by breakfast and the 10:00 a.m. conference. After the 11:15 a.m. Mass and dinner, the sisters were free until the 4:30 p.m. conference. Following supper at 6:00 p.m., sisters attended night prayers and Benediction. From 1946 through 1966, swimming in the ocean in front of the retreat house was prohibited by the Coast Guard because of the danger of unexploded mines still in the water from World War II. As a result, free time usually meant rest or walking or sitting on the porches, in silence.

A regular component of each retreat was Reverend Mother's visit and annual conference. In her conference, Reverend Mother encouraged the sisters to remain faithful to their communal spiritual life. One sister vividly recorded in the annals: "Reverend Mother's inspiring conferences to the sisters stressed the Common Life, with emphasis on prayers for perseverance . . ." Reverend Mother also emphasized the need to practice the vows with even greater fidelity and to be courteous in interactions with others within the local convent. She also warned about the dangers of secularism manifested in the overuse of such devices as the telephone, television, and radio. Each retreat also included the possibility for a sister to have an individual appointment with Reverend Mother and the sisters lined up on "Reverend Mother's porch" outside her room for this appointment.

Attendance at a particular retreat was determined, not by personal preference but by a sister's study schedule, role in the convent, or particular summer duties. Superiors always went on retreat together. The young sisters attending summer school also made retreat at a different time, and all those sisters who were temporary professed made retreat together. For years, this latter retreat was called the "Junior Retreat" since that was the appellation given to those with temporary vows. There was even a retreat just for the elder members of the Congregation—the "White Socks Retreat." This humorously affectionate title sprang from the almost universal wearing of white socks, not black socks, by retreatants who had foot problems.

Often several days of camaraderie during vacation at Cape May followed the solemn focus of retreats. The large community room and dining room became the setting for much creativity. There were movies—a 1956 sisters' hit was the *Magnificent Obsession*—or use of the restored piano, which was also a player piano. Many enjoyed the singing, dancing, one-act plays, three-act plays, long and short skits, of both a grand and comic nature. The three vacation days following the Junior Retreat were particularly renowned for their picnic suppers, party fun, singing and entertainment, and a baseball game in the sand courtyard, under the gaze of the statue of the Blessed Mother! Often the days culminated with virtually all 300 of the junior sisters' staging their adaptation of an original Broadway show to entertain Reverend Mother. The 1965 favorite was *Hello, Dolly,* where the juniors sang "Hello, Mother" instead.

Overall, the annual retreat provided a common, ongoing spiritual formation experience, in the spirituality of the Congregation. In some cases, the devotions and practices associated with retreat closely resembled those that had been part of every sister's initial formation period at the Motherhouse, thus creating a continuity and uniformity in the spiritual tradition of the Congregation.

Renovation

In 1959, the Sisters of Saint Joseph initiated a new kind of ongoing formation or spiritual development: Renovation. At the time, there were two particular opportunities for sisters to be renewed spiritually: the annual retreat and the monthly retreat day in the local community. However, in the mid- to late 1950s, the Sisters' Formation Movement not only raised concern about a sister's intellectual preparation for ministry but also her spiritual development. Renovation, as it was termed, became a vehicle for additional spiritual formation.

Mother Divine Shepherd announced in January 1959 that a spiritual renewal program would be initiated in the coming summer. She determined that every sister finally professed for 15 years was required to attend and no one was excused. Her letter defined this spiritual renewal as a month-long program conducted at Saint Joseph Academy, McSherrystown. It included a week of retreat followed by three weeks of meditation and conferences based on the *Constitutions* of the Sisters of Saint Joseph. Led by a Jesuit priest, it was intended to be a kind of second novitiate. During the month, sisters were to strive to restore in themselves the spirit of the Congregation, to attain a deeper understanding of their religious life, and to develop a more mature outlook on religious matters for the future. It also became a time for many to renew their "party" relationships by reconnecting during this special summer month with those who had been their first companions in the Congregation and in their early years of formation. One hardship that some experienced was that it canceled out a summer of their graduate studies.

Interpretation of the Vows

During the late 1940s through the 1960s, the Sisters of Saint Joseph continued to be shaped by an interpretation of the vows framed by renunciation of and separation from the world. By now the *Decrees* had become a kind of handbook for the *Holy Rule* (usually called the *Constitutions*) that specifically stated how vows were applied to daily life. The *Decrees* were updated after each Chapter, and each innovation or reiteration was reviewed in the letters and talks of the superior general, or reverend mother.

Obedience

Obedience for the Sisters of Saint Joseph, as for most other congregations at the time, "focused on a response to someone who holds authority in a community or as a renunciation of one's own will and judgment," according to Judith Merkle in her book on the vows (1998). The *Decrees* further explained that obedience meant a sister's life was regulated by directives from superiors, adherence to rules and customs, and attention to the order of day. During the decades following World War II, the *Decrees* of the General Chapters, held every six years, and the other directives issued from the same body did indeed regulate the sisters' lives, even to the point of directing how to keep the superior's feast or exhortations to be at community exercises at all times. Other restrictions limited their presence in the parishes, visiting with families and friends, attendance at family events such as funerals, the celebration of the sacraments, and even the graduations of former students. While the sisters recognized the importance of obedience and tried to follow the directives, there is ample anecdotal evidence that they were often able with common sense to navigate the narrow channel created by the apparent legalism of many directives and participate fully in the life of the parish.

Another aspect of the all-encompassing vow of obedience was the wearing of the habit. By the nineteenth century, the habit was no longer a simplified version of the widow's dress as it had been in the seventeenth century; it had become a distinctive garb that not only marked the sister as a member of a religious community but also separated her from the rest of the secular world. According to the *Decrees*, uniformity of appearance was required by obedience, and sisters were admonished not to change the habit. Their personal modifications often entailed an adjustment to the head band (legally 3½-inches high) so that it appeared even taller and was thrust forward, evoking the image of the prow of a ship. The cornet, starched linen surrounding the face, was another favorite subject for adaptation. Reverend Mother, in a letter to the local convents, declared that the cornet was not to be "puffed at the sides" and warned against the worldly spirit that was also evident in the wearing of matching nightgowns, robes and even slippers, especially when the garments were bright red!

Poverty

Poverty during this period stressed the monastic style of a uniform practice of sharing. Sisters held all in common and were not to receive or spend personal funds. The superior controlled all monies and used them for communal expenditures and the sister' more personal needs. There was virtually no independence accorded the sister, even in her choice of underwear, since many convents either bought from particular stores or asked local salesmen to bring wares directly to the convent. Sisters were warned not to spend money without permission or to ask for every new gadget on the market. Although this was only one aspect of the vow of poverty, it is clear that the focus tended to be on the avoidance of materialism and on the observation of minute details that equated dependency with the vow of poverty.

Chastity

The vow of chastity, like those of poverty and obedience, was also defined in somewhat legalistic terms and euphemistic expressions. The renunciation of marriage and the avoidance of "particular friendships" were the lynchpins of most interpretations of the vow, and specific details pertaining to these were scantily provided. Despite the cautions issued about exclusive friendships, many sisters did form deep, supportive relationships with their peers and others. Restrictions on attending movies or listening to radios and directives that discouraged the reading of novels were considered important for the practice of this vow. Obviously, the topic of sexuality was too uncomfortable to broach, and, as a result, the actual reasons behind the prohibitions were rarely, if ever, discussed. Consequently, chastity in the evangelical sense was not emphasized to the degree that avoidance of temptations against the vow was. This was compatible, though, with the basic monastic orientation toward renunciation of the world, since the practice of the vow was intended to safeguard the sister from "worldly" thoughts and desires. While sisters struggled at times with the restrictions and uniformity, many Sisters of Saint

Joseph found ways to temper the regulations and the formal structures with a spirit of care and common sense.

FORMATION

In keeping with the spirit of the times, and analogous to programs of other congregations of women religious, the Sisters of Saint Joseph had a prescribed regimen by which new members eventually became fully imbued in the spirit of the community and gradually assimilated in to the Congregation. This formation typically consisted of three stages: postulancy, novitiate, and juniorate.

Stage One: Postulancy

Since the Sisters of Saint Joseph had their origins in France, the term "party" (partie), rather than "group" or "band" was used to designate those young women who entered the Congregation at the same time. Expressions of solidarity—"She's our party"—or attempts to identify the age of a sister—"Whose party is she ?"—are still common today. The word itself suggests not only friendly camaraderie but a deeper sense of support and fidelity forged within the group by shared experiences. Some "parties" even had nicknames, often earned through reprimand but sometimes through more auspicious connections. There were "The Charmers" (1942) and "The Uncrushables" (1964), the former so named by Mother Marie Estelle Duggan, mistress of postulants and novices, for what she perceived as their overly friendly attitude toward the new postulants! The "Marian Year" party (1954) all received some form of Mary in their religious names in honor of the Blessed Mother.

During the 1940s to the 1960s, little, if anything, changed in the procedures that governed entrance into the Congregation. Most young women were eighteen, some older. Each had been mentored by a sponsor, a Sister of Saint Joseph who knew the young woman and who, in most cases, had taught her in grade school or in high school. On a designated date all postulants arrived at the Motherhouse dressed in the black garb and bonnet of postulancy. When the bell rang, the new postulants said farewell to their families and assembled for Benediction.

The postulancy lasted from six to seven months, and in the 1950s to mid-1960s the number of postulants ranged from 50 to 100. The young women attended classes in secular and spiritual subjects and learned the various communal prayers, the Ignation Method of meditation, and the *Maxims* of Father Médaille. They also had assigned charges at the Motherhouse and later at the Fontbonne Postulate when the building opened in 1960. One of the most tangible signs of the desire to instill uniformity of behavior into a diverse group like postulants was the etiquette class, which incorporated lessons on personal hygiene with a curriculum on manners that would have made Emily Post proud. How to make a bed, how to walk like a lady, and how to eat properly in formal style were several of the main lessons of the course.

Stage Two: Novitiate

Reception Day marked the transition from postulancy to novitiate; canonically, the two-year novitiate period began the Tuesday after Easter. Up until 1967, the Liturgy of Initiation into the Congregation focused on the theological concept of the sister as the Bride of Christ; consequently, the postulants to be received entered the Motherhouse Chapel dressed as brides but at a designated point in the ceremony exited the chapel and returned garbed in the habit. During this ceremony, each sister received a new, religious name to symbolize her new identity as a Sister of Saint Joseph.

The novitiate stage of formation was divided into two parts: the canonical year and the mission year. The canonical year was governed by precise canon laws pertaining to the necessary requirements imposed on religious congregations by the Church. During this phase, novices were instructed in the fine points of the *Constitutions* and the *Directory*, the theology and practice of the vows, and spiritual and historical heritage of the Congregation. Novices also spent additional periods of time in private prayer during adoration of the Blessed Sacrament, a feature of daily life in the novitiate.

At the conclusion of the canonical year, novices entered the second phase of the novitiate known as the mission year, so named because the novice would be assigned to a mission that September and become part of a local community. During the summer months, the mission novices received instruction in classroom management and techniques for teaching reading and math at the grade levels appropriate to the new assignments. The chief architects of this "crash course" in pedagogy were Sisters Felicitas and Clare Michael Keating, assisted by other teachers.

During the mission year, the novice was given full responsibility for a classroom, mentored by their principals and grade partners. They continued to be instructed in the spirituality of the Congregation and in the rules that governed community life at the local level. On Saturdays, novices went to Chestnut Hill College to continue receiving instruction in classroom methods. When June came and school ended, mission novices returned to the Motherhouse to begin a summer of spiritual preparation for the making of first vows. This program focused particularly on the study of the vows and the *Constitutions* of the Congregation and culminated in the initial vow profession referred to as "First Vows." The ritual was celebrated generally around August 15, the feast of the Assumption of Mary. During this profession ceremony, the novice promised to live her vows for one year and received her crucifix (bronze corpus on black wood), which she wore tucked into the bodice of the habit to distinguish her from the novices who had no crucifix and from the finally professed sisters who wore it openly. The mission novice was now a canonically vowed "temporary professed sister," a junior.

Stage Three: Juniorate

The period of temporary profession (juniorate) lasted five years. Formation continued but was conducted at the local level, with the superior of the convent assuming responsibility for the junior's instruction on the *Holy Rule* (*Constitutions*) and *Maxims of Perfection*. The mistress of juniors also met personally with each temporary professed sister. Juniors were required to attend the semi-annual meetings held at the Motherhouse.

The fifth and final year of the juniorate was called tertianship. At the end of the school year sisters in this stage of formation spent the summer in spiritual preparation for the profession of final vows. During the postwar years and through the 1960s, *Catechism of the Vows* by Peter Cotel SJ, was a standard text used by the formation personnel, in conjunction with the *Constitutions* of the Sisters of Saint Joseph. Traditionally, the tertians professed their perpetual vows on August 15 at a private Mass. Families arrived later for lunch and an afternoon visit. The newly professed wore a crown of flowers and displayed the profession crucifix openly.

Formation Personnel: Mistress of Novices and Assistants

For 34 years (1932–1966), Mother Marie Estelle was the sole person in charge of the spiritual formation of novices, and until 1960, she also oversaw the formation of postulants. Steeped in the heritage of the Congregation and dedicated to the Church in which she served, Mother Marie Estelle wisely and compassionately instructed both postulants and novices in the methods of prayer and personal devotions. She herself was a "Loving Holy Rule" whom young sisters could emulate. According to some who remembered her daily conferences, she was fond of saying "Keep the *Rule* and the *Rule* will keep you." Mother Marie Estelle also stressed love, not fear, as the motivating factor behind obedience to the *Rule* and was quoted as claiming that anyone should be able to understand what the *Rule* of the Sisters of Saint Joseph was by observing the actions of any one of its members. Her concept of spiritual formation focused on developing a personal relationship with God that would ideally be mirrored in the genuine relationships with others, marked by generosity and loving service. According to the testimony of many sisters who benefitted from her strong leadership, Mother Marie Estelle taught more by example than by directive, a hallmark of a truly great teacher.

Mother Marie Estelle was assisted in her position of novice mistress by a core staff of sisters who functioned as teachers and "house mothers." While formation had a spiritual focus, it also incorporated training in the ways of daily living in community. Since postulants and novices came from varied backgrounds and locales, the Congregation provided instruction in how to live a uniform lifestyle that would promote harmony, eliminate any potential divisiveness, and facilitate accomplishment of all the daily tasks involved in maintaining both the Motherhouse and the college. In order to do this, novices needed to assume responsibility for physical jobs like serving at table, buffing floors, and working the mangle in the laundry. Supervising and instructing in these areas were the roles of the novitiate professed sisters.

Several of these sisters began their formation ministry at the same time as Mother Marie Estelle, although three sisters predated the novice mistress's term: Sister Nicolita McCloskey (1912–1962), Sister Celestia Rawle (1918–1962), and Sister Martin Joseph McLaughlin (1922–1970), who taught music, conducted the choir, and supervised the reading in the dining room. No one who had personal experience with Sister Martin Joseph could ever forget her corrections of pronunciation, delivered in a "stage whisper" that could be heard across the dining room.

Other notable members of this group of assistants included Mother Marie Estelle's cousin, Sister Grace Stanislaus Duggan (1933–1970), keeper of the keys to the much coveted candy closet (among other duties), along with Sister Seumis Moore (1934–1958), seamstress in charge of habit-making, and Sister Helen de Chantal Callahan (1939–1969), a registered nurse in charge of the novitiate infirmary. In 1942, Sister Charisma Austin joined the formation staff, primarily to teach theology. Those whose skills in penmanship were somewhat inadequate, however, remember instruction in the Palmer Method. Securing a certificate in the Palmer Method was mandatory for every novice, and Sister Carisma took her job very seriously. Also part of the staff in 1942 (until 1964) was Sister Francis Louise Kuhn, who supervised the clothes room where the laundry arrived to be sorted.

In 1952, Sister Catherine Marie Montgomery became one of the novitiate professed, and her tenure lasted until 1970. Like Sister Carisma, she taught theology, but she was also in charge of the novices who carried trays to the infirmed sisters and worked in the diet kitchen of the Motherhouse infirmary. All of these sisters, along with those who followed them in the 1960s and later decades, were dedicated to the mission of forming postulants and novices in the traditions and heritage of the Sisters of Saint Joseph so that they, in their turn, could be examples of fidelity and service to the church, through their lives as vowed women religious.

Formation Personnel: Mistress of Juniors

Analogous to Mother Marie Estelle's position as mistress of postulants and novices was that of Mother Mary Andrew McCormick, Mistress of Juniors from 1944 to 1963. For nearly three decades she guided the temporary professed sisters' ongoing formation. As part of her duties, she met annually with each sister, a task that grew more daunting as the numbers grew from 182 (1946) to 290 (1962). Mother Mary Andrew's job also entailed counseling and guiding young sisters as they adjusted to local community living, especially in situations that could be challenging. Those who were attendees at her conferences recall her admonition to nurture the first fervor of the novitiate and not become jaded by routine or disillusioned by everyday realities.

Formation Personnel: Mistress of Postulants and Novices

In her annual reports to Reverend Mother and her reports to the General Chapters, Mother Marie Estelle repeatedly voiced her concern over the difficulty of providing a longer sustained period for developing the needed foundation in religious life for the postulants and novices in her care. She felt that an increasingly secular world exerted influences on the young women entering the Congregation and that much more time and energy needed to be expended upon the assimilation into the ways of religious life. Another factor compounding this situation was the increased number of entrants each year. Mother Marie Estelle's estimation of this issue was that "two groups . . . are very numerous, making it difficult to give adequate individual spiritual guidance." Her proposed solution—eliminating the mission novice phase and keeping novices at the Motherhouse for two years—was deemed impractical for two reasons, namely staffing concerns in schools and excessively large numbers in formation at the Motherhouse. In 1946, Mother Marie Estelle suggested subdividing the role and creating a mistress of postulants who would supervise the formation of those who were in the first phase (six to seven months long) that would culminate in reception. In 1960, this proposal was finally accepted and implemented, and Mother Francis Anita Gercke became the first mistress of postulants. That year, 109 young women entered the Congregation at the new location in the renovated Fontbonne Academy building on Sunset Avenue in Chestnut Hill.

Chapter 2
GOVERNANCE

The Superior General and Council

The governance structure of the Congregation at this time reflected the hierarchical patterns of most ecclesial institutions. There was a recognizable chain of command, a concept familiar to military as well as church organizations, and a large body of followers who received directives for ordering all aspects of their lives. Of the three evangelical vows, obedience appeared to take precedence, and submission to those in leadership roles was predicated on the belief that their commands represented God's will. The universality of this orientation toward compliance with authority was evident in secular life as well. With some exceptions, structures in Church, state, family, and workplace were all based on this hierarchical order, and in most congregations of women religious (and men), the major leadership position was that of superior general, a title taken from the Jesuits.

The superior general and her assistant (the Congregation's second-in-command) tended to the daily administrative duties of their offices. Dealing with the local ordinary of the diocese, communicating with the Vatican official in charge of religious congregations, consulting with local superiors, writing letters to the local houses, handling financial issues, visiting the local houses, accepting women into the Congregation, and attending the funeral of each sister were among the demands of their leadership roles.

Given the burgeoning size of the Congregation, the superior general, who was addressed by the title Reverend Mother, needed assistance in the complex governing and for this purpose had an elected assistant superior general and three elected councillors of the Institute. This group of five met six times a year and was available for consultation by telephone at other times. While the superior general and assistant lived at the Motherhouse, the three councillors lived in local convents. Usually the councillors were superiors of local houses, principals of elementary schools, or heads of departments of secondary schools. Because there were always an insufficient number of sisters to fill staffing needs, it was imperative that the councillors remain in an apostolate, even as they participated in the governance of the Congregation.

In order to maintain a direct connection to sisters at the local level, the superior general relied on letters to communicate directives to the local superiors and other sisters. These letters contained spiritual admonitions to be faithful to the *Holy Rule* and to be diligent in the ministry of teaching. In one of her letters to the sisters (1955), Mother Thecla exhorted the sisters to cherish their rules as teachers since "a teacher affects eternity."

The day-to-day operation of a large Congregation required the contributions of many persons, each working in her own sphere but communicating with the superior general and council. Among this group were the procuratrix general/bursar, the general secretary, school supervisors, college registrar, and formation directors. Of these, the role of procuratrix was crucial to the efficient management of all the buildings that composed the Motherhouse and Chestnut Hill College complex, as well as other congregational properties. It was this person who directed all building projects, supervised the workers, furnished new convents, and advised on all financial matters. Sister Francis Xavier McPeak held this position from 1946 to 1976. This extraordinarily talented woman personally directed the erection and repair of buildings, even joining in the labor herself. For many of the men who worked on the grounds of the Motherhouse and at the retreat house in Cape May Point, she was more of a mother than a boss, and her compassion and dedication were rewarded by their deep loyalty. Every novice also had the opportunity to benefit from Sister Francis Xavier's skills in the culinary line when a major feast day dinner was to be served. She instructed those waiting table in the exact etiquette of serving and removing dishes, and her dictum concerning the food was legendary: "Hot things hot and cold things cold."

The Local Superior

Despite the growth of the Congregation during the two decades following World War II, there had been no addition of midlevel governance structure, and as a result the local superior continued to be the next link in the chain of command between the superior general and Council and the sisters at large. Consequently, this was a position of great authority and power. It was the superior's primary role to assure that there was uniform religious observance in her local house as was expected in all houses of the Congregation, according to Mother Divine Shepherd in her report to Rome in 1961. In Mother Thecla's words, superiors are the "soul of the whole." The superior was to be a model of the bond of charity and reconciliation that should unite and characterize the local community. Mother Divine Shepherd summed up the role succinctly when she said that the superior is "the leader of her fellow religious in the ways of God." These words were clearly an expression of the ideal and, in many cases, an accurate description of the intentions of those who held this responsibility. During this time period, the superior was usually the leader at home and at work, since she also served as principal of the school. As one superior recalled: "I was superior, teaching second grade and principal." This same person also noted that "only big schools had nonteaching principals." Her experience was doubtless replicated throughout the Congregation, often complicating an already heavy burden of responsibility.

As the direct line between Reverend Mother and the local community, the superior communicated Reverend Mother's directives and, in turn, was the conduit through which each sister's educational needs, retreat plans, and personal concerns were relayed. The superior was also consulted regarding changes or transfers of a sister from one mission to another. All superiors attended retreat together at the Motherhouse, vacationed together at Cape May Point, and were delegates to the General Chapters that occurred every six years. Appointed for life, a superior would move from one local house to another when her six-year term in one convent had expired. Sometimes, the same two superiors would switch houses repeatedly throughout their tenures. This longevity, coupled with absolute authority, had the potential to become problematic, particularly if a superior's view of religious life was marked by rigid observance or colored by the force of her own personality. However, the 1950 General Chapter reaffirmed the lifetime term of the superior, with Mother Thecla declaring that this practice was supported by the *Holy Rule* itself. The rationale of the Chapter body was that "superiors who have been in office for some time have the experience to better guide . . . and administer the affairs of the convent and school."

The General Chapter

During these years the deliberations and decrees of the General Chapters seemed fairly uneventful for the ordinary sister on the mission. Only superiors were elected delegates and few sisters were nondelegate attendees. The distinction applied to voting rights (nondelegates could also vote on points for discussion) and assigned places (delegates first). The General Chapter was convened every six years and consisted of two parts: Chapter of Affairs and Chapter of Election. From 1946 until 1965 there were four General Chapters. In 1944, a special Chapter of Election was held to fill the vacancy created by the death of Reverend Mother Mary Berchmans Stoffel, but at this time there was no Chapter of Affairs.

The procedures of these Chapters followed a predictable pattern, and a typical report to the Chapter body included statistics on membership, information on formation, reports from the head of each congregationally owned institution and the school supervisors, and a financial report. The Chapter of Affairs lasted five to six days and included the superiors' retreat. Following the Chapter of Affairs was the Chapter of Election. Traditionally, the delegates re-elected the current members of the Administration if they had served only the first of two consecutive terms.

One of the only departures from the usual business of the Chapter, whose main task was to reaffirm the primacy of the *Holy Rule* in the daily lives of the sisters, came in 1956, when the issue of lay sisters taking rank was finalized. This meant that lay sisters received equal rights and responsibilities with the choir sisters with whom they entered. This vestige of monastic life disappeared on September 8, 1956, with the formal approbation of the Holy See. Although the Congregation had sought this elimination of class distinction in 1939, Cardinal Dougherty had advised against it, claiming that it would be unwise to petition Rome so soon after having submitted the revised *Constitutions*.

Participation in National Conferences of Women Religious

In 1950, Pope Pius XII convened the First International Congress of Religious in Rome. His goals were to facilitate unity among the various Congregations and foster sharing that would lead to renewal and adaptation of religious life to modern society. A direct result of the meeting was the First National Congress of Major Superiors in the United States, at the University of Notre Dame, August 9–13, 1952. Topics discussed at this meeting included the training of formation personnel, practice of the vows in modern times, theology for sisters, and professional preparation for the apostolate. In response to Rome's urging, the major superiors of 235 orders of women religious in the United States met in Chicago and established the Conference of Major Superiors of Women Religious (CMSW), later renamed the Leadership Conference of Women Religious (LCWR).

In 1952, Reverend Mother Thecla and Mother Divine Shepherd attended the Congress of Major Superiors in South Bend, Indiana. Mother Divine Shepherd's notes conveyed just a hint of the momentousness of the occasion. She recorded the numbers attending—2,000 sisters, 1,000 priests—and commented on the quality of the papers that were delivered to the group, especially the one given by Mother Rose Vincent McGuiness, SSJ, whose sister, Mother Mary Bethany, was a member of the Council. In 1956, both Mother Divine Shepherd and Mother Thecla attended the founding meeting of CMSW in Chicago, but this time the Superior General was Mother Divine Shepherd.

Despite these groundbreaking efforts at intercongregational dialogue, the hierarchical structures remained in place and little, if any, communication of the proceedings of these meetings was shared with the sisters. Even the informal beginnings of what would later become the Federation of the Sisters of Saint Joseph rated nothing more than a passing comment in the community annals: "many experiences and much to tell about the meeting, other communities' habits. It was indeed a profitable week." One tangible result of these conversations was the *Sisters of Saint Joseph Inter-Congregational Bulletin,* which was created to gather items which would bring about a closer association resulting in ever-growing appreciation of our saintly founders. It would be another decade before those tentative beginnings finally culminated in the establishment of the Federation of the Sisters of Saint Joseph in the United States.

Congregational Finances

During this time, the main source of revenue remained the stipend accorded each teaching sister and paid by either the parish or the diocese. In the late 1930s, some dioceses set a standard stipend for all sisters teaching in a diocesan school; however, not every pastor complied. By 1950, the allotted stipends ranged from $420 to $600, annually. Based on this income, the local house generated its operational budget and contributed a percentage of the monies received to the Motherhouse. Local houses were also assessed for the education of the sisters, and in February 1952 Reverend Mother Thecla asked the local superiors to begin paying for health insurance.

Financial decisions usually centered on the need to maintain congregational properties, which required shrewd planning and new fundraising endeavors. During the next two decades the Congregation undertook a number of major projects, necessitated in part by expanding numbers of those entering and those retiring.

Major Projects: Restoration and Expansion

One of the major projects undertaken during this time period was the full restoration of the Cape May Point Retreat House, Saint Mary by-the-Sea, for use by the sisters. During World War II, the Congregation leased the property to the US Coast Guard. In 1946, the Coast Guard returned it to the Congregation, but cleaning, painting, and repair work were needed to make it suitable for use. Extensive repairs to the heating system in both the Convent and Novitiate building at Chestnut Hill were costly, as were improvements to the Villa in Cheltenham. The redecoration of the Motherhouse Chapel was more a labor of love than a project, and it was funded by the donations and gifts Mother Thecla received on the occasion of her Golden Jubilee in 1955.

The first expansion program that would result in "heavy financial debt for the future," as Mother Divine Shepherd told the sisters in her January 1959 letter, was the erection of new buildings on the grounds of Chestnut Hill College and the Rex Farm property. These new structures included Logue Library, Fontbonne Hall Student Residence, and the new Mount Saint Joseph Academy. The renovation of the former Mount Saint Joseph Academy into Saint Joseph Hall (College) and reconfiguration of the former Fontbonne Academy (closed 1959) into the new Postulate Building were part of the expansion project.

In order to finance these undertakings, the Congregation mortgaged the Motherhouse property for $2.7 million. Over time, both the College and the Academy were to repay the loans. However, the Congregation still needed to meet the payment schedules, so Mother Divine Shepherd initiated what she called the Sacrifice Drive 1959. The intention was to increase the level of involvement of each sister to contribute to these projects by making modest acts of self-sacrifice, such as no gift-giving among themselves at Christmas, or asking families for monetary gifts, not personal ones. These small sacrifices accrued into larger sums, and sisters took pride in being a part of such a worthy enterprise.

In 1964, when Mother Divine Shepherd announced the decision to build a new Villa in Flourtown, rather than merely expand the existing one in Cheltenham, she extended the Sacrifice Drive to help defray the projected $5.3 million cost of the building. The Sacrifice Drive was augmented by other special fundraisers like the March 12, 1966, benefit concert at the Academy of Music in Philadelphia, featuring a chorus of 225 sisters, and by the establishment of the Villa Guild (1966) and the Villa Fair (1967). All of these attempts at fundraising were combined with a bank loan of $2.5 million in order to finance what was the most ambitious building program the Congregation had ever undertaken.

Portraits of Leadership:
Mother Thecla and Mother Divine Shepherd

For almost a quarter of a century two women held the position of superior general of the Sisters of Saint Joseph. When Mother Thecla was elected to that position, Mother Divine Shepherd was elected assistant. Twelve years (two terms) later, the roles were reversed, creating an opportunity for great stability and continuity of leadership. It was evident that these women worked well together, although they differed in temperament and style.

In 1945, Mother Thecla's quiet air of authority and keen insight fostered a much-needed sense of equanimity. Those who knew her claimed she had a "spiritual magnetism to draw people to love and serve God." She was also known for a kind of homey wisdom, disarming in its simplicity. She was also equally well known for her delicious soup! "Teeny Brennan," as her family called her, entered the Congregation in 1902, after serving as a lay teacher in a parish school in her native Orange, New Jersey. Her 25 years as an elementary school principal helped prepare her for the challenges of administration of an entire Congregation of women religious. During her tenure, her major theme was fidelity in little things and little things done with love. It was a motto she preached with her life, not only with her words.

Having served as assistant superior general to Mother Thecla, Mother Divine Shepherd was elected to succeed her in 1956. She also was known for her wisdom and intellect, but a quick, dry sense of humor was clearly part of her personality. Mother Divine Shepherd entered the Sisters of Saint Joseph in 1915 and taught in elementary school and at West Catholic High School for Girls. She studied full time at The Catholic University in Washington, DC (1933–1934), and was appointed mistress of juniors in 1940. She ministered in this capacity until her election as assistant to Mother Thecla in 1944. Mother Divine Shepherd was a risk-taker with a clear vision of the future of the Congregation, and she made the decisions necessary to expand and develop the Congregation's properties. One sister was quoted as saying Mother Divine Shepherd had "piercing blue eyes that looked right through you and out the other side; she was gifted with the ability to inspire."

Conclusion

The years to come would offer many challenges to the stability of life generated and sustained during the nearly 25 years of leadership provided by Mother Thecla and Mother Divine Shepherd. Tremendous upheaval in areas secular and sacred were on the horizon, but the Sisters of Saint Joseph had survived troublous times in the past, and, as a Congregation, they had tried to prepare for the future, while maintaining a steady gaze on the present mission.

PUBLISHED SOURCES

Augustein, John J. *Lighting the Way: The Early Years of Catholic School Superintendency.* Washington, DC: National Catholic Education Association, 1996.

Byrne, Patricia, CSJ. In the Parish and Not of It: Sisters. In *Transforming Parish Ministry,* by Jay P. Dolan, R. Scot Appleby, Patricia Byrne, and Debra Campbell. New York: Crossroad Publishing, 1990.

Connelly, James F. *The History of the Archdiocese of Philadelphia.* Wynnewood, PA: Unigraphics, 1976.

Dolan, Jay P. *The American Catholic Experience.* Garden City, NY: Doubleday and Company, 1985.

Hennessy, James, SJ. *American Catholics: A History of the Roman Catholic Community in the United States.* New York: Oxford University Press, 1981.

Kashuba, Mary Helen, SSJ. *Tradition and Risk.* Virginia Beach, VA: The Donning Company, 1999.

Logue, Maria Kostka, SSJ. *The Sisters of St. Joseph of Philadelphia.* Westminster, MD: The Newman Press, 1950. Although Sister Maria Kostka Logue edited the text, she relied largely on the contributions of Sisters Consuelo Maria Aherne, Margaret Rose Brown, Bernard Francis Loughery, and Juanita Morgan. While Logue, *Sisters of St. Joseph of Philadelphia,* was published in 1950, it addressed material only up to 1944.

Merkle, Judith A., SNDedN. *A Different Touch: A Study of the Vows in Religious Life.* Collegeville, MI: The Liturgical Press, 1998.

Meyers, Bertrande, DC. *Sisters for the 21st Century.* New York: Sheed and Ward, 1965.

Oates, Mary J. *The Catholic Philanthropic Tradition in America.* Bloomington, IN: Indiana University Press, 1995.

O'Brien, David. *Public Catholicism.* New York: Macmillan Publishing Company, 1989.

Quinonez, Lora Ann, CDP, and Mary Daniel Turner, SNDdeN. *The Transformation of American Catholic Sisters.* Philadelphia: Temple University Press, 1992.

Schneiders, Sandra M., IHM. *Selling All: Commitment, Consecrated Celibacy, and Community in Catholic Religious Life.* New York: Paulist Press, 2001.

ARCHIVAL SOURCES

Mount Saint Joseph Convent, Philadelphia, Pennsylvania
Primitive documents, records of General Chapters, personal papers, focus groups, and other records.

Chapter Three

Rediscovering Our Mission

1965–1969

The Second Vatican Council has ushered in major changes in the Catholic Church since its opening on October 11, 1962. With a steady, rapid pace, its major documents set forth a new direction for prayer rooted in liturgy (*Sacrosanctum Concilium,* December 1963), for understanding the Church as all the People of God (*Lumen Gentium,* November 1964), for the centrality of Sacred Scripture (*Dei Verbum,* November 1965), and for holiness found in union with the world (*Gaudium et Spes,* December 1965).

In addition to these documents, *Perfectae Caritatis*, which dealt specifically with the renewal of religious life, was a major influence on virtually all congregations of women religious. Attentive to the direction of Vatican II, in the mid to late 1960s Mother Divine Shepherd Flaherty initiated changes in the horarium and in devotional practices. For example, the Office of the Holy Ghost and the 1:00 prayers were omitted, and only three novenas (out of 11) were to be retained. Local houses were offered choices, such as whether dormitory prayers would be recited aloud by one sister or said privately, or whether spiritual reading (lecture) would be done communally or privately. Other practices like the examen became the responsibility of the individual sister. She eliminated monastic rituals like kissing the floor or the pew and in 1968 introduced the praying of the Divine Office. While this prayer of the Church became the primary communal text, the *Formulary* with its devotional prayers was maintained.

Some monastic practices related to the vow of obedience were also eliminated and a few new privileges granted. For the first time sisters were permitted to drive, but only if necessary and never alone. Some restrictions on family visitation were rescinded, and sisters could partake more freely in some family celebrations.

Mother Divine Shepherd's decision regarding the habit was to eliminate the cornet and guimpe and to slightly shorten the hem—in her words, "Nothing drastic." Careful drawings of the minute changes in sleeves, cincture, hemline, collar, and headpiece reveal that uniformity was critical. The first modifications consisted of replacing the linen cornet with a polyester cap covering the ears, and the hard celluloid guimpe with a smaller, soft, square bib-like Dacron collar. The celluloid headband was abandoned for a smaller pre-made plastic mold to support the veil. Finally, the doubled-over wide sleeve and undersleeve gave way to a simple single tapered sleeve.

By June 16, 1966, the Sisters of Saint Joseph were ready for their new habit. On that day all 2,600 sisters, with the exception of the canonical novices who had received the modified habit at their reception in April, donned the slightly modified habit. Since the date coincided with the first retreat at Cape May Point, this was the first large public gathering where the sisters saw each other in their new attire. Those on retreat, according to one eyewitness, were eager to share their tips on how to make the caps fit more snugly or arrange the underveil. While some advocated Velcro, the less adventurous favored safety pins! According to this same witness—the compiler of the Cape May Point album for 1966—everyone thought the molded headpiece was perfect. Perhaps this observer captured the essence of the experience when she declared that "A day that marked a required change without loss of identity became a day of cherished uniformity among Sisters of Saint Joseph of Chestnut Hill."

Other changes that stemmed from Vatican II involved revising the ceremonies of Reception and Profession of Vows. The Council documents stressed the public aspect of the Profession of Vows, and on August 14, 1967, the Final Vow ceremony of the Sisters of Saint Joseph became a public celebration. The following year, the Reception Ceremony was private and bridal gowns were not worn.

CHANGES IN GOVERNANCE STRUCTURES

Although the decision not to subdivide the Congregation into provinces had already been made in consultation with the Congregation for Religious in Rome, a feasible alternative was found in the construction of "regions" with regional superiors overseeing them. At a special meeting of local superiors on February 12, 1967, Mother Divine Shepherd simply stated that in the summer the Congregation would be divided into four regions of approximately 650 sisters each. In June, the first regional superiors were named: Mothers John Eudes Cooke, Miriam Gertrude Donohue, Gertrude Helene

McGraw, and Josephine Rosarii Burke. These sisters assumed their duties in the fall of 1967. The Congregation succeeded in satisfying Rome's desire for a more manageable governance structure, while preserving the unity of a centralized government.

Another modification in governance concerned the lifetime terms of superiors. Following the 1968 Chapter, as each superior completed her six-year term, she would go out of office for at least one year, before she could be considered for reappointment as a superior. This compromise ended the debate over the concept of superiors for life and promoted a greater sense of egalitarianism among sisters.

THE GENERAL CHAPTER OF 1968

According to Vatican II, renewal and adaptation of religious congregations was to take place through their General Chapters. A periodic governing assembly, the General Chapter was not only a legislative body but a vehicle to promote spiritual and apostolic vitality. Vatican II decreed that "the involvement and concern of all members" was essential for renewal and considered this total participation the basis for preparing, conducting, and implementing the General Chapter.

For the Sisters of Saint Joseph, the 1968 General Chapter became their Chapter of Renewal. Mother Divine Shepherd set in motion major changes affecting both the content of the Chapter and the composition of its delegates. One of the first steps in the process was consultation. While superiors had been consulted in summer 1966 about some changes in prayer, the first total congregational consultation began with a single item. In September 1966, sisters were asked to vote on where they wished to celebrate their jubilees: at Chestnut Hill or in a local house. The majority voted for the local mission. In October 1966, Mother Divine Shepherd established eight Committees for the 1968 Renewal Chapter: Prayer Life, Community Life, Apostolate Works, Obedience, Poverty-Chastity, Formation (novitiate), Formation (juniorate), and Administration. Since Vatican II decreed that "the religious habit, as a symbol of consecration, must be simple and modest, at once poor and becoming," the topic of habit was included in the Poverty-Chastity Committee. Sixteen superiors were appointed to chair the committees, and sisters were invited to send proposals to them. This invitation reflects a major change in the sisters' participation in a Chapter.

Rumors flourished as sisters worked feverishly to submit their proposals on time. Mother Divine Shepherd met the entire Congregation in five large group meetings at specified locations throughout the Congregation in February 1967. At each session, a discussion and question period followed a major presentation on renewal by speakers such as theologian Augustine Paul Hennessey CP. Although no records of these meetings exist, changes in leadership of the eight committees occurred on March 4, 1967, when sisters were invited to vote for 16 sister assistants (non-superiors) to help the appointed superiors with committee work.

The eight committees followed a prescribed format using the norms from Vatican II, other relevant resources, and the content of the sisters' proposals. Initially, committee reports were to be a set of interim directives for compilation in January 1968, with questionnaires for the delegates voting at the Chapter that summer.

Prominent among the resources for Chapter content was the congregational participation in the National Sisters' Survey, a seminal national study of American women religious. The Council of Major Superiors of Women (CMSW) sponsored this extensive, professional questionnaire in April 1967. Designed to ascertain sisters' beliefs about religious life and their perception of actual and anticipated changes, the survey provided each participating Congregation with a profile of its own membership as well as an aggregate national profile. The survey served as both a reliable measure of the sisters' current positions and an educative experience. Among the congregations of women religious who took the survey, the Sisters of Saint Joseph had an unusually high response rate of 89 percent (2,396 sisters), which proved beneficial and significant in pre-Chapter committee work and proposal writing

A new method of delegate selection was another critical aspect of Chapter preparation. On the advice of canonist Joseph F. Gallen SJ, Mother Divine Shepherd secured Rome's permission for a group system to replace the traditional election process based on the local houses. This method eliminated the expectation of superiors being the only delegates and enabled sisters to consider every finally professed sister in the Congregation as a potential delegate. In the new system, the sisters elected 15 delegates from each of the four groups based on rank or length of time since entrance. These groups were virtually age groups because of the predominant pattern of sisters entering directly after high school and were designed to be roughly equal in size. The sisters voted between January and March 1968. Much enthusiasm attended the new process, and speculation abounded as sisters chose delegates to enter a new Chapter experience. Sixty elected delegates joined the 11 ex officio members included because of their positions in the general Administration. Of the 60 elected, 39 were not superiors and had not previously been Chapter delegates.

1968 CHAPTER OF AFFAIRS: SESSION I

When the 71 delegates gathered at 3:30 p.m. on Friday, June 7, 1968, at the Postulate Auditorium for the convening of the Fifteenth General Chapter of the Sisters of Saint Joseph, all believed it was the beginning of a new time, but no one knew exactly what to expect. Mother Divine Shepherd, as chair ex officio of the Chapter proceedings, set the direction in her opening address. She stressed the role of the Chapter body in the renewal of the Congregation, identifying its primary goal of intensifying the spiritual life of each sister while focusing on the contemporary needs of the Congregation. She also emphasized the freedom, openness, and responsibility of each delegate.

Looking back at the event, one delegate summed up the sense of quiet revolution that was immediately triggered when Mother Divine Shepherd moved to the first item of business:

> We all sat in rank in this huge formidable looking room with our general superior and Council across the front. In the back were about ten of us who were in our early thirties. Mother Divine Shepherd had a beautiful speaking voice and impeccable English; she called the roll and I noticed a stack of blue copy books (the kind we use in universities for written exams) piled at each one's desk. After roll call, Mother . . . explained that the blue books were the work of the committees she assigned to do work for us prior to the Chapter. The first blue book on top of the pile was on "Chastity"; she was assured none of us had a problem with that. I think she expected all to nod and agree, and she would move to the next book. Suddenly about five or six hands (mine included) were raised in the back of the Chapter room. She seemed somewhat startled and began whispering to one of her councillors. We could hear a little since there was a microphone on their table; the councillor was suggesting that perhaps she ought to ask what was the problem. Mother Divine Shepherd called on Sister St. Pierre and asked what the young sisters wanted. Sister St. Pierre stood up, looked around at us, and advised Mother she did not know what we wanted, but she would like to read the blue book. We all nodded our heads; that was our concern too. Our sisters at Chestnut Hill College had educated us not to comment on anything we had not read!!!!
>
> To her undying credit, Mother Divine Shepherd then announced that the capitulars were to read the blue books and return the next day. . . . The following day the Chapter body returned. The young sisters had the books all marked up with suggestions to derogate, abrogate, change, supplement. They were not hesitant to raise their hands and ask questions, give opinions, and make suggestions. I think we took for granted that that was what a Chapter was all about. . . . Gradually, the Spirit took over. The rest of the body began to realize if they wanted their opinions included, they needed to get on their feet. This was particularly difficult for some of the senior sisters, as they had never been asked for their opinions. But they, too, were bright, alert and loved the institute. . . .

There are, of course, variations in the recollection of this event by other members of the 1968 Chapter. Some suggested that Mother Divine Shepherd was perhaps less influenced by the audacity of the "young Turks," as the younger sisters at the Chapter were dubbed, than by interventions in support of their request that came from more senior delegates.

From this momentous opening on June 7 through June 30, 1968 (*Session I*), the Chapter delegates engaged each other vigorously. Committee presentations, small group discussions, open floor debates, and personal conversations all became vehicles for educating, challenging, and stretching to renewal. As the momentum developed, more and more delegates took to the microphones. To accommodate the desire for full floor discussions, many more microphones were added, causing some delegates to exclaim that it "looked like the UN"!

Although there were dozens of separate items to be voted on, three critical topics came to dominate the proceedings. Two of these were major pre-Chapter Committee areas: prayer life and community life. The third was a seemingly small point of nomenclature. The Administration Committee proposed, among other recommendations, that superiors no longer be called "Mother." The Chapter first discussed prayer, then the Administration Committee's proposal, and then community life. While seemingly unrelated initially, it soon became clear that all three of these dominant issues revolved around questions of relationship.

Prayer Life Committee

On June 8, 1968, the second day of the 1968 Chapter, during the general discussion of the Prayer Committee's report, Sister Winifred Grelis (William Augustine) came to the microphone "urging a total re-thinking" of the concept of prayer life. She challenged the Chapter to envision a whole different way of relating to God in prayer. Rather than merely adjusting prayer practices as recommended by the committee report, she called the delegates to develop a direction for the sisters' life of prayer, centered on Mass and the Divine Office and the relationship between communal and personal prayer. Sister Winifred Grelis's presentation crystallized a dominant focus for the Chapter: the primacy of prayer life, both personal and communal, and her approach to the initial committee draft established the precedent of critiquing a committee's entire report, not merely focusing on the wording of practical recommendations.

For many, the discussions on prayer life were very painful yet also grace-filled. They struggled with how to move from the familiar life of devotional prayers to the less familiar formal prayer of the Church. Delegates endeavored to grasp the relationship between communal prayer centered on the Eucharist and Divine Office, with personal prayer rooted in mental prayer and contemplation. In contrast to an understanding of holiness as separation, they delineated the chief effect of all prayer as intensification of union with God and others.

Rethinking prayer touched the sensitive areas of personal choice and personal responsibility and raised hard questions. Why introduce this new dynamic to communal life? How much autonomy should be given? The delegates re-examined the value of ascetical practices, such as silence, penance, mortification, and self-denial.

From this struggle, key enactments emerged affirming the centrality of the prayer of the Church and a sister's personal prayer. Communal recitation of morning and evening prayer was to be complemented by each sister's hour of private personal prayer in a setting of her choosing. This time was to be safeguarded by the individual sister as well as by the community from the pressures of apostolic work, an implicit reference to the issue of "fitting prayers in" and to the struggles of the music sisters in particular. This private hour of prayer was also exclusive of Mass, Divine Office, and spiritual reading. Other options for creativity in prayer life were also provided, and devotions such as the Rosary and the Stations of the Cross were not negated but listed as choices for daily personal prayer. The Chapter also affirmed the major role of sacraments in the life of the Church, which led to granting sisters permission to attend a family member's reception of any sacrament.

Administration Committee

The Administration Committee chose Sister Ann Edward Bennis, the only committee member not a superior, to present the most controversial proposal: that all members of the Congregation use the title "Sister," reserving the title of "Mother" for the superior general only. When Sister Ann Edward, a member of the English Department of Chestnut Hill College, was asked *why* such a recommendation was being made, she replied: "Because the sisters asked for it."

This proposal was not just an exercise in semantics but symbolized a seismic shift in the membership's understanding of the vow of obedience, the role of superiors, and their own responses to authority. Many of the superiors at the Chapter rose to explain that they felt called to be mother to the sisters under their care, treating them with dignity but also with loving correction and evoking obedience without question. On the other side, there were delegates, some superiors among them, who urged the change of title in order to reflect the concept of collegiality, which was prominent in contemporary interpretations of Vatican II's vision of the Church. These delegates contended that the superior best exercised her office by being seen not as one *above* the sisters but as one *among* them, considering and honoring their input and inviting them to shared responsibility.

During the discussions, Mother Marie Emily Smith, the chair of the Administration Committee, analyzed the proposed change from another angle. She linked the recommendation with the results of the National Sisters' Survey, which showed dramatic differences between the superiors and the other sisters regarding the quality of communication and understanding of authority in local houses. Over 75 percent of the sisters saw the need for better communication while only 45 percent of the superiors supported this. In nearly all responses about aspects of communication, the superiors were 20 to 30 percent more positive than the sisters. Similar inequities surfaced regarding the authority of the local superior. On the survey, sisters reported that initiative was discouraged, personal service for a superior was expected, and superiors were distant from the sisters. Mother Marie Emily characterized the report as disgraceful, saying "we must do something about it." With a 76 percent majority, the Chapter body voted for the title change. The committee's final report captured both a hesitancy to accept and a desire to embrace the evolving concept of authority conveyed by the change of title. The local superior was to adopt the principle of subsidiarity to encourage prudent initiative and to care for the sisters' spiritual, physical, intellectual, and psychological needs. The superior maintained responsibility for final decisions, yet, she was to make them after consultation and dialogue with the sisters.

Community Life Committee

Proposals to the committees and responses to the National Sisters' Survey indicated significant support for increased personal responsibility. For example, sisters desired more variation in recreation, more free time, options for vacations, community sharing in decisions formerly left to superiors, a more varied horarium, and freedom to go out without a companion. They also wanted more freedom in the use of the telephone and the convent car and to be trusted with small amounts of money. These expressions for responsibility countered the prevailing monastic practices of seeking permissions and using rank (seniority) to determine one's status in the local house. At the same time, sisters identified certain essentials for their life in community, such as Eucharist, praying the Divine Office in common, providing meals and housekeeping for each other, talking seriously about spiritual matters, and sharing responsibilities for finances.

In laboring over the particulars—103 items under community life—and debating the underlying concepts, the delegates consistently found themselves discussing major questions. Who is truly responsible for the sisters' life together? What are the obstacles for participation? What are the essentials needed for preserving and enhancing a spirit of joy and unity with each other? From these debates the themes of personal responsibility, collegiality, and local group responsibility grounded in "faith in the integrity, sincerity, and idealism of the individual sister" gradually emerged. Local houses were given greater autonomy in formulating policies concerning the use of car and telephone and other matters of communal importance. These changes signaled the Congregation's transition from a monastic mode of life, in which "permission saved," to an ethos of personal responsibility for the quality of community life.

The Habit

Since there was no actual committee designated to study the issue of the habit, proposals came from the Poverty-Chastity and Community Life Committees. These were essentially moderate in nature and included simplifying the habit and headpiece, the possibility of having the habit made commercially, eliminating the side rosary, and permitting wristwatches. These committees also established a subcommittee to handle sisters' suggestions for further simplifications of the habit.

On June 21, 1968, Mother Divine Shepherd surprised the Chapter delegates by presenting a simplified habit, modeled by Sister Gerard Eileen Mehlman. She pointed to the results of the National Sister's Survey, which showed that 70 percent of responding Sisters of Saint Joseph opposed contemporary dress, as the rationale for her actions. Although the record of the day's proceedings offered few details of the delegates' responses, it was evident that Mother Divine Shepherd's tactical move "did not meet with general approval." Consequently, she appointed a separate committee to study the issue and communicated the desire for suggestions from all sisters.

By the end of the first session of the 1968 Chapter, the issue of the habit was still unresolved. Other than support for habits commercially made, one-third of the delegates opposed any change, while the remaining two-thirds supported consultation with the total Congregation regarding modified habits and a simple veil. The issue would be revisited in the second session of the Chapter in the fall 1968.

Confidentiality vs. Communication

While delegates were expected to keep the proceedings of daily Chapter meetings confidential, Mother Divine Shepherd and the Council needed to balance this with the essential involvement and concern of all members that was advocated by Vatican II. To accomplish this, Mother Divine Shepherd announced that a newsletter would be mailed, as often as possible, to the local houses in order to apprise the sisters of the Chapter proceedings. During the summer 1968 session, four Chapter summaries were distributed and four additional ones were mailed in spring 1969.

Another method of communication, "open windows," was a grassroots solution to the problem of confidentiality. Sisters who were not delegates simply positioned themselves near the open windows of the Chapter meeting room, so they could hear the deliberations. Pope John XXIII had opened the metaphorical windows of the Church to let the Spirit breathe where it willed, and these sisters simply took the directive literally!

Attendance of Non-Delegate Superiors

All superiors attended certain 1968 Chapter sessions. They were present on June 15 when Sister Helen Veronica McKenna, a psychologist, presented an interpretation of the results of National Sisters' Survey, and they all took home a copy of the results for their houses. All school supervisors and superiors, most of whom were principals or high school administrators, participated in the June 21 open meeting on sisters' education. The annual superiors' retreat was combined with the Chapter delegates' retreat, June 25 to July 2. During this retreat, the superiors joined the delegates on June 30 to hear Mother Divine Shepherd's directives for the follow-up to Chapter session I. On July 2, they prayed with the delegates at the Mass in preparation for the Chapter of Elections. This inclusion of all superiors, though partial, reflected the more traditional view of authority that recognized a definitive hierarchy within the Congregation.

Conclusion of Chapter of Affairs: Session I

The superior-delegate retreat should have marked the end of the 1968 Chapter of Affairs, but the work was far from complete. On June 29, delegates voted on the 383 particular items proposed by the committees. Only six of the 383 items were rejected while another 46 needed further consideration because they did not garner an absolute majority. Also, the revision of the committee reports explicating the underlying norms, rationale, and vision for renewal remained unfinished business. With the election of a new General Council scheduled for July 2, the first session of the Chapter of Affairs adjourned on June 30, 1968, but resumed the following June. The delegates then prepared for the Chapter of Election.

1968 CHAPTER OF ELECTION: SESSION 1

The atmosphere of the Chapter of Election was far more solemn than that of the Chapter of Affairs. Delegates were reminded to obey rigorously the structure set forth in the *Holy Rule*: "Sisters are gravely forbidden to speak among themselves of the election or the choice they intend to make." On the third ballot, the delegates elected Mother Alice Anita Murphy as Superior General.

This was the first time a sister without experience on the General Council had been elected Superior General. The delegates, however, reverted to the traditional pattern by choosing Mother Divine Shepherd, the outgoing Superior General, as the Assistant or First Councillor. The three remaining council seats were filled by the first-term elections of Mother Lilian Teresa McClain, Mother Francis Ines Moloney, and Sister Consuelo Maria Aherne. These five women, four of them in their first elected office, inherited the unprecedented situation of an incomplete Chapter of Affairs.

BETWEEN SESSIONS: JULY 1968 TO JUNE 1969

There was no lull between the two formal sessions of the 1968 Chapter; in fact, the momentum increased. The Congregation was engaged in education, experimentation, and consultation while the delegates forged ahead on unfinished Chapter business. Despite the demands of the apostolate and daily community life, all were participants in the process of renewal.

Superiors were the first target audience for education in the Chapter degrees. Seeing the local superiors as crucial to the success of renewal, Mother Alice Anita instituted superiors' workshops, as recommended by the Chapter. With just 10 days' notice, she convened a meeting of all superiors at Cape May Point, August 21–24, 1968. Jude Mead CP, a nationally recognized spiritual writer, spoke on the theme of community and personal dignity. The regional superiors organized panels and presentations about the exercise of authority with regard to obedience, communication, and subsidiarity. In the following spring, John McCall SJ, addressed another gathering of superiors about the need for mutual understanding, trust, closer relationships, and open communication in local communities. He later repeated this presentation for sisters preparing for first or final profession of vows and for sisters who had recently made final vows. Also that year, canonist Joseph F. Gallen SJ, spoke on obedience to separate groups of superiors, junior sisters, and sister students.

Education for renewal, however, was not restricted to superiors and the younger members. For the entire Congregation, the Administration arranged a series of presentations throughout the year on the theme of renewal as presented in the documents of Vatican II:

- October 13, 1968: Richard Murphy OMI, canonist, spoke on the meaning of renewal.
- October 26–27, 1968: Luis Dolan CP, missionary and founding member of For a Better World, presented on global themes.
- February 1–2, 1969: Sister Mary Emil Penet IHM, a leader in the Sister Formation Movement, focused on the sister as apostolic religious.

- March 1–2, 1969: Thomas Dubay SM, author and theologian, engaged themes of Church and prayer, such as ecclesial women and the relevance of contemplation for apostolic religious congregations.

The sisters seemed eager for the education and, despite a heavy snowstorm, 2,200 sisters attended Father Dubay's March weekend at Cardinal Dougherty High School in Philadelphia.

Practical education and new research on the Sisters of Saint Joseph heritage supported the implementation of the mandated changes in the sisters' prayer life. Guidelines were distributed providing the regulations for all community prayers and for understanding new distinctions. Samples of different prayer forms were also sent to local houses. As part of educating the sisters about the spirit of the founder, which was identified by Vatican II as an essential element for renewal of religious Congregations, a new translation of the original French *Constitutions* was sent to the houses on December 19, 1968. In her cover letter Mother Alice Anita identified joy, service, and unobtrusiveness as key elements of the spirit of Father Médaille.

During this interval between Chapter sessions, sisters were invited to submit further questions and suggestions. Items designated as needing further consideration were assigned as topics for weekly local community dialogues through January 1, 1969. The regional superiors received written reports from the houses by January 15 and forwarded them to the Chapter Committees later that month. Over 1,800 sisters replied "yes" or "no" to the 46 items needing more input.

Chapter delegates continued their committee work during this time, even though they continued to perform the duties connected to their full-time ministries. Between August 1968 and February 1969, the delegates met as a total body once a month. In these sessions, they broadened committee membership so that every delegate was now a committee member. An additional committee on the "Spirit of the Founder" was established, and the Poverty-Chastity Committee was divided into separate entities.

In spring 1969, the total Chapter body gathered again from Friday evening to Sunday afternoon on three consecutive weekends in March and another in late April 1969 to labor over the creation and revision of their reports in light of the feedback from their own meetings and local house reports. Chapter bulletins sent to all the houses described the breadth of the work and emotional tenor of the weekend sessions as exhausting but exhilarating.

In late autumn 1968, delegates traveled through the geographic regions of the Congregation from northern New Jersey to North Carolina, meeting with groups of sisters to continue gathering their observations. At the same time, Mother Alice Anita apprised the delegates of what was coming to her from the sisters—pain, anguish, and struggle:

Our every Sister loves her Community but [there is] much agony in the convent among our older sisters because of change in the way of life [and] with the younger sisters because the older are misinterpreting their ways. Many of us do not favor the proposals but are following the direction of the Holy Spirit to those who voted on them.

Mother Alice Anita urged all sisters to "have faith in one another and carry out the Chapter proposals in charity." In the presence of controversy, she advocated the need for compassion, understanding, and prayer.

A New Habit

In October 1968, the Habit Committee that had been appointed by Mother Divine Shepherd in the summer consulted the total congregation, via questionnaire on various components of habit modification. Using the results of a questionnaire, the earlier work of the Poverty-Chastity Committee, and that of the former General Council, the Habit Committee coordinated the development of 17 different models of the habit and various headpieces. On December 30 and 31, 1968, nearly all 2,000 sisters streamed to Mount Saint Joseph Academy for a "fashion show" featuring the 17 versions of the habit. During these two days of Christmas vacation, sisters modeled the different designs they had created, and the entire group indicated their preferences. Mother Alice Anita exhorted all to retain the dignity, the prudence, the loyalty, and the "style" of spirit for which we have been noted. She admonished the sisters to pray for the discernment of spirits so that the love of Christ might be the dominant impetus in all of our decisions. The habit design identified as number 17, a simple black mid-calf length dress with some resemblance to the current habit, received majority support. Since there was no clear majority favoring any of the headpiece designs, the issue remained unsettled and was tabled until the second session of Chapter.

CHAPTER OF AFFAIRS: SESSION II

The delegates reconvened formally for the second session of the 1968 Chapter of Affairs on June 15, 1969. For the next 10 days, they held final discussions and voted on all the proposals, retaining those tried experimentally and accepting many of the 46 that had needed further work. They also affirmed final drafts of the committee reports including norms and commentary. In a major departure from Chapter protocol, the delegates did not issue a series of degrees but formulated a document that included, unedited, the full reports of the committees. The explanations of the intentions and motivations behind the Chapter enactments could be used by the sisters for their ongoing prayer, study, dialogue, and decision making.

While there was accord with virtually all of the final committee work, there was none when the delegates returned to the habit controversy. The sisters' choice of habit design had been affirmed easily, but the headpiece posed problems. The delegates examined and wore eleven different models and engaged in soul-searching discussions. Unable to reach an agreement, the delegates voted to adapt the present headpiece rather than change to a different design. In communicating this decision, Mother Alice Anita described the delegates' concern for the general good of the Congregation and called the moment of decision one of "agonized unity."

Implementation

The delegates determined that the promulgation and implementation of their work was not solely the responsibility of Mother Alice Anita and her Council, and so a Coordinating Committee was formed to compile the committee reports into one document called *Design for Excellence.* Mother Alice Anita appointed Sisters Ann Edward and Anna Josephine Bennis, both 1968 Chapter delegates, as writers. The delegates also voted for the formation of standing committees to further the work of the Chapter. This directive to establish standing committees also specified that the time frame for the work of these groups be determined by the superior general and council.

Conclusion of the Chapter of Affairs: Session II

The final balloting of the 1968 Chapter took place on June 24, 1969. Superiors who were not delegates again joined the Chapter members for retreat with Luis Dolan CP, from June 25 to July 2. Afterward, the delegates personally reported to the sisters about the Chapter proceedings during the 46 meetings scheduled between July 8 and August 24. In committees or as panels, they met with sisters during retreat, summer school, or vacation at Cape May Point or the Motherhouse, the Novitiate, Chestnut Hill College, and Saint Joseph Villa.

On September 7, 1969, the 1968 Chapter was formally closed in an unprecedented public celebration. Every sister was invited to this event that was designed to symbolize the engagement of the whole Congregation in the call to renewal. Held at Cardinal O'Hara High School, the day's proceedings included liturgy, brunch, and a presentation by Jude Mead CP, on "Chapter and Renewal." That day, as Mother Alice Anita stood on the stage, she described being in awe of the profoundness of the sight of 2,000 dedicated Sisters of Saint Joseph who had come to celebrate this significant moment in the history of their Congregation.

CONCLUSION

Legacy of the 1968 Chapter

For the Sisters of Saint Joseph the 1968 Chapter had been their own "aggiornamento," opening the windows to the Spirit and new life. This extraordinary Chapter body encompassed elected leadership, newly appointed regional superiors, core leaders of the past, and sisters ranging in age and experience from some of the most senior to those still in their thirties. While they had divided moments, many later recalled the Chapter as not divisive overall because everyone really wanted what was right for the Congregation and did what they had to do to make the Congregation better.

Most important, the 1968 Chapter sowed the seeds of participative leadership where each sister assumed personal responsibility for the life of the Congregation. It modeled communal decision making where the leadership was willing to do what was needed, and the sisters were willing to contribute "their own piece of the truth." Embracing cautious and careful adaptation, the delegates laid a firm foundation by hammering out norms and principles for the process of renewal. Carefully discerning what should be kept, what should be abandoned, what changed, and what added, they opened the Congregation to new inspiration while preserving the vital traditions of the past. The Sisters of Saint Joseph had now embarked on the journey away from the monastic mode of religious life and toward a new identity as apostolic women religious, rooted in prayer and united through ministry with the People of God.

PUBLISHED SOURCES

Byrne, Patricia, CSJ. In the Parish and Not of It: Sisters. In *Transforming Parish Ministry* by Jay P. Dolan, R. Scot Appleby, Patricia Byrne, and Debra Campbell. New York: Crossroad Publishing, 1990.

Flannery, Austin, OP, ed. Norms for Implementing the Decree: On the Up-to-Date Renewal of Religious Life (Ecclesiae Sanctae). In *Vatican Council II: The Conciliar and Post Conciliar Documents*. Boston: Daughters of St. Paul, 1975.

Quinonez, Lora Ann, CDP, and Mary Daniel Turner, SNDdeN. *The Transformation of American Catholic Sisters*. Philadelphia: Temple University Press, 1992.

ARCHIVAL SOURCES

Mount Saint Joseph Convent, Philadelphia, Pennsylvania
Primitive documents, records of General Chapters, personal papers, focus groups, and other records.

Mount Saint Joseph Convent Chapel, Feast of Saint John Neumann 1977

Superiors General, Reverend Mother Divine Shepherd and Reverend Mother Thecla, Winston-Salem, North Carolina 1950

Saint Francis of Assisi School, Baltimore, Maryland 1960

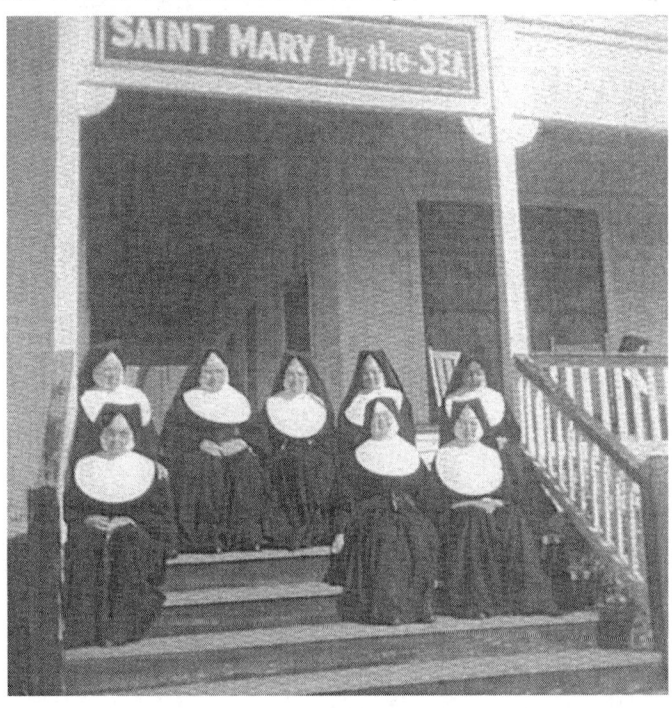

Sisters Vacation, St. Mary by-the-Sea, Cape May Point, New Jersey 1960

Reverend Mother Alice Anita 1968–1979

Local Community, Saint Leo Convent, Philadelphia, Pennsylvania 1968

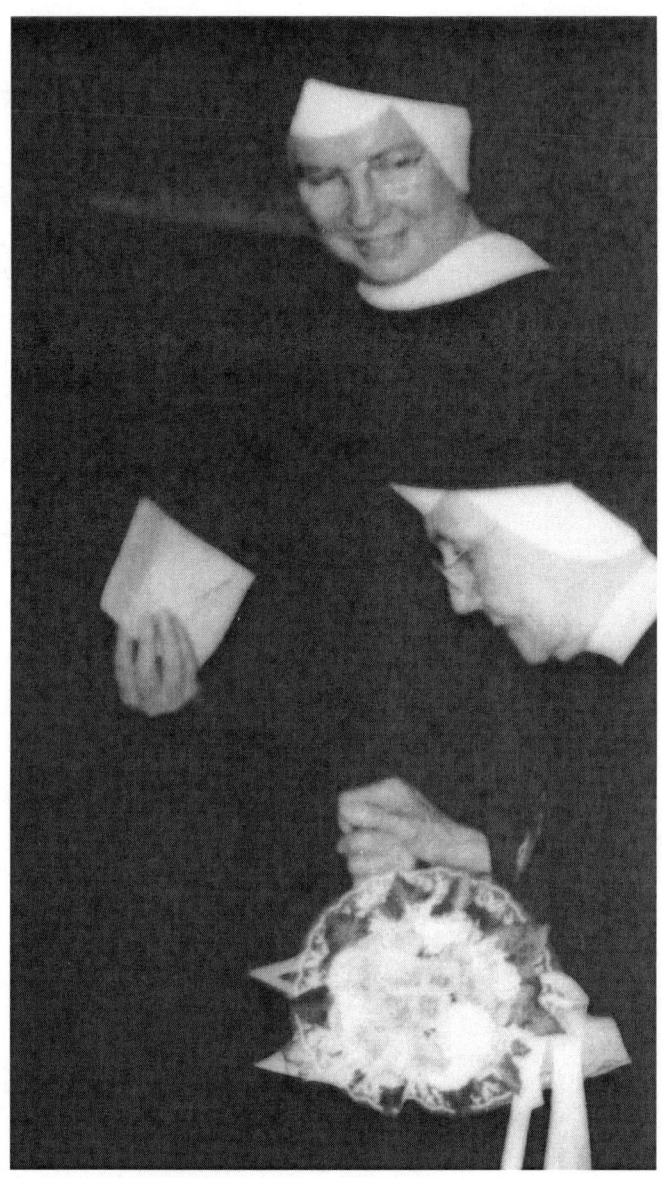

**Reverend Mother Alice Anita and Mother Marie Estelle,
Mistress of Postulants and Novices 1932–1966**

Closure of the Special Chapter of Affairs, Cardinal O'Hara High School, Springfield, Pennsylvania, Bishop Gerald V. McDevitt, celebrant 1969

Music Class, Sister Joanne Mongelli, West Philadelphia Catholic Girls High School, Philadelphia, Pennsylvania 1980

Sister Diane Marie Wolf, Archbishop Ryan School for Children with Hearing Impairment 1988

Final Vows, Reverend Mother Alice Anita, Sisters, Formation Personnel, and Archbishop William Borders 1978

Saint Joseph Villa, Flourtown, Pennsylvania

SSJ Associate Advisory Board Members, St. Mary by-the-Sea, Cape May Point, New Jersey: Donna Aceto, Sue Dufrasne, Ann Shott, Rosie Cleaver, Margot Zucarello, Sister Roberta Archibald and Judy Cute

Sister Dorothea Newell, Superior General 1979–1989

Literacy Project, Sisters Ann Beatrice Kelly and Eileen Marnien 1996

Monks of the Weston Priory Visit, Mount Saint Joseph Convent 1981

Directress of Novices, Sister Marie Gervase 1966–1976

Final Vows, Sisters, Mount Saint Joseph Convent Chapel 1979

Formation Team: Sisters Joan Reithmiller, Eleanor McNichol, and Maria McCoy 1992

General Council: Sisters Patricia Kelly, Annemarie Roche, Helen P. Clifton, Dorothy Apprich, and Sister Margaret Fleming, Superior General 1989–1994

SSJ Habits, Brother Michael O'Neill McGrath, OSFS 1997

Chapter Four

Renewing Our Mission

1969–1979

During the 1970s, the Sisters of Saint Joseph, like other American Catholics, contended with the aftermath of the great changes of the 1960s. The three presidential administrations of Richard Nixon, Gerald Ford, and Jimmy Carter seemed marred by cynicism and disillusionment. Nixon's resignation, the sense of defeat in the Vietnam War, and the severe financial crisis that resulted in the fuel shortages of the mid-1970s were contributing factors to this national malaise. At the same time, issues considered revolutionary in the 1960s such as women's rights, concern for the environment, racial justice, political accountability, and a desire for peace in a nuclear-age became mainstream in the 1970s. As the United States prepared to celebrate its 200th birthday in 1976, the country seemed poised at a significant crossroads—political, ideological, financial, and moral.

Within this cultural context, the *Documents of Vatican II* presented a radical shift in theology, liturgy, and biblical scholarship. Holiness was viewed primarily as incarnational as well as transcendent. It was founded on integration with rather than separation from the world and included social responsibility or social justice as well as a personal relationship with God, which was deemed indispensable. Also, the laity were now to be active participants rather than passive observers in parish life, which included ministry, governance structures, and liturgy. Even the definition of Church changed dramatically as the central foci became Scripture, the Eucharist as a communal celebration, and the Church as the People of God. The uniformity of the Latin Mass, devotionalism, and legalism gave way to a pluralism new to most Catholics. This was a time of energy and enthusiasm, but also a time of loss and confusion. As the Sisters of Saint Joseph attempted to comply with Vatican II's mandate for spiritual renewal, they faced the same paradoxes and challenges confronting the Church itself. The movements away from legalistic uniformity would require painful choices, and the sisters prepared for this transition by first embracing interior transformation.

SPIRITUALITY

Renewal of Prayer Life

The Congregation embarked on a 10-year process of re-evaluation of both communal and personal prayer during the 1970s. This process included workshops and lectures as well as directed and 30-day retreats often built on the *Spiritual Exercises of St. Ignatius of Loyola.* Following the dictates of Vatican II, the Congregation concentrated its efforts on the incorporation of Scripture as a vital constituent of individual prayer, replacing the previous emphasis on devotional prayers. In order to encourage the individual sisters to embrace these changes in traditional prayer modes, the Congregation offered weekend programs beginning in the fall of 1969.

For the next four years, Sacred Heart Hall in Cheltenham, Pennsylvania, became the site for more than 14 renewal weekends. Sisters were invited to attend by entrance groups, beginning with those sisters who had been in the Congregation for 40 years. These weekends offered a blend of spirituality and socialization, allowing sisters to enjoy time together, to renew relationships, and to pray. A sister who attended one of these weekends of spiritual renewal captured the essence of the experience: "We felt confirmed in the belief that life does flow in activity, in communication, but the life process itself is silent. It is prayer." By fall 1972 nearly 400 sisters had attended one of these weekends, which continued through 1973 but were eventually phased out as other renewal efforts were initiated.

In August 1968, Father Thomas Dubay SM, was the main speaker at the CMSW/LCWR Conference, and his message, coupled with his reputation for rigor, scholarship, and Catholic orthodoxy, impressed Mother Alice Anita Murphy who had recently been elected Superior General of the Congregation. She promptly engaged Father Dubay's services, and he became the director for spiritual renewal for the total Congregation from 1970 to 1973.

Father Dubay's seminars for the formation personnel, sisters in the local houses, and special groups such as those preparing for final profession had a strong academic thrust. Sisters read, studied, and discussed works such as *Leisure, the Basis of Culture* and *Happiness in Contemplation* by Joseph Peiper; *Prayer* by Hans Urs Von Balthsaar; Augustine's *Confessions;* Teresa of Avila's *Interior Castle*; John of the Cross's *Dark Night of the Soul*; Gregory of Nyssa's *From Glory to Glory*; and Sacred Scripture.

While the weekends offered renewal experiences with one's peers and Father Dubay's sessions provided more formal education, the 1968 Chapter's Standing Committee on prayer life became a major force in the integration of the Chapter directives within the personal and communal life of the sisters. Chaired by Sister Rose of Lima McDermott, the Prayer Life Committee maintained a strong commitment to the "education necessary for development of prayer life in the community." After providing the Congregation with 12 presentations in July and August, the committee consistently but sensitively nudged the sisters forward. They provided guidelines and suggestions for implementing changes in prayer, carefully worded to support choice and creativity and to minimize any threat the changes might trigger.

On March 2, 1972, the Prayer Life Committee received permission to send three sisters to a House of Prayer that summer. These attendees would then assist in the replication of this experience for the total Congregation in the summer of 1973 so that more sisters would become familiar with the concept prior to the 1974 Chapter. In launching the House of Prayer Experience (HOPE) in October 1972, Sister Winifred Grelis (William Augustine) created two models: the mini-HOPE and the summer HOPE. The mini-HOPE offered a taste of multiple prayer experiences over a three- to four-day period. The summer HOPE, lasting five to six weeks, was an immersion into a variety of prayer experiences in a communal setting. Three mini-HOPEs and one summer HOPE were slated for 1972–1973, and approximately 200 sisters of various ages requested information.

In the first year, 123 sisters participated in the program. An additional mini-Hope was scheduled for February to accommodate additional requests. A special mini-HOPE for the 25 novices included practices such as shared journaling, integrating prayer, writing, and sharing.

The summer HOPE of 1973 was conducted at four different locations, each in a different diocese, where sisters came together and formed a local community based on prayer as the primary shared value. These communities consisted of six to 10 sisters, none designated the superior, who made all decisions by consensus. Each group determined its own horarium, choice of apostolic service, daily household needs, prayer styles, and a name that would reflect the spiritual intention of the group.

The HOPE houses supported one another with weekly letters documenting each one's plans and experiences. Sister Winifred Grelis and Sister Jean Holtz (Charles Immaculate), pioneers in the program, provided education and advice to the groups. Finally, Mother Alice Anita personally visited each of the HOPEs to gain first-hand knowledge of the sisters' experiences.

Six months later, the 28 participants evaluated their experiences and identified several key elements: an appreciation of silence, a greater conviction of God's direction in one's life, the importance of prayer and mortification, and the necessity of quality communication for developing community. These sisters also agreed that the recognition of one's own talents and their use in the building of community were essential factors for fruitful communal living. The ultimate goal of the HOPE project–to experience contemplation flowing into action–had been achieved.

1974 Chapter

The 1974 Chapter reiterated the core communal prayer structure that had been outlined in 1968. One significant addition was the daily communal recitation of a new prayer reflecting our tradition as Sisters of Saint Joseph. By adding the salutation "Father" to the 1973 U.S. Federation statement, a group of delegates created what became known as the Community Prayer, which synthesized the charism of the Sisters of Saint Joseph. The Chapter also mandated that each sister could choose her own yearly retreat, compatible with her personal and spiritual needs.

SSJ Center for Spirituality

Perhaps one of the most innovative mandates of the 1974 Chapter was the establishment of a spiritual center. Within six months after the close of the 1974 Chapter, Sister Alice Anita announced the establishment of the SSJ Center for Spirituality designed to be a "controlled experiment." Sister Winifred Grelis was appointed the first director and her previous experience with the HOPE initiative, as well as her 1968 Chapter work on the Prayer Life Committee, seemed to support this choice. The other three sisters who comprised the staff were Sisters Dorothea Newell (Ignatius Loyola), Elizabeth O'Hara (James Augustine), and Ann Marks (Rose Genevieve). Sister Dorothea had been on the novitiate staff in the mid-1960s and served on the 1968 Chapter Formation Committee. Sister Elizabeth, a member of the 1968 Chapter Prayer Committee, had been recommended by the Congregation-at-large for the Sisters of Saint Joseph renewal team. Sister Ann, who had entered in 1963, was the youngest member of the staff.

From its inception, the Center attempted to weave itself into the life of the Congregation, and the diverse activities offered during the first year reflected its mission and style. The first program, which took place on September 28, 1975, was Come and See. It was based on the apostles' first encounter with Jesus as recorded in John's Gospel. The staff also offered programs at Saint Joseph Villa and conducted regular sharing times with the sister residents. In addition the Center staff collaborated with Sister Kathleen Kean (Helen Therese), Coordinator of Congregational Renewal. The staff directed a retreat for the tertians, presented a retreat day for the renovants, and hosted a day of prayer for Sisters of Saint Joseph on exclaustration or leave of absence. In August 1976, two staff members led a directed retreat for Sisters of Saint

Joseph at Weston Priory, Vermont. In fall 1977, the Center opened its retreats to other women religious and lay women.

During the late 1970s, the Center staff provided education on topics such as quiet prayer days, centering prayer, personal discernment, charismatic renewal, and the Liturgy of Hours. They engaged regional and national speakers, such as Ms. Carla de Sola, founder of New York City's Omega Liturgical Dance Company; Bernard P. Prusak, author and theologian; and George Aschenbrenner SJ, Jesuit novice master at Wernersville, Pennsylvania. The staff also continued to organize the summer HOPEs through 1977.

While diverse in its offerings, the Center rooted its efforts in Ignatian spirituality and sought support from the staff at the Jesuit Center of Spiritual Growth, Wernersville, Pennsylvania. Initially, the Center's weekend and summer retreats were available only at Chestnut Hill or in designated Sisters of Saint Joseph houses. In 1977 and 1978, sisters had choices for weekends of guided or directed prayer at various geographic locations.

Evaluations of the Center's work by participants in the programs revealed a high level of approbation and appreciation for their efforts. The data also revealed that the sisters liked having one of their own as a director, something their Jesuit advisors had not observed in other congregations. Individually, sisters described the impact of the Center's programs in a variety of ways. One wrote that "the Center's thrust of apostolic spirituality has helped me in integrating prayer with apostolic work." Another "felt confident enough to make a directed retreat." Having the Center as an official work of the Congregation validated the importance of a sister's prayer life, the value of spiritual direction, and an openness to multiple approaches to one's prayer life with primary emphasis on Scripture. Although some sisters questioned the wisdom of withdrawing much-needed personnel from the school ministry, the majority recognized the Center's integral role in the ongoing education and spiritual development of the sisters.

Innovations in Retreats and Renovation

In the early 1970s, the structure of retreat offerings at Cape May Point was in flux since sisters felt the need for different types of retreats to accommodate their individual styles of prayer. Consequently, retreats became hybrid forms of education for renewal, with a monastic schedule of rising bell, set times for recitation of the Divine Office, conferences, Mass, and free time. Retreat masters like Luis Dolan CP, Jude Mead CP, Jordan Auman OP, Augustine Hennessy CP, Rev. Joseph Galante, and Thomas Dubay SM produced opportunities for dialogue about building community. As a result, Cape May became too noisy for many sisters. In 1973, Mother Alice Anita Murphy addressed the issue. While she recognized the value of discussion, she determined that Cape May was to be strictly contemplative with talk permitted only at suppertime.

In the early 1970s, Renovation, a summer renewal program, shifted from a regimented novitiate style format to a more varied experiences, focusing on topics pertinent to renewal efforts in the Congregation. In 1972, renovants engaged in a variation of the national Passionist Institute'72, with input on the evolving theology of religious life and on personality development. Although these changes in the renovation program pleased many participants, other sisters registered dissatisfaction with the logistics of housing and the lack of attention to the individual's needs. Others cited disappointment with a perceived focus on party reunion to the detriment of spiritual renewal. Attentive to these concerns, Sister Marie Ellen Hegarty, the Councillor for Ongoing Formation, created new options for Renovation, redefining it as a time dedicated to deepening the sister's personal relationship with Christ and increasing her knowledge of the charism of the Sisters of Saint Joseph. Instead of limiting renovation to a particular party, any sister finally professed for five to 15 years could apply for participation in the program. Other options for this period of renovation were also available, including a HOPE, a 30-day retreat, or a three-week program at Brisson Seminary, Allentown, Pennsylvania. The response to these adaptations was positive, and by the end of the 1970s renovation seemed to be an integral part of the Congregation's spiritual renewal.

Creativity in Communal Prayer

During the 1970s the Sisters of Saint Joseph also endeavored to be more creative in their approaches to communal prayer. In 1977, Sister Kathleen Kean, Coordinator of Congregational Renewal, collaborated with over 200 hundred sisters in the creation of the local community development manual, which incorporated numerous samples of adaptations of the liturgy of the hours designed to celebrate feast days, birthdays, and other special occasions.

Another form of communal prayer endorsed by the 1974 Chapter was shared prayer or faith sharing. While sisters often used these terms interchangeably, there were some differences.

Shared prayer was based on a chosen Scripture passage, and participants offered their insights on this; faith sharing encompassed a much broader range of topics. Each form, though, had the same goal: personal spiritual enrichment and a deepened sense of community.

The Vows: Renewal According to Vatican II

The Vatican II decree, *Lumen Gentium,* dealt specifically with the role of religious congregations within the Church and clarified the position that religious life was not a midlevel state between those of the clerical and the lay; instead it emphasized that religious vows flowed from the baptismal commitment, enhanced genuine human development, and enabled religious to serve more effectively as means to and instruments of love. *Perfectae Caritatis* explained that sisters should "follow Christ, who virginal and poor, redeemed and sanctified men by obedience unto death." This definition gave primacy of place to the vow of chastity instead of obedience, and it paved the way for religious congregations and the Church to develop concrete ways to more closely model their lives on the image of Christ defined in the decree.

Despite the obvious spiritual intent of *Perfectae Caritatis*'s definition of vowed life, the Sisters of Saint Joseph were still using very specific guidelines that dictated exactly how relational a sister's interpretation of chastity could be. For example, sisters could now attend the religious celebration of the sacrament of matrimony but not the social reception. Professed sisters were permitted to visit relatives or friends four times a year and extend the summer visit to a week. However, some sisters opted for a more individualized interpretation of the rules, and a survey of local houses conducted in 1972 showed both responsibility and autonomy were desired. The mobility that accompanied the permission to drive in 1965, coupled with changing perceptions of relationships, had engendered a new phenomenon: convents emptying out on the weekends as sisters spent time with family, friends, and parishioners. Data from the 1973 CARA Survey reinforced the sisters' desire for greater personal responsibility and autonomy in relationships. In addition to the 60 percent who advocated for increased autonomy, 74 percent expressed a desire for education in human, specifically women's, sexuality. Clearly, education in the area of psychosexual development needed to be provided to help the large number of sisters (84 percent) who acknowledged a lack of understanding of this topic so that they could cope with the changing perceptions inherent in a relational understanding of the vow of chastity.

After the 1974 Chapter, immediate action for education was undertaken by Sister Marie Ellen, the Councillor for Ongoing Formation, and the committees on chastity and mental health. Workshops in the areas of biology, psychology, and spirituality were made available to all from September 1975 through February 1976. At the 1977 Interim Assembly, both the Chastity and Mental Health Committees reported affirmative feedback on the workshops. Future education would address a variety of topics such as the stages of life development and interpersonal relationships. The committees' recommendations also focused on education to assist local communities about being more open to psychological help, both proactive and remedial, in order to enhance the quality of communal living.

A byproduct of the new understanding of the vow of chastity was the return to the use of a sister's baptismal name. Theologically, baptism is the source of one's Christian identity, and the vocation to religious life is an outgrowth of this initial commitment. Hence, the use of one's baptismal name reinforces the primary Christian vocation and promotes greater unity among all the People of God. By June 1976, almost 800 sisters (a third of the Congregation) had returned to their baptismal names, and in subsequent years more sisters opted for the change. Young women entering the Congregation at this time were strongly encouraged to retain their baptismal names rather than adopt religious names when they became novices.

The 1974 Chapter legitimized communal expressions of obedience where both the superior and the sisters were equally responsible to attend to the Holy Spirit and to discern God's will; participation in dialogue, shared decision making, subsidiarity, and communal discernment were the proposed means of attaining these goals. In addition, local community development processes presented sisters with skills useful in both dialogue and consultation. However, the 1977 Interim Assembly survey report on obedience revealed mixed reactions to the effectiveness of these initiatives. Questions arose about accountability. Approximately 70 percent of the sisters reported attempting to participate in shared decision making, but with limited success. Others found the process difficult but fruitful, while another group reported no success at all.

Another aspect of apostolic religious life integrally related to the vow of obedience was the process of personnel assignments, traditionally called *changes* by most Sisters of Saint Joseph. In 1972, Superior General Mother Alice Anita offered the sisters an opportunity to participate in a limited way in this process. However, her invitation to express concern only applied to those who had been changed and did not involve consultation prior to the reassignment. The 1974 Chapter cautiously took the next step by mandating that the regional superiors consider consulting with a sister before a final decision was made. While some regional superiors had already done this, it would now be incumbent upon them to consult with a sister before reassigning her. Unfortunately this consultation process was not formalized and varied with the regional superior and sister involved.

Although the 1979 Chapter tried to clarify the meaning of authority, obedience, and responsibility, it offered no new direction or mandates concerning these issues. Instead, the Chapter body dealt mainly with roles and structures in governance intended to organize and support the interaction of authority and obedience, consequently leaving the Congregation with essentially the same guidelines previously determined by the mandates of the 1968 and 1974 Chapters.

Although *Perfectae Caritatis* reiterated the traditional understanding of the vow of poverty, albeit with an emphasis on communal responsibility, it was Pope Paul VI who in 1971 identified the vow of poverty with a commitment to social justice:

> How then will the cry of the poor find an echo in your lives? That cry must, first of all, bar you from whatever would be a compromise with any form of social injustice. It obliges you also to awaken consciences to the drama of misery and to the demand of social justice made by the Gospel and the Church. . . . It is necessary that in your daily lives you should give proof, even externally, of authentic poverty.

Consequently, the Sisters of Saint Joseph began to view the practice of poverty as inextricably linked to issues of communal responsibility, social justice, and simplicity of life.

The Sisters of Saint Joseph did not overtly seek out the movements of social justice, antipoverty, or civil rights during the late 1960s and early 1970s; but these movements enveloped nearly one-third of the 1,900 Sisters of Saint Joseph who taught in parish schools. During these years, over 600 sisters staffed 30 inner-city schools predominantly in Philadelphia, Newark, Baltimore, Washington, Bethlehem, Camden, and Harrisburg, enabling them to work with the African American and Hispanic populations who were often the victims of poverty and injustice.

Some sisters recalled that in these inner-city convents, books on racism became part of their spiritual reading and dinner tables buzzed with conversations about how to address the challenges of protests and even riots. Other sisters volunteered in antipoverty programs funded by the government in conjunction with agencies and offices in the various dioceses. Some did home visitation in urban or rural settings or served migrant workers, developing apostolic teams for Spanish-speaking people. Many sisters participated in inner-city play street programs and worked with local adult leaders.

Growing numbers of Sisters of Saint Joseph now saw firsthand the faces of the materially poor and encountered the effects of poverty, racism, and injustice. During the Poor People Campaign in the summer of 1968, Sister Helen Anthony Mayhew and four other sisters in Washington, DC, experienced the simplicity of the other participants amid the appalling conditions of Resurrection City, the shantytown of 3,000 people on the National Mall. When they offered to help at the daycare center, they met Coretta Scott King who thanked them and talked about her husband and children and also about the crucial work that teachers must do. They then witnessed the Solidarity March of 50,000 on June 19, which was "marked with dignity and a most striking quiet," as Sister Helen Anthony observed, where thousands of people had but one purpose—to show that they wanted help for the poor of whatever kind. It was an experience that these sisters would not forget.

The Results of Chapters 1974 and 1979

During the 1974 Chapter, members of the Poverty Committee urged the Congregation to take some small steps toward real poverty. They advocated adoption of a moderate- to low-income lifestyle as the communal standard. The committee further advocated a greater emphasis on an external expression of simplicity of life that was fundamental to living the vow of poverty. The Chapter also reiterated the importance of communally creating the local house budget in order to promote greater accountability for the monies and to model a moderate- to low-income household.

In tandem with the emphasis on simplicity of life, the Chapter body promoted greater sensitivity to issues of social justice. In February 1975, the Social Action Committee was formed under the leadership of Sister Consuelo Maria Aherne. Inspired by her vision, the committee of 29 members defined its purpose as "the heightening of social consciousness, underscored by an awareness of those issues most in need of social action." They learned from experts about caring for the elderly and the homeless and supporting groups such as the United Farm Workers (UFW). They assisted with mailings for the UFW and planned a hunger walk organized by Communities Responding to Overcome Poverty (CROP). Some committee members taught English as a second language to youth and adult groups; others taught prisoners and/or visited nursing homes. A few participated in Network, the Catholic lobbying organization in Washington, DC.

At the local level, the Social Action Committee focused on creating awareness through educational materials and suggestions for dialogue. In 1976, it invited local communities to hold a series of dinner dialogues about peace and justice issues. They collated the salient points of these conversations and incorporated them into the U.S. Federation of the Sisters of Saint Joseph's statement to the US Bishops during their national Bicentennial Conference. Beginning in 1976, the Social Action Committee also published biannually the minutes of their meetings in a *Social Action Newsletter* for each house. This was used as a vehicle for accountability and education for the sisters. In conjunction with education on social justice, the Interim Assembly recommended that the March 1978 CCR (Centers for Corporate Reflection) event focus on poverty/simplicity of life. Both the preparation in local communities and the CCR event itself offered further education on living a simple lifestyle. The Social Action Committee produced for the 1979 Chapter a study entitled *Poverty and Simplicity: A Holistic Approach*, written by Sister J. Roberta Rivello. While these measures supported the desire to embrace a simple lifestyle, it did not result in the regular practice of it. Consequently, poverty and simplicity of life became dominant themes of the 1979 Chapter.

The 1979 Chapter designated specific practices for each sister, local communities, and the congregational Administration. An experimental personal budget ($20–$25 monthly), intended to give each sister the experience of "the temporal realities of limits and choices" for a simple lifestyle, was mandated. This personal budget was used for items (soap, book, or gift) of the individual sister's choosing. The Chapter also voted to require each sister's participation in formulating the local house budget. In addition, the General Council was enjoined to "direct the course of the institute toward a lived-out stance of social justice" and established two new entities that would design, direct, and effect this implementation: the Financial Advisory Board (FAB) and the SSJ Commission for Justice.

The Habit

Although often considered a separate issue, the modification of the traditional religious garb was also related to the concept of simplicity of life and sometimes became a barometer of a Congregation's or an individual's "political affiliations." Retaining a traditional habit symbolized conservatism, while wearing secular clothing meant liberalism. These labels often led to division among congregations and tensions among individuals within a congregation.

Changes in the Sisters of Saint Joseph Habit

On August 31, 1969, the Sisters of Saint Joseph adopted the second habit change since Vatican II and the first that permitted an option. Based on the consultation and deliberation during the 1968 Chapter, the modified habit consisted of a dress and headpiece with veil. While wearing the adapted headpiece was mandated for all, sisters could opt for the new dress or retain the 1966 habit. Despite this modest step away from complete uniformity, the majority of the sisters opted for the proposed changes, evincing their basic desire for unity.

The wearing of headpiece and veil continued to be controversial, though, and in November 1972, the Poverty Committee requested a discussion on the subject of experimentation with the headpiece, including the choice of not wearing it in the convent. Mother Alice Anita responded quickly and decisively to this request by declaring that the headpiece was to be worn at all times. There would be no further discussion until the results of the 1973 Center for Applied Research in the Apostolate (CARA) Survey had been tabulated.

The CARA Survey captured the diversity of views and the strong feelings among the sisters about the habit. One-third wanted no change at all; one-third advocated some change; and one-third preferred very slight change. Those calling for change were not requesting the elimination of the habit and veil but modifications of the headpiece and options regarding when to wear it. The summary of the CARA Survey succinctly delineated the Sisters of Saint Joseph's dilemma: "It will come as no surprise that the question of the habit is a point of controversy. Feelings are strong in this regard, and it will probably be some time before a universally satisfactory solution is reached."

Mother Alice Anita and the Council wanted to resolve the issue of the headpiece before the opening of the 1974 Chapter. Eight veil styles that showed the hair were created and presented to the sisters. In spring 1974 sisters tried on the eight different headpieces and 2,268 sisters completed a questionnaire about these styles. The results showed that while 614 sisters wished to retain the traditional headpiece, the other 1,654 preferred styles with a simple black veil, with or without a white headband. On June 18, 1974, Chapter delegates affirmed the option for the new headpiece, which consisted of a simple headpiece with short black veil. However, instead of mandating a universal day for changing the headpiece, sisters could choose to retain the traditional veil or opt for the new version any time after August 7, 1974. Attentive to the potential impact of this change on both clergy and laity, Mother Alice Anita sent an official notification to all pastors explaining the change.

Ultimately, the 1974 Chapter passed enactments that reflected the complexity of the issue of the habit. It also reaffirmed the habit as a sign of religious consecration and mandated that any sister desiring to wear alterative clothing must request permission from the superior general. Finally, the Chapter also provided a two-year period of investigation into the possibilities of an even simpler style of habit, a summer habit, and appropriative alternatives to the habit.

Beginning in May 1975, a newly formed committee called the Committee for the Future conducted two congregational consultations about the summer habit, asked volunteers to experiment with samples, and offered three styles in four colors: solid blue, grey pinfeather, blue pinfeather, and beige. Reaction to these samples was largely negative, so Sister Alice Anita in consultation with the Council and regional superiors, chose a modification of the current black habit in a cream color. Sisters were permitted to wear the summer habit after Easter 1977.

Developing guidelines for religiously appropriate alternatives to the habit actually took nearly three years. Despite the urging of the regional superiors, Sister Alice Anita hesitated to act, remaining committed to the symbolism and witness value of the habit. Finally, in February 1977, guidelines were issued. Sisters could wear practical, inexpensive, simple, modest attire for leisure activities. The veil was to be worn in public and in the convent at times of communal prayer, meals, and formal occasions. In other circumstances such as vacation, sisters were expected to exercise good judgment; however, they were to wear the habit and veil at liturgical functions, in restaurants, and theaters, even when on vacation. Instead of clarity, these guidelines generated further ambiguity.

The 1979 pre-Chapter Survey revealed that 70 percent of the sisters valued the habit as an essential sign of their consecration and as a witness to simplicity of life. On the question of the veil, however, 46 percent felt that wearing it should be optional while 51 percent felt that it should be required. More than 50 percent of the sisters wanted to make their own choices about wearing the habit on occasions other than religious and professional. Because of these results, divisions among the sisters regarding the habit became apparent. The 1979 Chapter's committee on poverty and simplicity of life expressed concern regarding "judgmentalism" in the interpretation of habit guidelines.

Ultimately the 1979 Chapter passed four enactments regarding the habit. First, sisters would wear the habit and veil in apostolic ministry and on formal occasions. Second, responsible dialogue on issues of accountability, sensitivity to the motives and choices of others, and the effects of sisters' choices were to be ongoing. Third, in light of social justice and the call to a simple lifestyle, sisters were to adopt a nonconsumerist attitude, avoiding an accumulation of clothing. Fourth, a committee was to be formed to study options for a simpler, more modern habit.

Formation: The Early 1970s

On January 6, 1969, between Sessions I and II of the 1968 Chapter, *Renovationis Causam*, a seminal Vatican II document about the renewal of formation programs, was issued. Religious congregations were given general guidance rather than specific legislation about formation and supported experimentation. The document affirmed the need to adapt formation to the experience of younger generations and the demands of the apostolate. It counseled congregations to do this while remaining faithful to their own nature and special aim.

Renovationis Causam redefined the formation stages placing emphasis on flexibility. The pre-entrance phase was to be a time of spiritual and psychological adjustment rather than a radical severing from the world. The novitiate marked the *actual* entrance into religious life. For apostolic institutions, the novitiate prepared novices for a cohesive life that closely linked contemplation *and* apostolic activity. Temporary profession focused on achieving the spiritual maturity necessary for a lifetime commitment rather than completing a term of years as a junior member. For all these phases, *Renovationis Causam* advocated adapting to the person's individual pace of development rather than following a set time frame for proceeding to the next level.

In order to implement the changes in formation suggested by Vatican II, the Sisters of Saint Joseph initiated special training and education for members of the formation staff. In 1969–1970, Sisters Demetria Cleary and Winifred Grelis were sent to Rome to study formation. On their return, Sister

Demetria became Directress of Postulants (1970–1978) and Sister Winifred Grelis joined the novitiate staff (1970–1975). In 1972–1973, Sisters Anna Louise Schuck and Margaret Mary O'Connell (Ellen Patrick) studied in Rome at pontifical theological centers such as Regina Mundi, the Angelicum, and the Gregorianum. Sister Anna Louise then served as Directress of Pre-Entrance/Candidates and Vocations (1973–1980), while Sister Margaret Mary O'Connell was Directress of Juniors (1973–1982).

Four other sisters attended the Institute of Man at Duquesne University in Pittsburgh, Pennsylvania, a three-year graduate program culminating in a major in religion and personality with a concentration in personal and spiritual formation. Sister Mary Carboy (Joan Michael) studied there (1972–1975) before becoming Directress of Novices (1976–1982). Sisters Lillian Needham (Anne Michelle), Directress of Postulants (1978–1984) and Marcella Springer (Frederick Mary), Directress of Juniors (1977–1985) also completed this program.

This commitment to educating formation personnel signified a choice to personalize and individualize the approach to formation. Even as the number of applicants declined and the number of sisters available for full-time ministry slowly decreased, the leadership opted to have more trained sisters available for formation work, thus setting a precedent for future decisions about formation programs.

During the early 1970s, the numbers of applicants to the Congregation were consistently smaller, averaging about 30 women a year, but approximately 24 percent of these had taken some college courses or completed a bachelor's degree. Products of the post-Vatican II Church, these women were more conversant with the Bible and accustomed to prayer services, Bible vigils, folk Masses, and dialogue. They had also been part of the social and political revolution of the late 1960s and early 1970s and had been exposed to the issues of women's rights, the civil rights movement, and the Vietnam War protests. In addition they were also usually better informed about their own sexuality and issues related to psychosexual development.

In keeping with these changes in the profiles of applicants, the formation program emphasized education in theology and spirituality and exposed the young women to the rudiments of contemplative and communal prayer based on Scripture. The program also acknowledged the importance of the family in nurturing a religious vocation by permitting home visits during the postulancy and encouraging the inclusion of the family in the important phases of the postulant's new life.

In the early 1970s, adaptations in the novitiate program were made only in the first or canonical year, and these pertained to development in the spiritual life. Monthly spirituality conferences tapped into the best national resources for education in contemporary theology and spirituality. Intercongregational sharing also occurred. Connections with family and friends were maintained during the canonical year, albeit in a more limited way than during postulancy. Besides planned home visits at Christmas, individual novices could receive permission to attend special family celebrations. To gain apostolic experience, novices sometimes helped with CCD classes in nearby parishes. Occasionally, they took field trips to an art museum, the zoo, and music venues and had access to some of the resources and special lectures at Chestnut Hill College. All these opportunities enhanced the spiritual and personal growth of the individual and supported the ideas and goals expressed in *Renovationis Causam*.

In addition to the changes in formation programs for postulancy and novitiate, there were alterations and adaptations to the ongoing education of temporary professed. Each year, Mother Alice Anita initiated programs for these sisters consonant with the congregational focus on interior renewal. Each party had one or two designated weekends for renewal that began Saturday afternoon following college classes and lasted until late Sunday afternoon. The speakers were frequently priests like Father Thomas Dubay SM, who provided the input for the larger Congregation. Changes were also made in the location and structure of the junior retreat in order to provide a more silent atmosphere. In 1971, the retreat was held at Chestnut Hill College and from 1971 to 1974 at the Malvern Retreat Center.

Although part of the juniorate, the sisters who were in the final year of temporary profession (tertians) had a special period of preparation for final profession that included a separate retreat from that of the other juniors. In the early 1970s this program was held at McSherrystown, Pennsylvania, and was designed by the directress of tertians. In 1972, for example, Mother Alice Anita engaged the Passionists to conduct the program, which seemed to be well received.

Formation: Mid- to Late 1970s

During this period, the ideals of *Renovationis Causam* continued to influence the Congregation's vocation and formation programs. The 1974 Chapter mandated a formal vocation apostolate with a directress who would coordinate this with a pre-entrance program. Sister Anna Louise was named to fill this position and her goal was to involve the total Congregation in this project. She solicited the help of a contact person in each local house who would promote awareness of the new vocation ministry and network with her to conduct days of prayer in various geographic areas. The next innovation was the establishment of a volunteer vocation team (in September 1975) that consisted of about 20 sisters who met monthly within their own geographic region to promote awareness and assist with weekend programs for interested young women. In 1975–1976, retreats for women 16 years of age and older were held in local convents.

Special programs were also conducted at the Motherhouse, including the Third Sunday Program for high school girls and older that included Mass, brunch, prayer, and social interaction with the postulants and novices. In addition to these efforts, Sister Anna Louise's outreach included communication with vocation personnel in other dioceses and groups like the Serra Club and Newman Centers on college campuses. In her report to the 1977 Interim Assembly, Sister Anna Louise cited positive results during the three years of the program. Not only was the total Congregation more aware of the importance of vocation work, but Sister Anna Louise claimed that 18 young women who had participated in the weekend retreats were now part of the initial formation program of the Sisters of Saint Joseph or that of another religious congregation.

Congregational formation now consisted of four stages: pre-entrance, postulancy, novitiate (two years), and temporary profession (juniorate). The pre-entrance program focused primarily on discernment. Candidates met in small groups and individually with Sister Anna Louise each month. Since social action was becoming a major focus of the Congregation, candidates were encouraged to participate in service programs like those at Mercy Hospice or St. John's Hospice.

While many participants valued the pre-entrance experience, others found the time and travel pressures difficult. The personal challenges of self-reflection and the obstacles posed by participating in groups not of one's choosing were also cited as problematic. However, the overall response to the initiative was favorable.

While the pre-entrance program developed, the postulancy period was being reshaped as a more gradual spiritual and psychological adjustment of the candidate in a setting that evoked a deeper level of maturity. From 1974 to 1979, Sisters Demetria and Lillian Needham designed a program that combined formation classes, college or professional apostolic work, social action, and immersion in community life. Their professional work varied according to their pre-entrance backgrounds; for example, five postulants who had completed college taught at Sisters of Saint Joseph academies and parish elementary schools, while one postulant, an x-ray technician, gave part-time service at the Saint Joseph Villa. In 1977, the postulants formed their own band—"The Holy Smokes"—and entertained at a nearby nursing care facility. They even made guest appearances at jubilees and congregational events.

Despite the innovations, the need for a more distinct demarcation between postulancy and novitiate was necessary. One obstacle was the location of both postulancy and novitiate at the Motherhouse and the limitations this placed on community life experiences and apostolic involvement. In her report to the 1977 Interim Assembly, Sister Demetria (Directress of Postulants) suggested moving the postulate out of the Motherhouse, and in 1979

Sister Lillian Needham, Sister Demetria's successor, experimented with the location of the Postulate by dispersing the postulants into various local communities for six weeks; the postulants commuted to Chestnut Hill College for classes twice weekly and served as teaching assistants or student teachers the other three days. They shared fully in the communal life of the sisters in the local house, taking their turns cooking, driving, shopping, and doing household chores. On two weekends, they returned to the Motherhouse to evaluate the experience. The results of this experiment eventually led to the decision to move the postulate out of the Motherhouse in the early 1980s.

Just as it was during postulancy, the discernment process was the primary focus of the canonical year of the novitiate. Under the direction of Sister Mary Carboy, Directress of Novices, the young sisters integrated this process into every facet of their daily lives, including class work, social action, and decision making. They studied theology; spirituality and self-knowledge; and obstacles and aids to spiritual development. They learned essential practices in prayer and reflection, coupled with emerging forms and styles of prayer like hermit day or Poustinia Day. The novices occasionally joined other Sisters of Saint Joseph in programs sponsored by the SSJ Center for Spirituality.

While the new patterns of the canonical year of the novitiate seemed suitable to the continuing transformation from traditional monastic modes of spiritual life, the mission year (second year) of novitiate was harder to redefine and reshape. Since the Congregation continued to assume responsibility for staffing more schools, despite diminishing numbers, mission novices were desperately needed as teachers. Although the women entering the Congregation might have had more post-secondary education than applicants from preceding decades, less than one-fourth of each party of novices had any classroom teaching experience. In September 1976, the congregational leadership proposed a new model: 20 mission novices would be interns and gain opportunity for teacher training on the mission. During the first semester the novice was guided by a skilled junior professed sister-teacher. In January 1977, the novice then became the full-time teacher and the junior sister became a full-time student at the College so that she could complete her degree more quickly.

In 1977, even though all 12 novices had had classroom experiences prior to entrance, each was given a strong grade partner. In 1978, Sister Mary Scanlon (James Anthony) was assigned to assist novices and juniors in the teaching apostolate, so during the year she visited the novices in their schools and provided educational assistance. This arrangement, however, did not effect a definitive solution. Finally, in spring 1979, a formal novice internship was approved and plans were made to implement the program in the fall. This model for the second year of the novitiate seemed closest to the 1974 Chapter's vision of it as an initiation into the works of the community.

During the second half of the 1970s, the juniorate program became more consistent and comprehensive. The junior sisters now shared in all aspects of community life without a separate set of permissions or rules; however, they received the special support, guidance, and direction needed to help them internalize their vocations as Sisters of Saint Joseph.

Every four to six weeks, each junior sister met for guidance with her directress. A yearly program of instruction on the vows, reflection, and prayer was established in 1975, and a Summer of Spirituality was instituted for third-year juniors. This month-long program, which included retreat, was held in McSherrystown and provided the sisters with an opportunity for reflection and self-assessment.

Although many of the changes effected in the formation program during the 1970s seemed beneficial, ambivalence regarding their efficacy remained. The number of applicants to the Congregation was clearly declining, yet there seemed to be a disproportionate number of sisters involved in the formation process. These smaller numbers also led to greater individuation, and some veterans expressed concerns that novices had less of a traditional type of novitiate than those who had entered prior to 1970 had. Other sisters applauded the innovations and thought the more personalized approach to formation would help postulants and novices to develop a strong prayer life and a deeper understanding of their vocations. The pre-Chapter Survey of 1979 corroborated these perceptions with data that showed 50 percent of the membership endorsing changes in the formation programs and about 25 percent dissatisfied with the current system, while the other 25 percent were unsure. These results paved the way for further proposals from the Chapter concerning both formation and membership.

GOVERNANCE

Membership

During the late 1960s and the early 1970s, many congregations of women religious experienced diminishing numbers of applicants and increasing numbers of departures. In just two years—1965 to 1967—the number of losses in personnel went from 1,562 to 2,015 nationally, and in 1970 the number had more than doubled to 4,337. The impact of these diminished numbers was mitigated by the fact that the Congregation was still large and nearly half (44 percent) of the membership was under the age of 45. The fact that the Congregation continued to accept responsibility for the staffing of new schools contributed to the illusion that the Sisters of Saint Joseph had sufficient numbers to meet all their obligations in the teaching apostolate.

In 1976, the leadership issued a comprehensive report on the status of membership during the period from 1966 to 1975. The study also included a

10-year projection for the future. In 1973, the Congregation lost 62 sisters, 50 percent through death and 50 percent through departure. While the information contained in the report was clearly and accurately presented, the reality was difficult to digest. At the same time, the Congregation was engaged in a formal process to determine an apostolic direction for the immediate future, and this data would be a crucial part of any decision.

Congregational Leadership

The renewal of the Congregation in the decade that followed Vatican II was conducted under the leadership and guidance of Mother Alice Anita, ninth Superior General of the Sisters of Saint Joseph of Philadelphia. Her primary focus was on internal renewal, and she supported extensive educational programs aimed at the total membership, not only those in formation. Mother Alice Anita was comfortable being in the public eye and used her many talents and intellectual gifts to forge relationships between the Sisters of Saint Joseph and other congregations of women religious in the United States. She was an ecclesial woman, dedicated and loyal to the Church and its leaders, but also visionary in her goals for the Congregation. She was committed to the concept of dialogue and continually promoted its use at the local level. Mother Alice Anita eschewed the use of political labels like "conservative," or "moderate progressives"; instead, she believed that the Sisters of Saint Joseph were "one community" where love for one another was essential.

Portrait of Mother Alice Anita Murphy

From her youth, Mother Alice Anita Murphy, formerly Veronica Murphy, exuded much zeal and zest for God's work in her life and that of the Congregation. She described her own calling as the moment when "The Lord stepped in at a dance." She entered the Sisters of Saint Joseph in 1926 from St. Bridget's Parish in Philadelphia, Pennsylvania. Degreed in English, she taught at Saint Mary's Academy and Hallahan High School before becoming principal and superior of Holy Savior School in Linwood, Pennsylvania, and then Immaculate Conception School in Jenkintown, Pennsylvania, where the parishioners loved her. In 1963, she was appointed Mistress of Junior Sisters and then elected Superior General in 1968. Tall and stately, Mother Alice had a deep capacity for friendship and formed a great web of relationships with sisters, clergy, and laity. She attracted many with her gracious charm as much as her persuasive arguments. As one of her councillors later recalled, "She loved local community life; loved to dance . . . [and she had] great ability to work with people." While by no means a feminist in 1970s terms, she envisioned each sister of the Sisters of Saint Joseph striving to be a "valiant woman, nobly formed." Imbued with an historical stance, she saw these times as a "tremendous age for the Church" and constantly reminded perhaps herself and certainly the sisters of patience, for "God thinks in centuries."

As the head of a large Congregation, Mother Alice Anita was held in high regard nationally among American women religious congregations. Through 1976, she played a major role simultaneously with two divergent groups: The first was the Conference of Major Superiors of Women (CMSW), which had changed its name to the Leadership Conference of Women Religious (LCWR) in 1971. The second was the Consortium Perfectae Caritatis (CPC), formed in 1970–1971 by Conference members who preferred a more traditional approach. Basically, the two groups appeared to hold contradictory perspectives about religious life. In general, most LCWR members perceived apostolic religious life as a way for actively participating in the world, and so religious life evolved in its role and structures. The Consortium Perfectae Caritatis founders focused on the unchanging nature and components of religious life.

Mother Alice Anita's role in the dichotomy between the two groups began with her committee work in CMSW. In 1967, the CMSW began a revision of its by-laws that created a conflict regarding the group's purpose and its structural relationship within the hierarchy of the Catholic Church. Mother Alice Anita was a member of the bylaws committee for four years, beginning in 1969, and although a champion of renewal, she opposed many of the suggested changes in the CMSW bylaws. In 1970–1971 a small group within CMSW, uncomfortable with the direction of the majority, formed the CPC. Mother Alice Anita was one of the founders, along with Mother Claudia Honsberger IHM, the Superior General of Sister Servants of the Immaculate Heart of Mary, Immaculata, Pennsylvania.

Initially, Mother Alice Anita saw the CPC as having no competitive goals with CMSW but viewed it as a spiritual supplement to CMSW, which had become LCWR in 1971. In summer 1972, Mother Alice Anita wrote to the Congregation requesting their prayers and acts of mortification for the Holy Spirit's guidance during the CMSW meeting in Seattle where the vote would be taken on the new bylaws. At the conclusion of the meeting, she announced that "All went as well as one could expect." By winter 1974, however, the relationship between the two groups had become more adversarial and the Sacred Congregation of Religious called for a meeting between the two groups in Rome to work toward reconciliation. Although Mother Alice Anita informed the Congregation that she had been invited to the meeting, due to her congregational commitments for follow-up to the 1974 Chapter, she did not attend. At the conclusion of the meeting the press release stated that discussions had led to the reaffirmation by both the LCWR and the CPC of the essential values of religious life and greater acceptance of the principle of pluralism in unity. The Sacred Congregation of Religious urged the two groups to continue to dialogue.

As Superior General, Mother Alice Anita was largely responsible for the implementation of the 1968 Chapter enactments. There had been significant changes in governance, including the creation of regional superiors and the reconfigured roles of community school supervisors in the dioceses in which the Congregation administered schools. The regional superiors quickly acquired additional responsibilities, and beginning in August 1968 they participated in the ongoing formation of local superiors by staffing the annual superiors' workshops and special weekend meetings. They facilitated Chapter follow-up, hosting fall 1968 regional meetings to distribute the Chapter voting results, and in January 1969 they coordinated the dissemination of the results from local community dialogues to the Chapter committees. In their 1969–1970 visitations, the regionals offered to lead prayer and dialogue in each house concerning the Chapter implementations. As they gradually superseded the school supervisors in the process of personnel placement, the regionals were able to provide a broader context for ministry. Due to the expanding role of the regional superior, Mother Alice Anita in fall 1969 appointed four assistant regional superiors to help with the workload. These sisters assumed the duty of visiting some of the houses in their region while in their full-time ministry. The following sisters were appointed to this newly-created role: Sister Charlotte Therese McGrillis, Sister Mary De Paul McDonald, Sister Thomas Elizabeth Cavanaugh, and Sister Clare Leona Kern. By 1972, the number of regions was increased to eight, and the four assistants became full-time regional superiors.

Although the role of regional superior was conceived as that of a liaison between the superior general and the individual sisters, there was ambiguity regarding the nature and scope of the authority of the regional. Because the title "superior" was attached to the role, many sisters regarded the regionals as an authority figure; however, the extent of the regional's delegated authority had not been clearly determined. This lack of clarity was compounded since the regionals did not perform their duties in a uniform manner. This tendency toward individuation was sometimes perceived by the sisters as inconsistency. By the mid-1970s there was widespread confusion about the regionals' role and authority, and in the late 1970s, even though the regionals consulted formally with the sisters regarding personnel assignments and helped develop major renewal efforts, the ambiguity about their role continued. In fact the role of the regional superior continued to undergo various alterations during the next two decades.

Congregational Renewal

In November 1969, each sister received a personal copy of *Design for Excellence,* the complement to the *Holy Rule* that incorporated the work of 1968 Chapter. Although Mother Alice Anita planned to personally address the sisters about concerns over the 1968 Chapter enactments, demonstrations against the Vietnam War and winter storms prevented these meetings. However, on February 20, 1970, Mother Alice Anita sent each house a 14-page letter, accompanied by a questionnaire to help the sisters assimilate the information and directives received since the closing of Chapter. In February 1970, a wide-ranging plan for total immersion of the 2,600 Sisters of Saint Joseph in education for renewal was initiated. The plan divided the Congregation into 22 geographic areas for the purpose of studying *Design for Excellence.* By fall 1970, the plan incorporated renewal days led by Father Thomas Dubay SM. Each geographic area assembled monthly for education set within the context of prayer. To handle the vast quantities of paperwork generated by such an extensive renewal effort, a Coordinating Committee for renewal was created, linking subcommittees and standing committees from the 1968 Chapter. Topics including philosophy of education, adult education, urban community, retirement, re-editing the *Holy Rule*, liturgy, and mental health were focuses of these committees. At first, members of these committees were appointed, but over 500 sisters volunteered to serve when the invitation was issued in April 1971. The Coordinating Committee met twice annually with congregational leadership to help track the progress of the implementation.

When Mother Alice Anita had previously engaged Father Thomas Dubay SM, to direct the Sisters of Saint Joseph renewal, he had focused primarily on spirituality. From September 1970 through March 1971, he encountered 2,027 sisters through Theology of the Vows workshops conducted at various locations from New Jersey to North Carolina. In spring 1971, Father Dubay determined that he needed more input from the Congregation in order to facilitate further renewal. To accomplish this goal, he proposed a six-question "opinionnaire" that would survey attitudes toward communication and relationships vis-à-vis leadership, and the individual sisters. A response of 1,404 sisters reflected a potential for polarization within the Congregation.

On October 23, 1971, Father Dubay reported the findings at a congregational meeting held at Cardinal Dougherty High School in Philadelphia. Sisters arrived amid "negative rumors concerning the habit and authority." Father Dubay catalogued their strengths: prayerfulness, loyalty, unity, high-quality leadership, and fidelity to renewal. Then he summarized their most acute problems: difficulties with issues of authority, lack of poverty, lack of communication and trust, impersonalism, and polarization. In an open forum, several sisters expressed strong negativity about Mother Alice Anita's involvement in CPC. Reflecting on the day, Mother Alice Anita wrote:

> This meeting was, I think, the most crucial of my Administration. Despite the workshops on dialogue which the Community had experienced, the "touch" of Christian dialogue was still weak in the lives of some of the Sisters. The Administration returned home realizing that we still had "miles to go."

In February 1972, Father Dubay provided a second analysis after completing a series of weekend talks on the topic of Theological Background for Christian Dialogue. His observations corroborated his earlier concerns, and his conclusions were more dire. He warned the Administration that if no action was taken, some or even many good sisters may leave the Congregation, sisters who gave every evidence of sharing the Vatican II vision of religious life. He cited communication as the most serious issue and recommended procuring professional resources to help the sisters learn dialogue, as well as a professional survey to ascertain the thinking of all the sisters regarding the major problems as preparation for the next General Chapter.

At the March 4, 1972, Administration meeting with the renewal committee chairs, the participants advocated for improved communication with committees and Administration. They identified the need to distinguish between implementation and experimentation, noting that some houses considered the 1968 Chapter enactments as experimental ideas that sisters might or might not choose to adopt. Discussion at this meeting reiterated points about increased tension in superior-sister relationships and raised questions about the local house's commitment to engage in dialogue.

The Médaille Team: 1972–1975

By mid-February 1972, it appeared that the Sisters of Saint Joseph faced serious dilemmas, and the March 4 meeting of the renewal committees reinforced this. However, a letter to Sister Consuelo Maria from Sister Therese Liddy, who was studying at St. Bonaventure University and living with a group of Allegany Franciscans, opened the door to a new venture that proved to be a significant shift in the Congregation's approach to renewal. Sister Therese had met some of the Franciscans who were involved in the St. Louis Program for Corporate Renewal and had contact with the program's director, Dr. Nicholas Colarelli. In her letter, Sister Therese recommended the program to Sister Consuelo Maria. Mother Alice Anita authorized Sister Consuelo Maria to make inquiries and communication with the directors of the program ensued. While the program seemed promising, it would mean cutting back on school staffing needs to provide full-time personnel for training. Father Thomas Swift SJ, one of the program's directors, and Jesuit seminarian Thomas J. Porath were invited to Chestnut Hill to explain the program to Mother Alice Anita and the Council. The Administration decided to invest in the program, and a letter announcing this decision was sent to the Congregation on March 17, 1972. Mother Alice Anita later characterized this meeting "as one of the greatest graces given to her and the Congregation by the Holy Spirit."

The announcement about this corporate renewal program immediately solicited the sisters' participation. The Administration committed to investing in two teams to be trained by the Center for Planned Change from St. Louis. One was a six-member "grassroots" team, so called because the entire Congregation was invited to nominate sisters for this team. Using criteria suggested by the program's directors, the sisters submitted nearly 400 names. Named the Médaille Team, the selected six-member team of sisters was intended to represent the polar strengths of the Congregation. The sisters, ranging in age from 31 to 66, were Sisters Grace Pino (Maria Goretti), elementary school principal and music sister; Bernard Francis Loughery, former congregational school supervisor, now a principal; Marie Ellen and Michael Cecilia Walsh, secondary school teachers; Kathleen Kean, elementary school teacher; and Harriet Corrigan (Saint Pierre), college teacher. Deliberately chosen for their differences, they would learn to become a team and a local community. They would then move among the Sisters of Saint Joseph as peers, training them to do what the team had done: become one as a local community. A second team, composed of the eight regional superiors, was added in June 1972 and trained in St. Louis. Sister Miriam Gertrude retired that year, so five new regionals were appointed: Sisters Rita Bernadette Danks, Eugenie Madeleine Gaddi, Alma Celeste Gallagher, Clare Leona, and Adele Marie Toal.

During five weeks of intense training in the summer of 1972, both groups focused on discerning congregational strengths and perceived weaknesses. Many sisters shared the spiritual traditions learned during a formation under the tutelage of Mother Marie Estelle Duggan, former Director of Novices. Confronting problems directly was not a strong point for many, often due to the fear of hurting another's feelings. Whether a strength or a weakness, the Sisters of Saint Joseph typically moved cautiously preparing carefully prior to action and employing a gradual implementation of subsequent changes. Working quietly and diligently were also hallmarks of the Sisters of Saint Joseph. The task of the Médaille Team was to relate these discernments to the charism of the community and to formulate a corporate renewal strategy that could eventually be woven into the life of the Congregation, even after the teams had served their purpose and were phased out.

The Médaille Team's Work

From August 1972 through June 1975, the Médaille Team implemented three areas of corporate renewal. First, they stressed local community renewal by focusing on "quality of presence." Second, they initiated procedures for developing a broad base of sisters to serve as internal resources for leadership in renewal. Third, they created, with the Administration, a corporate reflection process, meetings called Centers for Corporate Reflection (CCR), to engage the Congregation's participation in decision making. During this time, the Médaille Team was directed and supported by the staff of the St. Louis Center for Planned Change.

In October 1972, the Médaille Team hosted fifteen area meetings to acquaint sisters with their program and offer their services to local communities. Two hundred local houses responded with invitations for the team to visit, and from mid-October through December 1972, every house was visited by a member of the original Médaille Team and a regional superior. Each pair answered questions about the renewal program, gathered information, and conducted a shared prayer session. Based on the data gathered from each local house, the team presented techniques that would foster "quality of presence." By the 1974 Chapter, the team had conducted local community training sessions with 89 houses. During 1974–1975, they met with the remaining houses in clustered groups.

To sustain renewal over the long term, the Médaille Team incorporated leadership development into their program. At first, they worked with particular groups: local superiors, sisters in formation, Villa personnel, and congregational Administration. They identified leadership as a function of the group, an integral part of creating the quality of presence requisite for local community life. After the 1974 Chapter, this leadership formation transitioned into a program called Local Community Development (LCD).

In November 1973 and in April 1974, the Centers for Corporate Reflection (CCR) were first implemented, with approximately 800 sisters in attendance. This part of the corporate renewal process was aimed at increasing the sisters' participation in congregational decision making. The input from each gathering or center constituted a consultation between the sisters and the congregational leadership. This process proved to be a viable way for sisters to be more intimately involved in such a large Congregation. The 1974 Chapter then designated the CCR model as the main vehicle for sisters' participation in the general governance of the Congregation. With the incorporation of the CCR process into the life of the Congregation, the Médaille Team's contributions to congregational renewal were firmly established.

1974 Chapter of Affairs

On June 16, 1974, Mother Alice Anita formally opened the 1974 Chapter with a critique of the present state of affairs in the Congregation:

> The efforts to carry the *Design for Excellence* from dialogue to living reality have been sincere and constant—but there are miles to live in achieving this reality. . . . "It takes deep prayer, Mary's faith, and loving sacrifice to BE an authentic consecrated woman in this historic period." She enjoined the delegates to be guided by the Holy Spirit in all their deliberations, since their task was to preserve the essence of the Congregation while perpetuating "its adaptation to the needs of the times."

Usually, the Chapter of Affairs was a closed proceeding, but delegates raised the possibility of opening the proceedings to sister-observers. While this proposal prompted debate, a compromise was reached:

> Except for proceedings in executive sessions, all transitions of the Chapter of Affairs are exempt from the structures of confidentially; transactions of the Chapter of Election, as specified in our Holy Rule, are matters of conscientious secrecy.

The delegates then voted to have observers present at the general Chapter sessions and to make audio tapes of these available. During the nine weeks of the Chapter of Affairs, over 1,000 sisters observed the proceedings.

Enactments of 1974 Chapter

The delegates tried to avoid the ambiguity surrounding the 1968 Chapter directives by clarifying whether enactments were for *experimentation, implementation,* or *consideration*. They also decided to authorize a second edition of *Design for Excellence* that would integrate the applicable norms and directives/revisions of the 1974 Chapter.

During the nine weeks of the Chapter of Affairs, delegates debated a total of 11 topics but identified two key issues: the quality of presence in community life and the nature of governance during this period of renewal. The need for increased personal and communal responsibility, advocated by delegates in 1968, was reaffirmed in 1974. The results of the 1973 CARA Survey noted the majority of sisters favored more personal autonomy and a greater degree of participation in local and congregational decision making. Although the Chapter delegates encouraged shared decision making in the local houses, they still determined that the final decision rested with the superior. Other issues were handled in similar fashion. The proposal for a small discretionary budget for each sister emerged as a suggestion for a small amount of money for emergencies or incidentals. The problem of the so-called weekend-clearout that occurred in some local houses was not the subject of any legislation, but the delegates encouraged sisters to assume personal responsibility for the building of community.

With regard to administration, the delegates passed 52 enactments requiring action and 13 requiring consideration. They expanded the number of councillors from four to six, with four residing full time at the Motherhouse, and eliminated all special titles including that of Reverend Mother; everyone was now called *sister*. In addition the delegates delineated specific roles for councillors, assigned additional duties to regional superiors, created new responsibilities for local superiors, mandated new administrative committees, and authorized the use of Centers for Corporate Reflection (CCR) for participation in general governance. Delegates determined that future Chapters would be held every five years, not six, thereby reducing the term of the superior general and council. They mandated an interim assembly in the third year following the General Chapter when the delegates would reassemble to evaluate the implementation of enactments and plan for the next Chapter. The result of these decisions produced conflict within the Chapter body since some delegates interpreted the specificity of the enactments as a sign of distrust in congregational leadership, while others regarded it as an ongoing evolution of the process begun in the 1968 Chapter.

1974 Chapter of Election

The 1974 Chapter of Election was held August 15, 1974. Those nominated for councillor were given the option of stating a preference for being councillor at the Motherhouse or councillor-at-large, and a list of nominees for each category was generated. The superior general and six councillors were elected for a five-year term, and the first four council members elected were those who would live at the Motherhouse, exercising full-time duties as outlined by the Chapter of Affairs; the other two would live on a mission. Sister Alice Anita was reelected Superior General, and Sister Consuelo Maria, First Councillor and Assistant, was also reelected to a second term. The three full-time council members elected were Sister Agnes Marie Gunn, Sister Clare Michael Keating, and Sister Marie Ellen.

The Councillors-at-Large were Sister Mary Thomas Murphy and Sister Saint Ursula Egan. Initially, Sister Mary Thomas remained as principal at Saint Mark High School, Wilmington, Delaware, and then, in 1975, became administrator of Saint Joseph Villa. Sister Saint Ursula continued as administrator of the Catholic Home in Philadelphia, Pennsylvania.

Implementing the 1974 Chapter

Unlike the 1968 Chapter, the 1974 Chapter had no standing committees to continue its work, so the systematic implementation of its enactments became the task of the General Council, the regional superiors, and the offices or committees assigned by the Chapter. To facilitate initial congregational support for the Chapter's enactments, Sister Alice Anita and Council inaugurated a program to educate the sisters in the theological basis and implications of the Chapter's decisions. Ten Chapter education days at multiple locations were scheduled for late October 1974. These days were intended to create a mini-experience of the total Chapter process. For local community follow-up during the year, the regional superiors created a format for monthly dialogues on Chapter principles and decrees. Each sister also received *Design II,* the compilation of the 1974 Chapter's work.

Using the directives of the 1974 Chapter, a new governance model of the General Council was adopted. The four full-time councillors resided at the Motherhouse and assumed specific tasks. Sister Consuelo Maria continued as treasurer with oversight of financial and temporal matters of the Congregation and responsibility for the Social Action Committee. Sister Agnes Marie Gunn directed the sisters' education in collaboration with the Councillors for Formation and Apostolic Works, Sisters Marie Ellen and Clare Michael. Sister Marie Ellen's specific area of responsibility was expanded from that of retirement /Saint Joseph Villa to continuing formation. Sister Marie Ellen also worked with the Mental Health and Chastity Committees.

The two Councillors-at-Large, Sisters Mary Thomas and Saint Ursula, assumed responsibility for the formation of the Committee for the Future, which conducted studies and experimentation on issues such as vacations for sisters, local houses as communal discernment communities, the election of superiors by the local community, and the feasibility of a model for total parish education. Sister Saint Ursula also served on the Social Action and Urban Committees.

Additional roles and offices supported the Council's work, creating a more layered governance. Sister Loretta Hogan (Joan Loretta) as Coordinator of Schools and Sister Antoinette Munafo (Antonia) as Coordinator of Religious Education filled two new staff positions mandated by the 1974 Chapter to assist the councillor for apostolic works. The work of the Médaille Team continued under the auspices of the newly created Renewal Office (1975) coordinated by former team member Sister Kathleen Kean. In 1977, Sister Barbara Hogan (Catherine Christine) assumed this post when Sister Kathleen Kean was appointed regional superior. This office developed the Local Community Development (LCD) program and the Centers for Corporate Reflection (CCR). It also coordinated the work of various committees and task forces, providing a common background and vocabulary for initiatives and policies developed by the new Council offices. A new communications center opened under Father Joseph Breslin was expected to work with the secretary general to explore new methods of communication.

These major changes created new images of congregational government. The changes involved individual councillors to communicate with the sisters regarding initiatives in their own sphere of influence; however it also led to a proliferation of communications from the Motherhouse regarding policies and procedures germane to each councillor's area. The congregational governance structure was becoming more bureaucratic in size, nature, and scope. However, the sisters' desire for increased participation in the decision-making processes of the Congregation was being addressed by the multiplicity of committees, workshops, surveys, and other means of soliciting input from the grassroots.

Congregational Finances

The 1974 Chapter established a direction which would place responsibility for all financial matters into the hands of the councillor in charge. At this time, the position was held by Sister Consuelo Maria. Using communication and consultation, Sister Consuelo Maria began to reshape the Congregation's financial operations with more standardized processes and policy development. With input from the Financial Advisory Committee and the local superiors, she regularly provided financial memos for the local houses, question-and-answers sheets, and reminders about how to handle financial concerns. Sister Consuelo Maria annually conducted workshops for superiors and house treasurers. The March 27, 1976, session of the Financial Advisory Committee reported on the fiscal state of the Congregation with a focus on the Villa debt, the General Fund, Social Security, and the Retirement Fund. It also held a group discussion on the Congregation's use of house assessment monies, and it educated houses on budgeting, accounting, reconciling bank statements, and maintaining accuracy in record keeping for local house finances.

Attuned to the longstanding practice of the fiscal autonomy of the local house, Sister Consuelo Maria cautiously implemented more congregational oversight while educating the sisters about the evolving interrelationship of local and congregational finances. To conduct the annual audit of house accounts, as directed by the 1974 Chapter, she recruited the Financial Advisory Committee, who employed a peer review approach. The committee's observations often identified topics for future workshops and memos. She stressed the importance of accurate house accounts for the financial health of the Congregation when she observed that "our auditors compile the cost per-sister-per-month form, the annual reports of our local houses, and from them establish the fair-market value for food and clothing on which our Social

Security taxes are levied. If our records are inaccurate we may pay more or less than we should."

In the summer of 1975, Sister Consuelo Maria provided concrete evidence of the impact of sound local house finances on the total Congregation in a letter announcing that in 23 months the Congregation was able to pay the $1.5 million owed in retroactive Social Security taxes. This move guaranteed that most sisters would be eligible to receive Social Security payments when they reached the appropriate age. In January 1978, she explained the benefits of the comprehensive approach to medical insurance adopted by the Congregation, and established the policy that provided a $75 vacation allowance for each sister. A "vacation for all" general account was established for those houses that lacked adequate funds for this modest sum for each sister.

Local Community Development (LCD)

The Local Community Development (LCD) program offered systematic formation in new processes and structures for renewal in the local community. In the early 1970s, the Médaille Team focused on quality of presence, but the LCD went further and deeper. LCD processes taught the sisters in local community to diagnose the climate of the house and to identify and address obstacles to renewal. With the LCD, the sisters utilized practices like goal setting and weekly house meetings to establish a closer bond within the local community.

In spring 1975, 20 sisters trained as resource persons piloted the LCD program in 16 houses. Simultaneously, the 200 local superiors attended seminars on the process. In August, during a week-long training another 40 resource sisters learned how to assist houses with LCD. In the fall, the 58 newly appointed superiors were trained. By early September 1975, over 300 sisters had received initial formation in LCD.

In its first full year of implementation (1975–1976), LCD focused on local house climate and goal setting. Evaluations of the first year were less than enthusiastic. Sister Alice Anita must have anticipated this resistance because in October 1975 she wrote that "difficulties and repugnance to the process will be experienced by some." However, she expected sisters to engage in the program since it was intended as a learning experience. By fall each house had its own LCD resource person who attended the training session. With over 200 sister volunteers, Sister Kathleen Kean facilitated the creation of an LCD manual containing worksheets and checklists for assessing house climate, conducting house meetings, making decisions, and setting goals. There were even models for creating communal prayer services.

Centers for Corporate Reflection (CCR)

While LCD used the process of corporate reflection in local community, the phrase *corporate reflection* was also associated with the Congregation structure known as Centers for Corporate Reflection (CCR). Envisioned by the 1974 Chapter as a vehicle for sisters' participation in the governance of the Congregation, the CCR process examined "issues in light of Gospel values, the Church documents, the spirit of the founder, and the signs of the times." The 1973–1974 pilot CCRs had demonstrated their potential, and between April 1975 and March 1979 the entire Congregation of over 2,400 sisters attended eleven CCRs, some of which lasted two days. Eight of these focused on apostolic direction (April 1977 through October 1977), one on the topic of poverty and simplicity of life (March 1978), and two on preparation for the 1979 Chapter (October 1978 and March 1979).

CCRs were both a location and a process. Going to the CCR meant that the entire Congregation assembled simultaneously in 27 different geographic locations spread across thirteen dioceses. Sisters from five to 15 houses typically met at their assigned CCR location to share the fruits of local house discussions, to receive input, and to provide feedback to the congregational leadership. Modified versions were held for the sisters at Saint Joseph Villa. After the local CCR, each director compiled the center's feedback and the directors met again in a follow-up CCR with the Superior General and Council. This group worked to discern themes in the feedback received from all of the centers. Usually, the congregational leadership reported the overall CCR results to the local houses.

Conducting the CCRs, particularly at their inception, was a mammoth undertaking. For the first CCRs held in spring 1975, 28 sisters were trained as directors. They were instructed in the theory behind corporate reflection and in the processes for leadership, group behavior management, and consensus development. In April 1975, 203 sisters received similar training as facilitators, one for each of the small groups in each center. At each site sisters served as local contact persons, leaders of prayer, and volunteers to handle the logistics. As a result of this training and planning, more than 700 sisters were prepared to assume responsibility for the CCRs.

In the 1979 pre-Chapter survey, many sisters affirmed the efforts of both the LCD and CCR. Nearly 74 percent found the CCR a helpful way of participating in congregational decision making, and 61 percent reported that they had been enriched by house meetings. Still, 44 percent reported that issues that might produce conflict in local community were being avoided.

1977 Interim Assembly

The 1974 Chapter body reconvened in an Interim Assembly from August 5, 1977, through August 19, 1977, to conduct "a corporate conscience examen," as Sister Alice Anita described it. Mandated by the 1974 Chapter, this body had no legislative powers but had two purposes: assess the 1974 Chapter's implementation of enactments, and plan for the 1979 Chapter. Using the Ignatian practice of the examen, Sister Alice Anita set the focus of the group's deliberations on prayerful communal discernment about the Congregation's growth and needs. The 1974 Coordinating Committee and topic committees solicited feedback from the sisters by sending out a questionnaire with sections developed by each committee, and approximately 1,200 sisters responded. Specific committees collected additional data through conversations, interviews, and small group discussions. The reports from the committees suggested a spirit of renewal evolving within the Congregation. Nearly all the 1974 Chapter enactments were being implemented in some fashion—even amid difficulties. The recommendations highlighted the need for ongoing discussion on *how* to be apostolic religious. The delegates stressed greater attention to purposes, more reflection in choice making, and more specific study in concepts like simplicity of life, which became the topic of the March 1978 CCR.

The delegates to the Interim Assembly and the congregational leadership proposed changes in the selection of Chapter delegates that would broaden participation in the 1979 Chapter. Ideas for the process had been solicited from canonists, the sisters, other religious, and professional consultants. The method was finalized in May 1978. The Interim Assembly also suggested that the 1979 Chapter be limited to the areas of congregational life in need of immediate attention. This limitation in scope was in marked contrast to both the 1968 and 1974 Chapters.

Preparations for the 1979 Chapter: Participation

Expanded roles, a new Chapter newsletter, and the use of the various consultation modes provided key avenues for every sister's involvement in the 1979 Chapter. Sisters had the opportunity to assume one of several roles: elected delegate, occasional observer, participant observer, House of Prayer member, and supporter through daily prayer. After considerable review and study by a seven-person task force, which included two consultations with the Congregation, Sister Alice Anita and the Council announced a new approach to delegate elections. Before the voting, a sister now had the opportunity to withdraw her name from consideration. Then in a rather complicated process, the sisters voted for 10 delegates from her own rank/age group, six from her region, and nine more from the total listing. The sisters elected 102 delegates who, with the seven ex officio members (Sister Alice Anita and the six councillors), formed a Chapter body of 109, with another 15 elected alternate delegates who had participated in committee and Chapter work. Of the 109 capitulars, 56 percent had been delegates for at least one previous renewal Chapter.

Eight hundred occasional observers viewed the proceedings or listened to tapes of previous sessions. The 85 sisters who were participant observers attended all Chapter sessions. A House of Intercessory Prayer was established at Sacred Heart Hall, Cheltenham, Pennsylvania, and 29 sisters engaged in fasting, reflection, and communal and personal prayer around the clock, to intercede for the revelation of the Lord's plan. In addition, some 1,450 Sisters of Saint Joseph pledged their participation through prayer and sacrifice.

To further enhance participation, a professionally produced document, *The Chapter,* was created. Edited by Sister Arleen Ronollo (Anne Robert), a trained journalist, it combined the brevity of a bulletin with the format of a newsletter. *The Chapter,* employing more than 20 sisters, offered information and commentary on Chapter proceedings and captured, for the whole Congregation, the extensive engagement of the sisters in Chapter work.

1979 Chapter

A short Chapter by previous standards, the 1979 Chapter of Affairs opened July 1, and concluded July 13. The Chapter of Elections took place on July 16, preceded by two days of spiritual preparation by the delegates. The Chapters of Affairs had also been preceded by a week-long retreat. Directed by Jesuit theologian, Father Paul Molinari, the delegates received further input and inspiration from Passionist Jude Mead and Bishop Fulton J. Sheen, who communicated via taped message.

Sister Alice Anita opened the 1979 Chapter by invoking the biblical image of Moses leading the Israelites through "desert uncertainties." She defined the Chapter experience as a paschal celebration, calling the sisters to a "deep, and perhaps painful, search for God's way" that would ultimately lead to a "new creation of the spirit . . . a sensation of freshness in the church." In Ignatian terms, she challenged them to become one body of unity and strength in order to design a future for the "greater glory of God" and for the good of the neighbor, "locally and globally." One of the main themes of the Chapter was based on Pope Paul VI's apostolic exhortation *Evangelii Nuntiandi* (Evangelization in the Modern World). This theme would be explored in terms of the relationship between community affairs and the broader context of the mission of the church. Combined with an emphasis on poverty and simplicity of life, this focus on mission would help determine the direction of ministry in the next decade. Based on input from the October

1978 CCR, discussion on formation/membership, community life, and administration (governance) would also be part of the Chapter of Affairs.

As the Chapter proceeded, the topic of governance consumed much time and energy. The delegates affirmed the principle that "Government begins with each sister" and that the purpose of this structure was to free sisters for mission. The delegates also identified the necessary constituents of effective governance: unity, collegiality, delegation, consultation, subsidiarity, and accountability. Some of the concrete results of the discussion were reduction of the general council to five persons, expansion of the role of regional superior, separation of the position of treasurer from the Council, establishment of the Office of Personnel Services, and transformation of the Renewal Office into the Office of Research and Planning. Although not an enactment, the possibility of the local community electing its own superior was introduced by the delegates. Ironically, this idea had not been highly supported by the sisters who responded to the pre-Chapter survey.

The Chapter body affirmed the apostolic direction of Corporate Ecclesial Commitment to People (CECP) and expanded the individual's responsibility for decision making by establishing a personal budget and granting each sister the right to make limited choices about wearing the habit. The delegates further encouraged every sister to embrace the Gospel values of social justice and simplicity of life. Another outcome of the Chapter was the clarification of the membership of the Sisters of Saint Joseph in the LCWR and CPC. Although Sister Alice Anita had tried to retain membership in both groups, she eventually felt compelled to leave the CPC and remain with the LCWR. While personally drawn to some of the more conservative values of the CPC, Sister Alice Anita believed that membership in the LCWR would provide greater support as the Sisters of Saint Joseph continued to journey toward a more apostolic, relational mode of community life and ministry.

On July 16, the Chapter delegates elected Sister Dorothea Newell as Superior General of the Congregation. The four Council members elected were Sisters Agnes Marie Gunn (Assistant), Eugenie Madeleine, Saint Ursula, and Margaret Fleming (William Marguerite). Now at the end of a decade, a new Administration team would continue to lead the Sisters of Saint Joseph in their next stage of growth as apostolic women religious dedicated to serving the People of God and committed to deepening their own interior renewal.

MINISTRY

Professional Education of the Sisters

During the 1970s, the Sisters of Saint Joseph made major decisions about ministry, but these were largely internal, specifically related to the professional education of sisters. Emphasizing the need for professional competence in the apostolate, the Congregation provided abundant opportunities for sisters' education through undergraduate and graduate study, certification, and enrichment. The 1968 Chapter set definitive goals in sisters' education by decreeing that a definite schedule for sisters completing their undergraduate degrees should be established. The Chapter also mandated a new position, Director of Sisters Education, who would consult with the sisters to help them match their personal aptitudes with the needs of the Congregation.

In July 1971, Mother Alice Anita authorized the release from full-time ministry of 39 sisters so that they could complete their undergraduate studies in a more timely fashion. These sister-students formed a local community at the Postulate and commuted to Chestnut Hill College for class. Fourteen sisters were assigned to postgraduate studies related to the needs of Chestnut Hill College, Saint Joseph Villa, and Norwood-Fontbonne Academy. By the end of the 1970s, assigning sisters to full-time study had become the accepted norm rather than just an experimental initiative.

However, this practice was expensive for the Congregation in terms of both personnel and finances. In June 1971, the Congregation had assigned 53 sisters to study while it faced the loss of 73 sisters from the teaching ministry through attrition, retirement, or death.

Consequently, in this same year, the Congregation had 126 fewer stipended sisters in ministry, seriously impacting congregational finances. By February 1972, the projected cost of educating sister-students resulted in a $71,000 deficit. The decision to increase the local house financial assessment to cover this need underscored the sacrifice required to provide sisters with a good education, thus shifting some responsibility for this expense to the local house.

To further expedite the completion of their undergraduate degrees, sisters missioned at a distance from Chestnut Hill College were encouraged to study at nearby colleges. Since the Motherhouse, not the local community, was paying the tuition, this became a viable option. In January 1973, Sister George Edward Conway announced that sister-undergraduates would be interviewed by the department head of their major just as all other matriculating students were, thus aligning the degree requirement for sisters with those of all other students.

Within five years (1969 to 1974), nearly 700 sisters graduated from Chestnut Hill College. The remaining 200 sister-undergraduates were those who entered after the mid-1960s. By 1979, the number of sister-undergraduates was about 100. Though this statistic reflected a decrease in the number of sisters entering the Congregation, it also demonstrated the success of the plan, since a significantly larger number of sisters had completed their undergraduate degree programs.

Beginning in the early 1970s, the Congregation also developed a new strategy regarding graduate study. Pursuing a master's degree was now a possibility for more sisters, since this future study was no longer dependent upon invitation from the congregational leadership. Recommended by the 1968 Chapter, the Council established the Office of Sisters' Graduate Education in the early 1970s. From 1970 to 1975, the following sisters in succession occupied this post: Sisters Francis Ines Moloney, Lilian Teresa McClain, Rosalie Marie Funchion, Marie Emily Smith, and Consuelo Maria. The 1974 Chapter confirmed the role of Councillor for Sisters' Education, and Sister Agnes Marie Gunn then led the office for the next 10 years.

Sister Agnes Marie Gunn endorsed the emphasis placed on education by the *Holy Rule* which stated: "On the education of women largely depends the future of society." Her educational policies were rooted in the theology of religious life, and as sisters pursued the "intellectual life as religious women" they were encouraged to accept "the asceticism and apostolic service" study involved. Most sisters affirmed the process used by Sister Agnes Marie Gunn as beneficial because it engaged them in prayer, reflection, dialogue, and collaborative decision making about their own education. For many sisters, this approach to their education provided the first opportunity to identify and realize their potential contribution to those they served. For others, dialogue with a member of the General Council actually brought them to the heart of the Congregation, and they felt a confirmation of their personal worth.

In all her communications with individuals and with the Congregation-at-large, Sister Agnes Marie Gunn emphasized the model of shared responsibility for the productivity of the $500,000 annual investment in sisters' education. The self-evaluation of the academic program helped determine its efficacy in relation to the cost. The evaluative instrument provided feedback on academic rigor, professional, social, and spiritual support, as well as logistics of meals, room conditions, and atmosphere for study. These evaluations also became a useful resource for future choices concerning institutions and academic programs.

Between 1974 and 1979, Sisters of Saint Joseph studied at 87 colleges and universities across the United States. Nearly 400 sister-students moved into a different rhythm of life as they left the local convents in June to live in college dorms and apartments for the summer session. For those sisters who had entered directly from high school, this was their first experience living outside the convent. They were expected to manage their own schedules and monies and make their own decisions about social and professional activities. Those sisters who studied on Catholic campuses, such as The Catholic University in Washington, DC, were often exposed to some of the greatest American theologians of the day. These sisters also had opportunities to become more aware of and participate in social justice organizations and initiatives. Those who studied at secular universities sometimes faced challenges regarding their religious identity.

The 1974 Chapter also advocated the pursuit of professional credentials, since teaching certification and updated religious studies were necessary to continue teaching in many schools. Sister Agnes Marie Gunn collaborated with Sister Clare Michael, Councillor for Apostolic Works, in the attainment of this goal, and beginning in 1976 approximately 46 sisters annually studied for state certification, while another 50 took enrichment courses in a variety of educational fields. Through the late 1970s, Sister Loretta Hogan, Coordinator of Schools, conducted annual seminars on contemporary themes in school leadership, and in 1977 she negotiated with Chestnut Hill College and Villanova University to create a joint graduate program for Catholic school administrators. During the next two summers, more than 40 sisters enrolled in the foundational courses, and one-fourth of these matriculated in the masters program, thus satisfying the Congregation's requirement (1979) that all newly appointed principals must have six credits in Catholic school administration.

Viewing the principalship as a specialized work with particular professional demands and skills paved the way for separating that role from the traditional combined roles of superior and principal. The 1974 Chapter recommended that "by the time of the next Chapter [1979], the role of superior and principal or (secondary school) coordinator be separated, where at all possible." The separation of roles also supported the view that each ministry, whether teaching or administrative, was of equal value and that neither position was accompanied by power or authority beyond the ministry itself.

Religious Studies

In 1974, the Chapter mandated the establishment of an Office for Religious Education to meet the needs of sisters requiring certification in the teaching of religion. New ministries in religious education were opening up, and by 1979 the number of sisters engaged in religious studies had nearly tripled since the early 1970s. Sisters were pursuing degrees in a broad spectrum of subjects: liturgy, pastoral ministry, urban ministry, youth ministry, spirituality, applied spirituality, parish social ministry, and sacred science.

To facilitate this growing number of sisters engaged in religious studies, the Congregation appointed Sister Antoinette Munafo (Antonia) to the position of Coordinator of Religious Education in 1975. Using a model established after the 1968 Chapter, Sister Antoinette annually sponsored the SSJ Summer Institutes in Religious Studies, first at Sacred Heart Hall in Cheltenham and then at Chestnut Hill College. These four-week enrichment programs nurtured both personal and ministerial development. Sessions offered in 1978 included such topics as music in liturgy, Old Testament themes, and methods of catechesis. Sister Antoinette also initiated LaSalle Day, an enrichment day cosponsored by LaSalle College (now University) that drew over 400 sisters and lay colleagues from local schools and parishes. Twice a year, Sister Antoinette produced the *SSJ Religious Education Information Sheet,* a publication designed as a resource instrument, and a calendar of events, which highlighted the work of leading thinkers and writers and the new trends in religious education.

By 1979, 40 percent of Sisters of Saint Joseph had earned a master's degree, while another 14 percent were studying for one. The range of subjects had also broadened from English or mathematics to religious studies and educational fields such as guidance, Individually Guided Education, and the Montessori approach. The 1979 studies list showed 11 sisters taking classes in clinical pastoral education, which prepared them for ministry with the sick or homebound. Despite the mounting cost of such education, the Congregation made the investment so that the sisters would be better prepared for all forms of ministry.

Changing Trends and Demographics in Catholic Education

During the 1970s, as Catholic schools—particularly those in urban areas—faced radical changes in demographics, the Sisters of Saint Joseph remained steadfast in their commitment to the educational ministry with 82 percent of the sisters serving in schools. Catholic school enrollment peaked in 1965 and was decreasing by the early 1970s. The decline in the national birth rate, the exodus from city to suburbs, the choice of public education by Catholic parents, and rising tuition costs were some of the critical factors in this declining enrollment. Approximately 3,100 Catholic schools nationwide closed between 1965 and 1974. Those that remained faced the challenges of mounting costs driven by the high inflation rate and demand for higher salaries for lay teachers who, by 1979, comprised 75 percent of the schools' staffs. Steadily rising tuition also contributed to the problem of decreasing student enrollment. In response to this problem, the American bishops in their pastoral entitled *To Teach as Jesus Did (1972)* advocated new models of leadership in the diocese, parish life, and the school.

In the 1970s, at the diocesan level, merging schools with declining enrollments was one response to the problem. For example, Saint Augustine and Saint Patrick schools in Philadelphia were closed due to rezoning of these parts of the city into commercial areas, and the students were accommodated at Saint Mary Inter-Parochial School (5th and Locust Sts.), along with the populations of three other schools. Another response initiated by the Philadelphia Archdiocese and some dioceses in other states was the creation of regional schools. Some of these schools utilized two campuses, making use of all buildings. Examples of this restructuring were Ambler Catholic (Ambler, Pennsylvania) and Catholic Community School of Baltimore (Baltimore, Maryland). In Camden, New Jersey, several struggling schools were consolidated in order to meet the needs of the Latino and African American communities.

The new educational configurations often created both logistical difficulties and personal stress. Sacramental programs in multiple parishes had to be coordinated. Participation of pastors needed to be encouraged. Fiscal responsibility had to be shared among participating parishes, and, on occasion, reallocation of properties was necessitated. When this occurred, it was often the local convent that was involved, and sisters from different schools merged to form a single local community at one site, thus requiring the other group to commute to their ministry site. While sisters endeavored to be fully present to the needs of their particular parish community, the limitations engendered by commuting sometimes militated against full engagement in parish and school activities.

Urban Schools

Another result of declining enrollment in urban Catholic schools was the reduced number of Catholic students enrolled. Catholic neighborhoods were experiencing an influx of African Americans who were traditionally Protestant but wanted to avail themselves of the quality education offered by the Catholic schools. Thus the student populations of Catholic city schools were becoming increasingly non-Catholic. In addition, much of the population was living at or below the poverty level. For the more than 600 sisters ministering in 30 city schools in various metropolitan areas, this shift presented both challenges and opportunity. There were difficult questions regarding the primary purpose of the Catholic school and the equally pressing need to serve those who were poor, regardless of their race or creed. Building Catholic leadership and responsible citizens had always been the goal of the parish elementary school and diocesan secondary school. Now the emphasis was also on social justice and evangelization.

Amid the tough questions, the sisters serving in the inner city tried to understand and adapt to a culture not their own. In West and North Philadelphia, sisters scheduled cluster meetings among themselves for prayer and support, and eventually these groups expanded to include the priests of the parishes. Some sisters took specialized course work in African American history and in psychology using the resources of the Josephite Fathers at Howard University. Others became involved in neighborhood initiatives like the tutoring program operated by Rev. Leon Sullivan at Zion Baptist Church.

Other Educational Initiatives

During the 1970s, experimentation was part of the educational arena as it was in practically every other facet of American life. Individualized education contracts, team teaching, and other such initiatives were utilized by the Sisters of Saint Joseph in both elementary and secondary schools. The open classroom, nongraded education, and modular scheduling were other examples of a diversified approach to education. Honors courses, multiple elective options, independent study programs, and pairing with public vo-tech schools were often characteristic of high schools in the 1970s. In Philadelphia, several inner-city elementary schools staffed by the Sisters of Saint Joseph adopted the approach known as Individually Prescribed Instruction (IPI), and St. Gregory School was recognized nationally by Research for Better Schools as an IPI demonstration school.

Sisters also utilized many government-supported programs initiated in the 1970s, since federal and state funding often meant additional teaching resources and shared educational programs with the public schools. As they navigated the maze of red tape characteristic of both state and federal bureaucracy, the sisters not only secured money and other resources but forged alliances, both professional and personal, with the staff members of various government agencies, thus ensuring continued support for their educational ventures.

Parish Schools as Communities of Faith

The US bishops' document *To Teach as Jesus Did* urged Catholic schools to develop a community of faith, forge new partnerships with parents, and become integrated with parish-wide religious education. Based on their understanding of the bishops' document, sisters learned that building a strong faith community in school necessitated relating to the laity in a way that entailed shared responsibility and nurturing community. This community building drew sisters into closer relationship with their colleagues and fostered professional growth.

Adapting to New Models of Education in the Institutional Setting

The trends towards individualization, the need for restructuring, and the changing perceptions regarding institutional life significantly impacted the sisters involvement in social work during the 1970s. Two institutions staffed by the Sisters of Saint Joseph for over 100 years closed: St. John's Orphanage for Boys (1976) and St. Ann's Widow Asylum /Villa Laboure (1976). Foster homes and other institutions accommodated the 28 boys from St. John's, and the new Immaculate Mary Nursing Home in northeast Philadelphia provided care for the ladies of Villa Laboure.

By the early 1970s the sisters working at the Paradise School for Boys (Abbottstown, Pennsylvania) and the Catholic Home for Girls (Philadelphia) were now ministering to young people with severe social and emotional problems. In both cases, the sisters collaborated with Catholic Social Services and with community-based services of the Department of Public Welfare. The Paradise School, formerly a long-term institutional care facility, shifted to one with limited residential care but more intensive therapeutic intervention. The sisters who ministered there joined the first lay administrator, Mr. Thomas M. Kostelac, in establishing the team method of clinical treatment. Some sisters worked as child care workers collaborating with other team professionals on individualized programs for the boys, while others staffed the small group home on the Paradise grounds where young men were prepared for independent living.

At the Catholic Home, the Sisters of Saint Joseph created a fundamentally new approach in the structure of the facility and the programs offered. In 1972, both the Catholic Home and the Saint Vincent Residence for pregnant teenagers occupied the Woodland Avenue facility of the Catholic Home. By the mid-1970s Sister Saint Ursula became the first Sister of Saint Joseph to earn a master's degree in social work. Using a new structural model, the Catholic Home for Girls opened three group homes, one of which, Eugenie House, was staffed by the Sisters of Saint Joseph. This group home was named in honor of Sister Eugenie Marie Lynn who had ministered at Catholic Home for Girls for 34 years.

Sponsored Works: Institutions of Education

During the 1970s, the Congregation created new policies on personnel ratios (religious to lay) and finances in all of its own elementary, secondary, and collegiate facilities. From 50 percent to 75 percent of the teaching staff was now lay, with Sisters of Saint Joseph in administrative roles. In 1972, each institution separated its financial accounts from those of the local convent. Because of the changes in the demographics in Mt. Airy and other nearby neighborhoods in Philadelphia, Cecilian Academy evolved into a school for young African American women. In 1972, it was separated into an upper and lower school with approximately 200 girls in each. Consequently, the curriculum expanded its concentration on the arts to include a more comprehensive study of African American culture.

In 1972, under the leadership of Sister Mary Scanlon (James Anthony), a new entity, Norwood-Fontbonne Academy (NFA), was created from the merger of the former boys' and girls' schools. Rooted in both an individually guided program and in Montessori education, Norwood-Fontbonne Academy gained regional recognition as it piloted the new Middles States Accreditation process for elementary schools. By 1979, Norwood-Fontbonne Academy boasted an enrollment of over 600 students.

At the secondary level, Holy Family Academy in Bayonne, New Jersey, traditionally offered a college preparatory education for young women of diverse backgrounds and continued to do so throughout the 1970s. Meanwhile, Mount Saint Joseph Academy in Flourtown, Pennsylvania, experimented with part-time college coursework, mini-course intersessions, and an early admissions arrangement with Chestnut Hill College. A campus ministry program also grew under the combined efforts of sisters and laity.

St. Joseph Academy in McSherrystown, Pennsylvania, unlike those in Flourtown and Bayonne, struggled to remain open. During the 1970s, the sisters steadfastly tried to maintain the coed elementary program and the day and residential high school for girls. The Congregation financed new learning centers and a dormitory to supplement necessary improvements. Three factors, though, led to the close of the secondary school in 1978 and of the elementary school in 1979. First, this rural area of southern Pennsylvania had a low school-age population. Second, Delone Catholic High School and the five parish elementary schools adequately served the existing student population at a tuition rate nearly 75 percent lower than that charged at the Academy. Third, the families already had a relationship with the Sisters of Saint Joseph, since they staffed all five grade schools and Delone Catholic as well. The closing of the school, however, was not the end of the institution itself or of the sisters' connection to it, because a completely new use was found for the property: a senior citizen day care center and Head Start preschool. While the endeavors were distinct entities, the sisters created programs that united the young children with the senior citizens, thus utilizing the skills and talents of sisters in full-time and auxiliary ministry.

For Chestnut Hill College, the post-Vatican years meant reassessment and new directions. Sister Mary Xavier Kirby, the fourth president, steered the College through the crises of enrollment, governance, and finances that many American colleges faced. In addition the College's enrollment declined as the local men's colleges (St. Joseph, Villanova, and LaSalle) went coed. The number of sister-students dropped from 643 in 1969 to 113 in 1979. While maintaining its status as a liberal arts institution, Chestnut Hill adapted to the career needs of full-time and part-time students. Options such as the Women in Management program, internships, affiliations with other institutions like Thomas Jefferson University School of Allied Health Sciences, computer programming, and a new major in economics were instituted, along with a plan to offer graduate degrees. To stabilize governance, the Congregation amended the early 1871 Charter to assure the continued ownership by the Sisters of Saint Joseph and to expand the board of directors by adding lay members. Financially, the College practiced austerity in budgeting, set up an Investment Committee to develop its portfolio, and paid off its $1.5 million mortgage. By 1979, the College had recovered its enrollment, enjoyed a brighter financial outlook, broadened its involvement with the local Chestnut Hill Community, increased its recruitment of minority women, and established a new outreach in social justice.

Saint Joseph Villa

Saint Joseph Villa, Flourtown, provided expanded opportunities for ministry beyond that of the primary ministry of prayer of the 230 sister-residents. Although not originally intended for this purpose, building Saint Joseph Villa paved the way for the Congregation's entrance into the health care ministry. Every year, new sisters were assigned as Villa staff to meet the ever-increasing demands of clerical work, physical therapy, and skilled care of the residents. Increased personnel, though, did not completely solve every problem, and it became clear that a new model of administration was needed to effectively operate such a large, state-of-the-art facility.

To expedite this process, the 1974 Chapter designated retirement of the sisters and the administration of the Villa as areas of responsibility for a particular councillor. In August 1975, Sister Michael Cecelia became resident superior and Sister Alice Dolores Kane, Administrator. Sister Charles Consilii Anderson was appointed Director of Nurses, Sister Mary Thomas, Coordinator of Clinical Services, and Sister Celestine McCartan, Consultant. The result of the comprehensive evaluation of the Villa (1977) completed by 400 staff members and residents indicated a need for more personal involvement by the Congregation in the lives of the sister-residents. In response, four additional superiors were appointed, and by the late 1970s the full-time staff of the Villa included 50 Sisters of Saint Joseph.

Expanding Frontiers in Ministry

The Sisters of Saint Joseph have traditionally ministered, primarily in the education of children, at both the elementary and secondary levels. However, during the 1970s, other ministries were gradually emerging including youth ministry, family ministry, liturgy development, spiritual direction, and chaplaincies. While unwavering in her commitment to schools, Mother Alice Anita opened the door to other types of ministry:

> The Sisters of Saint Joseph will retain as their primary apostolate the education of children.... The Sisters will also engage, after proper professional training, in the relatively new frontiers of the Church's Apostolate of Education ... in the Confraternity of Christian Doctrine programs, in Adult Education, Special Education, and the Campus Apostolate.

By 1979, 31 sisters served as DREs (Directors of Religious Education), primarily in suburban parishes where Sisters of Saint Joseph were already established in the school. In 1967, Sister Kathleen O'Neill (Columba) became Coordinator of Parish Religion Programs at Saint Pius X, Bowie, Maryland. Her responsibilities consisted of coordinating the religious education of the parish school, administering CCD for 1,957 students in grades one through six, supervising the teaching techniques, planning parish adult religious education programs, teaching high school CCD (and some religion classes in the parish school), and attending all meetings connected to her work. Gradually, DREs began to serve neighboring parishes that had no schools. In 1974, Sister Mary Janet McGoldrick and Sister Agnes Bernadette Wagner established the religious education program for St. Bernadette, Northfield, New Jersey, in the Diocese of Camden.

Other sisters moved into even more diverse ministries. Sister Marie Therese Liddy became campus minister at Temple University's Newman Center (1973), and in 1974 Sister Leona Tucker (Elizabeth Leona), former principal of St. Joseph Special Education School in Pottsville, Pennsylvania, began serving as chaplain at the new Woodhaven Center in Philadelphia for mentally challenged and emotionally disturbed persons. In 1977, three sisters began pastoral care services in Spring Hill and Largo, Florida. In some diocesan offices, Sisters of Saint Joseph assumed leadership roles in education, while Sister Margaret Mary Culbert (Silvanus) (Archdiocese of Washington) and Sister Rose of Lima (Archdiocese of Philadelphia) served as Assistant Vicars for Religious. In the Archdiocese of Newark, Sister Anastasia Hearne was named Secretary for Parish Life and assistant to the chancellor in 1978.

While relatively few sisters served in these "alternative ministries," complex issues involving ministry and local community living arose. Sisters in alternative ministries sometimes seemed more isolated, having different schedules and separate cars for their use. At times, sisters in school ministry felt more confined and regimented, while sisters in other ministries who worked alone felt that their work was less valued by the other sisters. In some cases the Médaille Team and the Local Community Development (LCD) program helped sisters strengthen the bonds of local community and explore new ways of relating to one another.

Exploring Apostolic Directions

During the decade of the 1970s, the Sisters of Saint Joseph gradually expanded their range of ministries beyond the classroom as a response to emerging congregational and ecclesial needs. As far back as 1955, statistics revealed a discrepancy in the number of personnel available to staff the schools and the number actually required. In 1967, 19 novices had to "break" their canonical year and go out to teach so the congregation could honor its commitments. This radical solution clarified the severity of the personnel problem and presaged what would become evident in the next decade: the number of candidates to religious communities had reached its peak. An interior study was conducted in 1970, but the basic policy of maintaining commitment to staff a school—unless extraordinary situations forced a withdrawal—remained. The Congregation worked with the bishops in several dioceses to agree upon a fair ratio of sisters to lay teachers in order to continue serving in all schools to which it was committed, but none of these was tenable for any length of time. By 1977, the basic of the ratio had shifted to total enrollment, so that the personnel allotment was one sister per 80 students, and by 1979 that had increased to one sister per 100 students. Despite the obvious import of these statistics, the congregational leadership agreed to staff 20 new schools that year, exacerbating an already critical problem.

Meeting with bishops and pastors yielded no solutions to the staffing dilemma, so the Congregation attempted to deal with the situation internally. Using the Centers for Corporate Reflection (CCR), the congregational leadership engaged all the sisters in establishing criteria for apostolic planning that would incorporate the spirit of the founder, Gospel values, and the signs of the times. While the 1974 Chapter had affirmed education as the Congregation's primary apostolic outreach, it also advocated that sisters be open to the future, to new forms and new programs.

Since the number of sisters engaged in what had been called "alternative forms of the apostolate" was increasing, the need to plan for the future, rather than allow circumstances to dictate it, was critical. Sisters discussed a wide range of topics which resulted in five basic questions that needed to be resolved:

- Whom should we serve?
- What should be the form of service?
- What are the resources required to support these forms of service?
- What do we need from those we serve?
- What kind of community life must we have to support our service?

During the summer of 1975, a task force investigated each question and compiled a comprehensive study packet of reflection points based on national and congregational statistics, Scripture, congregational documents, Vatican II references, and research on contemporary trends in society and the church. During 1975–1976, sisters dialogued in local community and in three CCRs on the five questions and formulated responses. In the summer of 1976, a second task force distilled the results of the responses and created four possible directions for the future. A booklet on each identified its implications for ministry, resources, and local community living. The directions were:

- CC—Corporate Collaborative: The Congregation makes a corporate commitment to work in a collaborative way with clergy and laity.
- IC—Individual Choice: Each sister makes/discerns her own individual choice of apostolate
- CP—Commitment to People: The Congregation makes a corporate commitment to people rather than a particular work and discerns best ways to serve the People of God.
- CW—Commitment to Works: The Congregation makes a corporate commitment to apostolate of education supplemented by related educational, social, and spiritual ministries.

From September 1976 through April 1977, sisters probed the meanings of the four apostolic directions, or modes of commitment. Soon the titles IC, CC, CP, and CW became household acronyms!

In April 1976, the Council dialogued with the bishops superiors, principals, and pastors. Feedback from these groups was available to the task force and to the Congregation before the sisters' final CCR in April 1977. The two top choices, according to the CCR results, were CP (Commitment to People) and CC (Collaborative Commitment). In June 1977, Sister Alice Anita announced that Commitment to People would be the apostolic direction of the Sisters of Saint Joseph. Later, this was officially titled Corporate Ecclesial Commitment to People (CECP) with the insertion of *Ecclesial* emphasizing the dimension of Church.

Conclusion

In choosing CECP, the Sisters of Saint Joseph affirmed the vision of their founder. The sisters were to be contemplatives in action, practicing all the spiritual and corporal works of mercy. Endorsing CECP the sisters did not mean abandoned Catholic schools but emphasized the relational aspect of service to people. In fact, they perhaps became more convinced that they themselves were the greatest gift they had to offer to those they served.

At the 1979 Chapter, the delegates mandated the actions necessary to implement CECP. First, the delegates affirmed it as compatible with the Congregation's charism, the sisters' capabilities, and the Chapter theme of evangelization. Second, the congregational Administration asked to initiate the restructuring of works and re-allocation of personnel in order to make CECP a viable reality. This daunting task would require ingenuity and stamina, as well as planning and education. The fruits of interior renewal would now become evident in this new direction which would lead the Sisters of Saint Joseph into new forms of apostolic ministry.

PUBLISHED SOURCES

Byrne, Patricia, CSJ. In the Parish and Not of It: Sisters. In *Transforming Parish Ministry* by Jay P. Dolan, R. Scot Appleby, Patricia Byrne, and Debra Campbell. New York: Crossroad Publishing, 1990.

Convey, John J. *Catholic Schools Make a Difference.* Washington, DC: National Catholic Education Association, 1992.

Dolan, Jay P. *The American Catholic Experience.* Garden City, NY: Doubleday and Company, 1985.

Flannery, Austin, OP, ed. Dogmatic Constitution on the Church (Lumen Gentium). In *Vatican Council II: The Conciliar and Post Conciliar Documents.* Boston: Daughters of St. Paul, 1975.

Quinonez, Lora Ann, CDP, and Mary Daniel Turner, SNDdeN. *The Transformation of American Catholic Sisters.* Philadelphia: Temple University Press, 1992.

ARCHIVAL SOURCES

Mount Saint Joseph Convent, Philadelphia, Pennsylvania

Primitive documents, records of General Chapters, personal papers, focus groups, and other records.

Chapter Five

Expanding Our Vision

1980–1989

Following the uncertainty of the 1970s, many Americans welcomed stability as Ronald Reagan's presidency ushered in a conservative era. Personal computers, minivans, video games, and designer clothes signaled a return to affluence, even amid a recession and a growing deficit fueled by new large military costs. Increased homelessness, the spread of AIDS, escalating medical expenses, and the use of a new drug, crack, clouded the American sense of well-being. Internationally, Premier Mikhail Gorbachev's reforms in the Soviet Union spurred rapid change in Eastern Europe, effectively ending the Cold War by 1989 as the Berlin Wall fell. After 40 years of threats, America stood alone as a superpower. There was a new world order.

Within a concurrent societal turn to religious conservatism, the Church took on many faces. Led by Joseph Cardinal Bernardin, the American bishops spoke out boldly for social justice and against war in the nuclear age; for economic justice and against abortion; for cultural pluralism and for racial equality. Pope John Paul II, elected in 1978, delivered the same messages globally during his world travels. Within the Church, he focused on restoration and centralization while the new *Code of Canon Law* (1983) captured the Vatican II concepts of consultation and subsidiarity. For American Catholics, a diversity of traditions in prayer, liturgy, and devotions was now commonplace. African American and Hispanic ethnic influences, a resurgence of older devotional practices, and Vatican II changes fit comfortably and sometimes not so comfortably into the mosaic of Catholic life.

Chapter 5
MINISTRY

During the 1970s, the Sisters of Saint Joseph effected changes in their apostolic ministry that would continue to have ramifications into the 1980s. In fall 1980, Sister Dorothea Newell (Ignatius Loyola), Superior General, invoked the biblical image of God as potter, reshaping the Congregation in matters of ministry, spirituality, and even governance in order to meet the challenges of the time—both ecclesial and secular. The 1979 Chapter mandated the restructuring of works and re-allocation of personnel; the leadership had to develop criteria to guide this process.

From spring 1980 through spring 1982, the entire Congregation was engaged in a data-gathering process that ultimately formed the basis for decision making regarding ministry commitments and personnel allocation. Studies were conducted in the 187 parish elementary schools staffed by the Sisters of Saint Joseph, eliciting feedback from parents, teachers, staff, pastors, and students. Next, local communities, collaborating with the Commission for Justice, developed 24 value statements reflecting the charism of the Sisters of Saint Joseph, including their philosophy of education, and the previously chosen apostolic direction, Corporate Ecclesial Commitment to People (CECP).These statements eventually became the criteria used to evaluate the viability of current commitments and to make decisions regarding future apostolic works. In addition to this data, sisters were asked to complete a survey on apostolic priorities (1981). One of the major issues that arose from this was whether to continue staffing schools that now had a largely non-Catholic enrollment. Since many of these schools were in poor urban areas, withdrawing meant abandoning the very people the Congregation, in its social justice initiatives, had pledged to serve. In these parish schools, evangelization had also become a major outreach; consequently, the withdrawal of the sisters would impact many other programs that were tangential to the education of the students and welfare of their families. After reviewing all the data, Sister Dorothea Newell and the Council decided not to use percentages of non-Catholics as a criteria for withdrawal from a school.

Since 56 percent of the sisters served in 187 parish elementary schools, these commitments became the primary focus of the restructuring of ministry and reallocation of personnel. The title given to this process was Project: Withdrawal/Recommitment (PWR). Each year a percentage of the parish-staffed elementary schools was studied. Based on the results, the leadership determined whether to withdraw from a school or recommit to it for a limited number of years. Each recommitment necessitated an ongoing review. Usually, the withdrawal of sisters occurred one year after the decision was made. However, in schools with five or more full-time sisters a gradual withdrawal was offered. This meant that half the sisters left one year after the decision had been made to withdraw, while the other half remained for two more years. This process was painful for all parties involved, and, perhaps to avoid it, some parishes, when told of the eventual withdrawal, opted for a complete withdrawal of the sisters at the end of the year.

The difficulty of trying to retain a partial presence was compounded by the leadership's unwillingness to assign only a principal to a school since the number of principals was diminishing. However, the Congregation would honor any request for a Director of Religious Education, and this allowed the sisters to remain with the parish, even if they could no longer staff the school.

Supporting the sisters also remained a primary goal of the Administration as the Congregation struggled through the process of PWR. In two sets of congregational cluster meetings, the leadership engaged the sisters in prayer, education, and dialogue. More than 1,450 sisters at 40 cluster sites in fall 1982 listened to and questioned the Administration about the implementation of PWR. Sisters were stunned by the facts of the Congregation's diminished numbers, disputed decisions about individual schools, wondered how to enable lay leadership, feared unemployment, and worried how PWR would impact future vocations. At the fall 1985 cluster, the Administration met with sister-principals and vice principals to encourage them to assume a leadership role in facilitating the empowerment of the laity in those schools from which the Congregation needed to withdraw in order to continue the charism of the Sisters of Saint Joseph.

By the time of the next Chapter (1984), the Congregation had withdrawn from 37 schools and recommitted to 46. This did little to alleviate the critical shortage of personnel, since the actual process often resulted in gaining sisters from a withdrawal, but more were needed to staff other existing commitments. For example, in 1983, 35 sisters were withdrawn from schools, but 77 sisters were needed for the Congregation's commitments in other elementary schools.

Traditionally, parish convents housed the sisters who served in school ministry. Between 1979 and 1983, the Sisters of Saint Joseph moved out of 34 convents due to school withdrawals or convent consolidations. The sisters who ministered in these schools were responsible for completely cleaning and preparing the facilities for new occupants or for closure. In the past, the sisters were excited to open new convents, but now, there was a sense of loss, both personal and communal.

1984 Chapter and Project Withdraw/Recommitment

During the 1984 Chapter, PWR was one of 13 issues for study and discussion. After considerable analysis and consultation, the Chapter's Withdrawal/ Recommitment Committee affirmed the need for PWR, stating, "The information gathered, the facts found, and the statistics learned, made it very obvious that the reality remains—we are diminishing in resources and there is an urgent need for us to continue to deal with that reality." The committee's recommendations underscored the undeniability of the facts and critical problem of continued loss of personnel. The delegates unanimously passed enactments that authorized the Administration to continue the withdrawals but created a committee to determine whether PWR was the most effective instrument to effect the necessary changes. In its January 1985 report, the ad hoc committee on PWR did not recommend an alternative method; in fact, the committee viewed the next five years as the "second wave of PWR," stressing that it was not a question of which schools would be studied but when each school commitment would undergo scrutiny.

As of September 1989, the sisters remained in 99 parish elementary schools, representing a virtual 50 percent reduction from 1980. The decisions, which would be reviewed in 1992, reflected a remarkable proportionality, since the sisters were now serving in parish elementary schools in the same 15 dioceses as they had been in 1980, with the same distribution across socioeconomic groups. On the secondary school level, re-allocation was effected through attrition, and in 1989 the 228 sisters serving in 45 high schools represented a decrease of 43 percent from 1980 when 400 sisters were involved in secondary education.

Ministries in Sponsored Works

While PWR was the vehicle for determining future commitments in parish and diocesan institutions, the Congregation needed to address the problem of diminishing personnel as it affected the institutions owned and operated by the Sisters of Saint Joseph. In 1984, nearly 10 percent (130) of the sisters in educational ministry served in these institutions. Historically, Chestnut Hill College and the five academies had functioned fairly autonomously, with the College having the most integral relationship with the congregational Administration because the superior general chaired the College Board of Trustees and some members of the General Council were also members. In the 1984 Chapter Report, the General Council provided, for the first time, a detailed report on these institutions, and periodic meetings were then held with their administrators to discuss a shared vision rooted in the Congregation's mission and philosophy of education. On September 24, 1987, the administrators of the elementary and secondary academies met with Sisters Kathleen Kean (Helen Therese) and Eugenie Madeleine Gaddi, Councillors, and with staff from the Offices of Apostolic Works and Finances to discuss the purpose of these schools, their finances, their accountability to the Congregation, and their constituencies. In 1987, a manual outlining some common expectations was created, and the Coordinators of Ministry conducted regular supervisory visits to the academies assessing Sister of Saint Joseph identity, social justice efforts, and financial viability. Formerly, each institution had evaluated itself, but supervision was now under the auspices of the Coordinators of Ministry for Elementary Education: Sisters Mary Helen Beirne (Helen Eugene), Regina Bell (Francis Regina), Deborah Hughes (Patrick Edward), and Mary Scanlon (James Anthony). With regard to the College, Sister Frances Maureen Hoffman, appointed Coordinator of Ministry for Higher Education in 1985, dealt with the College administration and with the sisters on staff.

Due to the low enrollment, the decision to close Cecilian Academy's Upper School was made in October 1988. The Lower School was allowed to remain open because its predominantly African American student population remained stable. Holy Family Academy in Bayonne, New Jersey, suffered a steep decline in enrollment from 546 to 284 (1984–1989) and had incurred a significant debt. Attributing some of the school's difficulties to the decision of its neighbor, Marist High School, to go coeducational, the Congregation supplied additional financial support and provided more sisters on staff. Unlike Cecilian or Holy Family, Mount Saint Joseph Academy and Norwood-Fontbonne Academy continued to thrive. Enrollment in both was increasing and new programs were being piloted. Mount Saint Joseph closed its home economics department and focused on becoming a leading college preparatory school for young women. Computers were installed, and an exchange student program with France was initiated. Norwood-Fontbonne Academy, now a coeducational facility, continued to enhance its Montessori program.

During the presidency of Sister Matthew Anita MacDonald, Chestnut Hill College developed more programs to complement the traditional liberal arts regimen and initiated a graduate program in 1980. In 1988, amid considerable financial concerns, the College undertook its first capital campaign to increase its endowment and to bolster student financial aid, salaries, instructional needs, and improvements to the physical plant. To support this venture, the Congregation invested personnel in the College where contributed services provided essential support.

Saint Joseph Villa

Although not an educational facility, Saint Joseph Villa, Flourtown, Pennsylvania, was also studied and evaluated in an effort to enhance the facility and transform it into a full-service, professional health care institution. Several changes were made in the early 1980s that preceded the restructuring of the Villa. Advised by health care consultants Sisters Gerard Hartney CSC, of Washington, DC, and Mary Logan CSJ, of Brentwood, New York, the Congregation expanded the Villa's services to increase efficiency. When space was available, the Villa admitted members of other religious communities and lay persons. In addition, an adult day care center was established.

In 1983, the General Council took the significant risk of hiring a lay administrator for the Villa because the Congregation had no sister trained as a professional health care administrator. On the recommendation of the search committee, Mr. Terry C. Tressler, who had served as a consultant during the *Third Age* review, was hired to replace Sister Celestine McCartan. During the next four years, Mr. Tressler inaugurated a series of changes in policies, procedures, and services intended to align Saint Joseph Villa with the current standards of a multifaceted health care facility. For example, services formerly provided by the sisters such as those of the dietary and pharmacy departments were outsourced. New professional staff positions now required more formalized employee policies and procedures. A quality assurance program and patient profiling analysis system were implemented. A mission statement was developed, a residents' council established, and a professional pastoral care department instituted to ensure Saint Joseph Villa's social and spiritual character.

Amid all the modifications, one, in particular, brought a most difficult adjustment. Because of the new patient profiling analysis and the regrouping of services, a sister's medical needs for skilled, intermediate, personal, or residential care now determined her room and floor location. To institute this restructuring, 86 sisters changed their rooms in a single day, leaving behind familiar surroundings, faces, and patterns in the transfer to a new location. In their own way, the sisters at the Villa shared the pain and the challenge of PWR that pervaded the Congregation.

Early in 1987, Sister Marie Rudegeair (Madeleine Sophie), a trained secondary school administrator, completed her studies in health care administration and was appointed Assistant Administrator. In December 1988, she succeeded Mr. Tressler as Saint Joseph Villa's Administrator. In that same year, the Congregation agreed to supply additional sisters as nursing assistants to offset the impact of the national nursing shortage. The Council's reports to both the 1984 and 1989 Chapters highlighted the financial profile, listing the annual expenditures for Saint Joseph Villa in 1980 at $2.2 million. By 1988 this figure had risen to $2.9 million.

Subsidized Senior Housing Facilities

While initiating changes at the Saint Joseph Villa, the Sisters of Saint Joseph ventured into a new form of service to the elderly and infirmed: housing facilities and services. This new ministry implemented the 1979 Chapter directive to respond to the housing and personal needs of the elderly, particularly sisters' parents, but such service also enabled the Congregation to utilize unused buildings or properties. Staffing such residences did not require many sisters, but effectively elicited the skills that sisters had developed in educational ministry. On December 23, 1980, the General Council established the Saint Joseph Housing Corporation. Its mission was "to provide elderly and handicapped persons with housing facilities and services specially designed to meet their physical, social, and psychological needs, and to promote their health, security, happiness, and usefulness in longer living."

During the 1980s, the Congregation undertook three housing projects, two at Saint Joseph Academy in McSherrystown, Pennsylvania, where housing for low-income elders was greatly needed, and one on the property adjacent to Saint Joseph Villa. In 1982, renovations turned two buildings into Academy Village, comprised of five two-bedroom apartments providing senior citizens in McSherrystown with subsidies for their rents. Building on the success of Academy Village, the Congregation leased two more school buildings and their grounds for the establishment, in 1987, of the McSherrystown Interfaith Village, a 47-unit apartment complex. The third housing development in Flourtown was part of a Department of Housing and Urban Development (HUD) project called Bethlehem Village that had opened in fall 1984 with 109 residents, including some with special needs. These new ways of providing for the needs of the "dear neighbor" gave renewed vigor to Father Médaille's vision that the sisters should meet the needs of the people.

New Support for Sisters

In the 1980s, the Office of Apostolic Works (OAW) expanded both in size and direction. The two-person staff of Sister Loretta Hogan (Joan Lorretta) and Sister Antoinette Munafo (Antonia), established in 1975, was increased to two full-time Coordinators of Elementary Education, two part-time Coordinators for Secondary Education, a Coordinator for Religious Education, and a Director of Personnel Services. The purpose of this enlarged staff was to revitalize the Congregation's commitment to quality educational ministry and to facilitate the creation of "a process of personal assessment."

Between 1981 and 1983, Sister Catherine Knobbs (Agnes Leonard), Director of Personnel Services, interviewed 134 sisters about their apostolic potential. Between 1982 and 1984, she offered a workshop—The Resume: A Tool for Self-Assessment—25 times; nearly 500 sisters attended. She also conducted the Congregation's career counseling, which included pre-retirement counseling, aptitude testing, and individualized preparation for ministry interviews. In the mid-1980s, the Office of Apostolic Works (OAW) was firmly committed to focusing on personnel rather than works. The 1984 Chapter mandated the appointment of coordinators of ministry to "promote a spirit of vitality and accountability" in ministry. Coordinators of ministry were to oversee specific ministries: elementary education, secondary education, and varied ministry.

Third World Ministry

In 1982 the General Council opted to send a few sisters to serve in Third World countries. Considering the apparent personnel shortage, this decision seemed paradoxical, but the Administration cited the papal appeals of both Pius XII and John XXIII for increased missionary efforts. Unlike some other congregations, the Sisters of Saint Joseph had no established foreign missions, nor did the Congregation have the financial or personnel resources to initiate such a commitment. Nevertheless, some believed that the call to social justice impelled the Congregation to embrace a global vision of the kingdom and to actively participate in it. Using the rationale that "where one of us is we all are," the General Council decided to send three to five sisters to Third World countries to join the efforts of other SSJ/CSJ Congregations that had pre-existing commitments.

Forty sisters responded to the General Council's invitation and five were chosen. Sister Mary Corbett (Anne Charles) became a pastoral minister in Marcona, Peru. Sister Kathleen Duffy (Miriam Matthew) taught physics at Ateneo de Manila University in the Philippines. Sister Catherine Lengle (James Laboure) became the principal at St. Joseph School in Greenville, Liberia, in West Africa. Sister Marie Isabel Manning became a pastoral minister in Chimbote, Peru. And Sister Winifred Grelis (William Augustine) joined Sister Catherine Lengle in Liberia as a spiritual minister. These missionaries shared their experiences via letters to the entire Congregation, enabling sisters to better understand the challenges and joys of this form of apostolic witness.

Summer Ministry

Another form of missionary activity was available to sisters through a variety of summer ministries, many of which involved service to the poor. In the 1980s, these ministries actively became testing grounds where sisters might experience a new type of apostolic service that could help them discern future choices about ministry. Many of these summer assignments took sisters as far as New Mexico, or as close as Holmsburg Prison, Philadelphia. The process of choosing a summer ministry involved both self-reflection and self-assessment, two aspects of a sister's personal involvement in the missioning process.

Changing Ministries

As a result of several factors—including PWR, education for non-school-related ministries, and involvement in missionary activity—the Congregation established a policy in 1982 to provide a structure for those sisters who felt called to serve in nontraditional ministries. Simply called the Change of

Apostolate Policy, this instrument gave sisters an opportunity to discern a change in ministry in a more formal manner.

The Change of Apostolate Policy was not a fast track for transition to another ministry; in fact, the policy included some potentially formidable hurdles. The Congregation still had numerous school positions to fill each year, so huge numbers of sisters could not be permitted to leave education. Since communal living required a convent, housing was another issue that needed to be considered. In addition to these concerns were the need for proper professional training—which could be costly—and the necessity of a stipend commensurate with that paid to those in school ministry. Even if a sister's request was approved, the actual transfer to another ministry could take up to two years to complete.

This process actually kept the number of sisters in non–school-related ministry fairly small. For example, many sisters requested hospital ministry, yet few paid openings were found in areas where the Congregation currently served and had available housing in a local community. By the 1984 Chapter, only 152 sisters were in stipended non-school ministries, and most of these were Directors of Religious Education, parish ministers, or pastoral musicians. Some held diocesan-level positions in social work, vocation work, vicars' offices, and parish renewal efforts, and a very limited number worked in ministries directly connected with social justice. Still, the Change of Apostolate Policy provided structure to the Congregation's effort to balance personal discernment and corporate needs.

Changing Demographics in Ministry

By the end of the 1980s, the Sisters of Saint Joseph had begun to serve in many alternative forms of ministry while statistics demonstrated that the number of sisters still engaged in the Congregation's corporate apostolic work of education was decreasing. While the number of full-time teaching sisters was dwindling, the number in auxiliary services was on the rise. In 1988, 349 sisters were ministering in schools while 146 were working in services at Saint Joseph Villa and local convents in an auxiliary capacity. In preparation for the 1989 Chapter, the Coordinators of Ministry for Elementary Education asked each sister involved to project her future time commitment to the elementary school apostolate. The report to the Chapter indicated the sisters' desire to provide quality and excellence in the classroom but cited diminished energy due to age and health issues. Approximately 63 percent (450) of the sisters projected full-time service for one to five years, while 37 percent (264) projected five to 10 years.

In addition to these factors, the creation of new positions of leadership and service within the Congregation also contributed to a lesser degree to the diminishing number of available educational personnel. Sister Catherine

Knobbs was appointed the first Director of Personnel Services, adding another dimension to the OAW (Office of Apostolic Works). In 1983, Sister Roberta Archibald (Robert Andrew) became the first director of the SSJ Associates in Mission, and in 1988, Sister Mary Elizabeth Clark (John Victoria) was appointed the first Social Justice Coordinator. Also in 1988, Sister Madeline Franze (Teresa Joseph) became the first Development Director. In that same year, eight sisters were assigned to Saint Joseph Villa as nursing assistants, and three others were appointed to the administrative staff of Bethlehem Retirement Village.

Not only was the Congregation investing personnel in internal services, but, following a 1984 Chapter enactment regarding ministry to the socially and materially poor within the United States, more sisters were permitted to serve in designated mission areas. Three ministered in parts of Kentucky, while others went to West Virginia and to Montana. In Philadelphia, two sisters became members of the staff of Women of Hope, a homeless shelter sponsored by the Sisters of Mercy. Although these ministries were consonant with the charism of the Sisters of Saint Joseph, they were costly in terms of monetary subsidies and personnel resources.

Personnel Services and the Missioning Process

Under the direction of Sister Catherine Knobbs, personnel services encompassed a wide range of initiatives. Sister Catherine was instrumental in drafting new policies and procedures for electing local superiors, changing apostolates, and a sister's preparation for new ministry. She organized and disseminated requests for personnel from dioceses, parishes, and other agencies. As a result of the 1984 Chapter-mandated missioning board, she was able to effectively network all the constituent parties of the OAW to facilitate the missioning process.

The missioning board became the vehicle for coordinating the evolving missioning process. This structure formalized some of the practices that had developed internally since 1979 and became the locus for implementing and assessing the elements prescribed by the 1984 Chapter. It officially brought together the area delegates, the coordinators of ministry, and the director of personnel services as the board members. After consultation with the sisters, the board made recommendations to the superior general for personnel assignments.

To handle the differences between assigning sisters for corporate commitments (schools) and individual commitments, the missioning board actually managed two different processes for the approximately 360 sisters needing placement each year. Each sister received an individual assignment letter, eliminating the much anticipated—sometimes dreaded—Summer Change List. In 1987, the Administration eliminated the official moving day for all those in transition and further individualized the process by offering sisters a period of 10 days (August 1–10) to move to their new missions.

Conclusion

Despite all the changes that had been made regarding the missioning process, missioning continued to be a critical issue demanding attention at the 1989 Chapter. The results of the 20 CCR Centers in March 1988 all identified missioning as a major topic for discussion. At the conclusion of deliberations, the Chapter mandated that the "Administration in collaboration with membership, examine and adjust our evolving missioning process so that each sister bring to her obedience, qualities of initiative, judgment, and personal responsibility." The Chapter further mandated that there would be a single missioning process and advocated the ongoing evaluation of the advantages and disadvantages of corporate commitments. During the next decade, the feasibility of corporate commitments would continue to be an issue, especially as more sisters transitioned from the teaching ministry into other apostolic endeavors that required personal discernment, professional preparation, and an individual specific application process.

SPIRITUALITY

Personal and Communal Prayer Resources and Experiences

Affirmed by the 1979 Chapter, the SSJ Center for Spirituality's programs provided an array of opportunities for growth in prayer, self-knowledge, and spirituality. In a decade when sisters were struggling with diminishing numbers and withdrawal from schools, the Center offered weekends on Ignatian discernment. Programs on the Enneagram, based on the Sufi system of nine personality types, helped sisters to understand personal blocks to conversion and aided them in their quest for health and holiness.

Although the SSJ Center for Spirituality provided diverse opportunities for prayer and reflection during the year, the annual retreat was still the mainstay in the spiritual life of each sister. During the 1980s, changes in the retreat offerings and schedules enhanced the experience for many sisters. One sign of change was the welcoming retreat brochure sent to every local house beginning in 1980. Replacing the traditional list of retreat dates, the new flyer included a description of each retreat's theme. It also contained a letter from Sister Dorothea Newell, Superior General, inviting sisters to make retreat choices that fit them personally. Congregational retreats also began to integrate the types previously given only through the SSJ Center for Spirituality.

At Saint Mary by-the-Sea, Cape May Point, women were introduced as retreat directors and several of these were Sisters of Saint Joseph. In 1983, Sister Grace Pino (Maria Goretti), worked with Rev. John Carboy SJ, on a liturgical retreat; and in 1984, Sister Eleanor McNichol (Eleanor Thomas) led an eight-day guided retreat on SSJ heritage and spirituality. Beginning in 1986, Sister Virginia Sampson SUSC, conducted the Enneagram retreats. The sisters who staffed the SSJ Center for Spirituality also provided both directed and guided retreats at Cape May Point. These initiatives were instrumental in encouraging women religious, especially the Sisters of Saint Joseph, to assume roles in spiritual development alongside their male counterparts.

In the 1980s, small-scale renovations at Cape May Point provided sisters with more privacy and enhanced their retreat experiences. In 1983, the third-floor dormitories were converted into 20 small rooms, and nine more single bedrooms were created the following summer. These new rooms actually had electricity, which in the past had only been installed in common area and corridors. After some debate about the proper way to renovate the worship space, changes in the layout of the chapel were made. In 1986, after some compromise, the pews were reconfigured in a u-shape with a simple wooden altar, designed by Sister Mary Julia Daly, as the focal point. The Blessed Sacrament was reserved in the tabernacle in a private prayer space where the original altar had been; weavings by Sister Lilian Virginia Lane cordoned off the area, creating a private prayer space. Sister Catherine Ann Meighan designed new Stations of the Cross for the assembly area. The overall effect of these renovations in Saint Mary by-the-Sea enriched the retreat experience from both a spiritual and aesthetic perspective.

Since Vatican II, communal prayer was comprised of morning and evening prayer based on the Liturgy of the Hours and faith sharing, or shared prayer as it was often called. Local communities endeavored to remain faithful to the established horarium, but the increasing diversity in sisters' personal schedules made this difficult. In order to accommodate these variations, local houses experimented with flexibility in scheduling. By the mid- to late 1980s, some local communities were also using different forms of the Liturgy of the Hours, such as *The New Companion to the Breviary*, which had a contemporary translation of the psalms that utilized inclusive language. In an attempt to strengthen the spiritual bond between the sisters in the convent and those to whom they ministered, sisters created prayer cards or sent letters to parishioners and coworkers to let them know that they were being remembered in the prayers in the local community. Such gestures were a tangible sign of the Mission of the Sisters of Saint Joseph: "That all may be one."

The terms *faith sharing* and *shared prayer* were—and still are—often used interchangeably; however, slight differences actually exist. Faith sharing did not necessarily have to be Scripture-based, while shared prayer revolved around reflection on a particular passage that all participants read and pondered before sharing insights aloud within the group. For some, faith sharing seemed to intrude on a person's private space, or at least demand a level of interpersonal trust that some sisters found difficult. In any event, controversy persisted, although most local convents attempted to include the practice in their weekly horarium. In 1984, a presentation was made to the Chapter regarding *Sharing the State of the House*, a term attributed to Father Médaille who intended the sisters to share more deeply with each other. The 1984 Chapter consequently affirmed the importance of the concept of shared prayer, faith sharing, or Sharing the State of the House, when it decreed: "True to the tradition of our early sisters, each local community creates an atmosphere and encourages a time for sharing life and faith."

During the 1980s, another innovation related to the adaptions made to both communal and personal prayer was the creation of a new position: congregational liturgist. The increasing number of communal gatherings at the Motherhouse, where large numbers of sisters participated in liturgies and/or para-liturgies to celebrate events like Ministry Day or Constitutions Day, required the kind of coordination and planning that could only be provided by someone with appropriate training and organizational skills. The first Congregational Liturgist, Sister Charlotte Zalot, was appointed by Sister Dorothea Newell in 1982. Sister Charlotte introduced aspects such as liturgical dance, inclusive language, and multicultural elements to the liturgies at the Motherhouse. In 1986, Sister Grace Pino became the liturgist. Sister focused her energies on education in local community prayer and enhanced liturgical prayer at the Motherhouse and at Saint Joseph Villa.

While the congregational liturgist enhanced congregational prayer experiences and educated the sisters in proper liturgical practices, those working in spiritual direction created a program that linked personal and communal prayer as integrated ways for sharing faith. The General Council affirmed this suggestion and in 1986 authorized the development of the program Living Waters, which consisted of five booklets, each with a different theme, that viewed the *Spiritual Exercises of Saint Ignatius* through the lens of the *Constitutions* of the Sisters of Saint Joseph. During the period of its implementation, a number of sisters affirmed its effectiveness and felt that it promoted a deeper consciousness of corporate identity.

The Vows

In the draft of the new *Constitutions*, the three vows were perceived as interwoven:

> These vows form one single movement of charity which frees us to give ourselves at one and the same time to Christ, and with him to others in a covenant of love accepted and received through the ministry of this Church.

The vow of chastity was now defined as a loving, positive relational response, in which love for Christ included love for all persons. Obedience was interpreted as the interior freedom to respond actively to God's will, not merely blind submission. The sisters brought initiative, judgment, and personal responsibility to decision making as well as a heart ready to go beyond personal ideas and preferences in view of the common good. The vow of poverty, instead of emphasizing material renunciation, called each sister to live ever more simply, to express moderation in all things, and to value all creation as a gift. Living the vow of poverty readied a sister's heart to hear the cry of the poor and oppressed and to accept her interdependence with the entire human community.

In order to help sisters internalize these newer interpretations of the vows, the Congregation sponsored workshops and seminars on topics such as drug and alcohol dependency in family, ministry, personal life, and community. Holistic Living days (celebrated in 1984, 1986, and 1989) also invited sisters to reflect upon and nurture personal growth and interpersonal relationships. Many of the former restrictions on visiting family and friends had been removed, but sisters needed to find ways to improve the quality of the communal life and nourish that primary bond of the local community. Sharing cars and managing modest sums of personal budget money presented some challenges that needed to be overcome, both communally and personally. With the added dimension of increased personal responsibility came the necessary accountability for nurturing the common life. Living the vows became a much more dynamic process, better suited to the apostolic mode of religious life in the 1980s.

Social Justice Initiatives

As an integral part of the vow of poverty in particular, the concept of social justice needed to be incorporated into the spiritual life of the Congregation in personal and tangible ways. To this end, on March 19, 1980, the feast of Saint Joseph, the Superior General and Council inaugurated the SSJ Commission for Justice. The appointed members of the commission were Sisters Joan Marie Berk (Regina Assumption), Mary Elizabeth Clark, Catherine Donohue (Marie Josephine), Kathleen Duffy, Judith Dwyer (James Mary) (chair), Maureen Erdlen (Francis Marguerite), Agnes Maurice LeCalvez, and Virginia Maria Stanton. The group was charged with facilitating, both personally and congregationally, the movement toward greater justice in living the Gospel daily. Along with Sister Saint Ursula Egan, Council liaison, they focused their efforts on changing hearts, through education and action, so that the message of social justice could be heard by all sisters.

In order to reach more people, the SSJ Commission for Justice created five subcommittees: education, networking, communication, local community development, and think-tank. By spring 1982, 70 sisters were serving on these committees. The education subcommittee sponsored workshops with national speakers such as Father Thomas Berry CP, and Sister Amata Miller IHM, while the networking group disseminated information via phone chain and local contact persons. The communication subcommittee provided topics for the congregational hotline and was responsible for publicity and videotaping all workshops. The local community subcommittee created prayer services for special occasions, such as Election Day and the liturgical seasons of Advent, Christmas, and Lent. The think-tank, which served as a resource for applying principles of social justice to congregational policies, studied global trends and helped to critique congregational policies. One such policy was the process for taking a corporate stand on a justice issue. With the assistance of Sister Maria Augusta Neal SND, the think-tank group developed the SSJ Commission for Justice Survey as a resource for the 1984 Chapter.

During the mid- to late 1980s, the Congregation moved beyond an internal acceptance of the doctrine of social justice and toward a more sustained and public commitment to its principles. As advocated by the 1984 Chapter, the General Council strengthened support for the Commission for Justice and for direct service to those who are poor. In 1985, Sister Annemarie Roche (Thomas Veronica) was appointed Coordinator of Ongoing Formation and Justice. In May 1988, Sister Mary Elizabeth Clark succeeded her as the first full-time Coordinator for Justice. During these years, the SSJ Commission for Justice extended many of its previous efforts, establishing a weekly justice hotline and re-aligning the justice network with local congressional districts. The General Council also assigned eight sisters to cross-cultural ministry and shared letters from the five sisters engaged in Third World ministry with the Congregation. In 1986, at the request of Sister Kathleen Duffy from Manila, over 70 local communities joined in prayer and fasting for the Philippine people and government during the period leading to the peaceful overthrow of the Marcos regime.

In response to questions from several sisters about civil disobedience, the General Council, in May 1987, introduced a policy regarding the appropriate uses of civil disobedience by an individual sister or by a group. Guidelines for initiating or participating in an act of civil disobedience included dialogue with the General Council, research into possible legal and financial ramifications, and communication with other members of the local community. The issue itself had to be directly related to peace or justice and of sufficient gravity to warrant such a radical action. Those who were not going to engage in the act of civil disobedience were still encouraged to offer prayer and moral support.

The Congregation initiated the taking of a "Corporate Stand," which had the potential to involve all of the sisters. Using resources from LCWR, the Council in fall 1987 defined a corporate stand in the following terms: "A Corporate Stand is a deliberate public statement and/ or action by a group with regard to an issue of human concerns, gospel values, and/ or ecclesial, societal systems. The stand, expressed non-violently, may be one of assent or dissent."

As part of the dialogue concerning the value and efficacy of the corporate stand, sisters posed questions about which issues would be chosen and what financial and legal burdens might be incurred. The Commission for Justice responded by explaining that the concept of corporate stand was rooted in Scripture, the documents of Vatican II, and the Congregation's Mission. The corporate stand could only be taken if a quorum (two-thirds) of the total Congregation was reached. They acknowledged the possibility for divisiveness yet believed the experience would lead to greater unity among the sisters. The commission also acknowledged the possible impact on the Congregation's benefactor pool, since a corporate stand was a public declaration that was usually at odds with a prevailing societal norm or view. However, the Commission concluded that, "In a Corporate Stand our union with the poor challenges us to give up our security and status as we become one with the victims of oppression. The severity of the critical situation moves us to speak publicly."

The issue chosen for the first congregational Corporate Stand was that of apartheid. After following the prescribed process in May 1988, the Congregation voted. Of the 1,804 sisters in the Congregation, 82.5 percent voted on the apartheid issue. Of these, 80 percent (1,188) supported the stand and 20 percent were opposed. The results of the voting were announced on June 22, 1988, and the official promulgation was made September 14, 1988. Sister Dorothea Newell communicated the decision to bishops in the 16 dioceses where the Congregation served, all senators and representatives in those districts, all secular newspapers, and radio and television stations. President Ronald Reagan, Pope John Paul II, and Anglican Archbishop Desmund Tutu of South Africa were also notified. In response, the Congregation received many letters of support. The Philadelphia City Council honored the Congregation on December 8, 1988, with a resolution citing its commitment to oppose racism.

Implementation of the Corporate Stand was a multifaceted process. The Council co-filed shareholder resolutions with IBM and Chevron corporations calling for the withdrawal of sales and services from South Africa. Following the advice of the Interfaith Center on Corporate Responsibility to boycott Mobil and Shell Oil companies because of their involvement in South Africa, the Council then recalled the Mobil credit cards used to fuel approximately 35 congregationally owned cars. While this might not have had a great financial impact on Mobil Oil, it provided tangible proof to the sisters about the seriousness of the Corporate Stand.

In support of the Congregation's financial actions, many local communities ritualized the boycott of Mobil and Shell in a prayer service during which they cut up the credit cards and mailed them back to the companies. Some houses decided to also boycott Coca-Cola for its refusal to comply with the call for divestment. Individual sisters signed petitions for the freeing of Nelson Mandela, while others focused on prayer or writing to Congress urging legislation on comprehensive sanctions against South Africa. The justice coordinator traveled with two interfaith delegations to South Africa to advocate for an end to apartheid and racism.

By 1989, the Sisters of Saint Joseph realized that they had had significant formation in social justice as essential for their vow of poverty. For ten years, they had learned to live social justice in prayer, reflection, education, and action. For many, taking the corporate stand in 1988 symbolized the Congregation's transformation. At their 1989 Chapter, the SSJs solidified their rootedness in social justice as a constitutive element of their mission. They explicitly expected each other to consciously live their mission of unity with a special preference for the poor. As the Sisters of Saint Joseph embraced the tenets of social justice, they expanded their original mission with renewed vigor.

The Habit

Since the mid-1960s, the habit had been a controversial issue and continued to present concerns through the 1980s. In the context of spirituality, the habit was considered a visible sign of membership in the Congregation and commitment to the mission. What were the indispensable elements of the religious garb that would represent fidelity to the origins of the Sisters of Saint Joseph?

The chairperson of the Habit Committee for the 1984 Chapter, Sister Catherine Pisarczyk (Marie Andrew), defined these essentials:

> We dress in a manner which reflects both the directives of the Church for active apostolic religious and the unassuming spirit of our Little Institute. Our garb, then, is simple, modest, and becoming. Although we realize that our vowed life in community involves a visible religious presence, our primary sign of unity is our expression of Christian love and service as Sisters of St. Joseph.

Based on these parameters, the committee proposed two new models—A and B—which represented distinct differences in the interpretation of ecclesial directives, congregational origins, and relationship to the world. Simply stated, Model A was a traditional habit with a veil and crucifix and signified adherence to Rome's insistence on a nonsecular dress for women religious. Included in the rationale for adopting the model was its fidelity to Father Médaille's use of the dress of widows as a distinctive mark of separation from secular styles of dress worn by married or single women in the seventeenth century. Model B, in contrast, proposed options for personal choice of appropriate dress, such as a suit, a simple dress, or alternate styles of habit. Father Médaille's vision of unity was invoked in support of the modernized form of habit; the revised *Code of Canon Law* (1983) that supported a Congregation's own proper law with regard to dress was also cited.

After much debate, including a motion to let the membership, not the Chapter body, have the final say on the habit, the delegates determined to keep the issue a Chapter decision. With this choice, the Chapter chose an understanding of their early sisters and primitive documents that focused on unity of purpose rather than uniformity of dress. On July 16, 1984, Model B was accepted with the required simple majority. The habit would now consist of the traditional dress, or any of the proposed alternates, the veil, and profession crucifix or congregational insignia.

Since the Sisters of Saint Joseph did not have an insignia, one needed to be designed. More than 80 suggestions were submitted to the committee, and the final product was an amalgam of several ideas. The cross, superimposed on a lined globe, was the expression of unity with Christ and the world; or, as Sister Dorothea Newell so aptly observed, "Our insignia is a statement of the Paschal Mystery and of our particular call to be with God in that mystery."

Formation

Another critical issue integrally connected to spirituality was that of initial formation, which in turn was influenced by the number of candidates seeking admission to the Congregation. From 1979 to 1984, there was a 40 percent drop in the number of candidates (88 to 63). By the latter part of the 1980s, there was a further 50 percent decrease, so that in fall 1988, there were 33 women in formation, with no postulants. While the Congregation continued to invest a significant number of sisters in vocation/formation ministry, the precipitous decline in candidates resulted in fewer sisters assigned to this ministry. By fall 1989, Sisters Mary Barrar (George Mary) and Maria McCoy (Kathleen Patrick) were the directors for all those in formation, while Sister Geraldine Muller (George Kathleen) was in full-time vocation ministry.

Changes in each stage of initial formation were also made during the 1980s. The period of postulancy was adapted to accommodate the changing trends and demographics. For example, some women spent this period in their own homes or in a local convent. In 1980, the congregational postulate was integrated within the local community at St. Michael Convent, Philadelphia. Young women could now live in community and be involved in ministry. The same personalized approach about the length of the candidacy was now applied to the postulancy. It could last from six months to two years.

In the 1980s, the novitiate was more explicitly defined as the as the formal initiation into religious life. It was to be a time of relative withdrawal from one's previous life in order to be with the One who calls. Guided by Sister Joan Riethmiller (Richard Christi), novices in this canonical year took classes, received spiritual direction, and experienced various forms of prayer to help them cultivate intimacy with Jesus Christ and learn the essentials of religious life. For most Sisters of Saint Joseph, these adaptations matched their image of the novitiate as a time of immersion in religious life, though for many the focus on conversion for them was less explicit and the separation more dramatic. Eventually, the novitiate was incorporated into the Emmaus Community, one of several local communities within the Motherhouse. After many experiments in the 1970s, a new plan for the mission year (the second year of the novitiate) was inaugurated in 1980. The mission year was traditionally the period the novice spent in a local convent, engaged in the apostolic work of the Congregation. Depending on her education and skills, a mission novice was assigned either to full-time ministry or to an internship. In 1980, mission novices were assigned as full-time teachers (3), a diocesan office worker (1), and as classroom interns (3). Now that the number of novices was relatively small, the program could be more flexible.

The final stage now called temporary profession was a time for internalizing the spirituality and mission of the Congregation. Sisters Marcella Springer (Frederick Mary) and Maria McCoy, the directors, emphasized the need for individual discernment about readiness to make final vows, since the individual sister could make profession after four, five, or six years. Throughout the 1980s, as the Sisters of Saint Joseph faced new realities in the decline in new members, the Administration with the formation personnel used various avenues of communication to engage the sisters in understanding how the changes reflected these realities and the needs of the women in formation. After struggling with these significant developments, most sisters came to accept and support the changes in formation by the end of the decade.

SSJ Associates in Mission

Associate relationship has a rich history with the Sisters of Saint Joseph. Their founders envisioned the sisters' bonding with others who were spiritual companions and coworkers while they continued in their own lifestyle as married, widowed, or single persons. The sisters' renewal efforts in the 1970s planted seeds for reclaiming association with persons who discerned a call to a mission of union. The Chapter of 1979 formally approved a proposal to explore this movement.

In the late 1970s, Sister Demetria Cleary had begun to meet with a number of former members and others who felt called to live their shared mission with intention. In 1983, committee members who had researched and studied the renewal of associate relationship in Saint Joseph congregations recommended offering three ways of being in associate relationship: as a Friend of the Congregation, a Member of a Christian Growth Group, and a Full-time Lay Volunteer.

The following year, with the leadership of Sister Roberta Archibald, the Congregation initiated a ministry to develop associate relationship. In December 1984, an advisory board comprised of six sisters and six associates held the first information session; two hundred interested persons and sisters attended. Sister Kathleen Szpila (Stephen Christopher) designed a logo for the associates—a cross and globe with three stylized persons. This design was later used as the basis for a pin given to associates at their commitment ritual. Sister Therese Benedict McGuire designed the pin.

GOVERNANCE

Congregational Governance

As directed by the 1979 Chapter, Sister Dorothea Newell with four full-time councillors, while retaining their individual areas of responsibility, presented themselves as a leadership team. As a result, memos, updates, and directives were sent from "the Council" rather than from the superior general alone. Each councillor assumed leadership in a major area of governance but networked with each other, the superior general, and committee or task force members. Sister Agnes Marie Gunn, Assistant Superior General or First Councillor, continued with the Office of Sisters' Education and chaired the Constitutions Committee. Sister Eugenie Madeline was in charge of congregational finances. Sister Saint Ursula's role as Councillor for the Office of Apostolic Works also included the Commission for Justice, and Sister Margaret Fleming (William Marguerite) led the Office of Formation.

Reaching out to the sisters in local houses, the General Council adopted ways for involving them in congregational life with new kinds of committees and task forces. Ad hoc committees studied the habit, the Cape May retreat house chapel, methods for electing chapter delegates, and residences for senior sisters. Advisory committees included the Constitutions Committee, Vowed Life Committee, Commission for Justice, and Financial Advisory Board. For both the Commission for Justice and Vocation Office, sisters volunteered as local house contacts. All of these groups along with search committees and special event committees worked closely with one or more members of the General Council.

The General Council tried to improve the quality of presence and communication with the membership, nearly 1,900 sisters, by creating new methods for disseminating information. As recommended by the communications task force, the Council initiated a telephone hotline of weekly recorded updates and short news items, a pulse line for receiving sisters' concerns or issues, and a revised version of the chain call system notifying houses quickly about a sister's death. They also formulated a congregational newsletter, *FOCUS*, to inform and educate sisters about the Council's work and other pertinent issues in the Congregation and in the Church.

In addition, the Council arranged area meetings at several geographic locales to engage sisters in dialogue on such topics as the *Constitutions* or PWR (Project Withdrawal/Recommitment). They also hosted large-scale celebrations at Chestnut Hill and, whenever possible, accepted invitations to celebrations from local communities. In the broader sphere, the General Council maintained and enhanced relationships with other congregations both within and outside the Federation. In fact, Sister Agnes Marie Gunn's election as CSJ Federation President (1980) signaled a time ripe for more networking and deeper bonding . . . among SSJ/CSJ Congregations, since this was the first time a Sister of Saint Joseph of Philadelphia had ever held this position.

The General Council further adapted its administrative structures and congregational processes to expand participation and consultation with the membership. New or redesigned staff positions included Sister Margaret Mary Smith (Leo Francis) as staff researcher within the Office of Research and Planning, and Sisters Anna Josephine Bennis, Mary Helen Beirne, and Kathleen Kean as additional personnel in the Offices of Sisters' Education, Apostolic Works, and Continuing Formation, respectively. Sister Catherine Knobbs became Coordinator of Personnel Services, Sister Terence Marie Harte Coordinator of Office Services, Sister Gabriella Drummy Director of Secretarial Services, and Sister Theresa Connor (Martin Therese) Congregational Treasurer. The role of the regional superior remained essentially the same, although these sisters now had monthly sessions with the Council and served as that group's primary resource for congregational planning.

Local Community Life

Governance changes in structure and attitude at the congregational level had obvious implications for community life at the local level. The 1979 Chapter Community Life Committee identified "the challenge of developing components of a relational community life" as inherent in the transition from a monastic mode of life to an apostolic model; and in August 1981 the General

Council developed a set of 15 assumptions about the meaning of apostolic community life. Sisters were urged to take time to listen and be ready to both offer and lay aside their own preferences for the general good. In spring 1982, as local communities responded to the General Council's directives, the Community Life Committee assessed the progress of this transition to an apostolic style by using a survey based on the assumptions about community life. Approximately 89 percent of the 160 local communities responded to the survey, which contained questions about experiences in local community and degree of shared vision. The results of the survey (May 1983) showed that sisters prayed together yet struggled with diverse forms of prayer. Sisters were present to each other, shared responsibility, appreciated each other, and supported one another; yet they sometimes still had trouble addressing conflict. Most sisters were engaging in weekly meetings and shared decision making but were not finding it easy. The committee concluded that a shared vision crucial to good community life was not present in many local communities.

One method used to promote greater unity within the Congregation and to provide material for dialogue, discussion, and prayer in local houses was the adoption of a congregational theme for the year. For instance, in 1982–1983, the theme was Think Globally; Act Locally. To assist the local community in organizing and conducting productive house meetings, the Council also proposed four types of weekly meetings per month, each with a different focus: (1) local decision making, (2) dialogue on Chapter enactments, (3) congregational topics, and (4) celebration/social. Since the council had affirmed the primacy of the local house meeting as the key structure of governance at the local level, it was crucial for the sisters to engage each other in this forum in an honest and trusting manner.

Another concept aimed at creating greater internal unity within the local community was the "intentional community." Already initiated by a number of congregations of apostolic women religious, this experiment in communal living was designed to foster a deeper bond among the sisters by identifying a purpose or intention and then forming a local community of individuals who wanted to espouse that intention. These could include hospitality, prayer, or a simple lifestyle. Although it was similar to the process of goal setting used since the late 1970s, the intention would be identified before missioning took place, and sisters committed to the intention would choose to live together rather than be randomly missioned. Since sisters would probably not be ministering in the same place, there would be a need for a new personnel placement process. An experiment of this nature aroused concerns and prompted debate over potential divisiveness or elitism. Practical aspects of finance, housing, and personnel needed to be examined. The results of the March CCR feedback identified key elements for consideration: more information and the desire to experiment.

A facet of local community governance that required the exercise of personal responsibility and accountability was the monthly sum of money allocated to each sister for personal use. From 1979 to 1982, sisters experimented with a monthly allotment of $20–$25 to cover such things as recreation and personal needs. The Financial Advisory Board invited the sisters' input. Using this feedback, as well as research conducted by other religious congregations, the board recommended an annual budget that gave sisters more flexibility. In 1982, the annual amount was set at $540. By 1984 each sister received a maximum of $815 to cover spiritual enrichment, vacation, and all personal needs.

The board also supported local community budgeting efforts and trained local treasurers, superiors, and sisters about topics such as health benefits, aspects of tax-exempt status, accounting procedures, and methods for projecting a budget. With materials designed to promote dialogue and decision making about financial matters, the board encouraged sisters to identify and dialogue about issues that arose from the use of cars in local communities. The 1979 Chapter delegates had previously claimed that the car represented both independence and power. Sharing a vehicle in a local community setting proved logistically and personally challenging as sisters tried to balance their own needs and desires with those of others in the local community.

Throughout the remainder of the 1980s, local communities continued to grapple with developing a shared vision. Engaging each other in the development of the personal budget, the corporate decision making in house budget, the use of cars, and the handling of congregational topics for CCRs fostered its growth. For many, increased personal and local community responsibility enabled them to etch out a shared vision as they made conscious choices for a simpler lifestyle and became more cognizant of the needs of others.

Writing New Constitutions

Central to the changes in governance during the 1980s was the rewriting of the *Constitutions*, the document that embodied the vision of the founder, the charism of the Institute, and the Congregation's relationship to the Church and the world. The content for this profound revision came from the *Holy Rule* (1939), *Design for Excellence I and II* (1968 and 1974), and the *Core Constitutions* of the CSSJ Federation. In order to accomplish this task, the Constitutions Coordinating Committee engaged the sisters in numerous Congregation-wide consultations and also gathered input from external sources. The committee itself was composed of five members: Sisters Agnes Marie Gunn (writer), Rose of Lima McDermott (canonist), Judith Dwyer (theologian), Harriet Corrigan (Saint Pierre) (historian), and Mary Helen Kashuba (French language consultant). Each of these sisters brought a wealth of knowledge and experience to the process of rewriting the *Constitutions*.

For four years, the Constitutions Coordinating Committee focused on writing *Constitutions* rooted in the life of every sister, as expressed by the 1979 Chapter delegates: "The Congregation was not constituted once for all historically; rather it is created every day, every moment of our lives by our lived out acceptance of our vocation." Maintaining this focus, the entire Congregation worked through two drafts of the document using a comprehensive consultation process. When the consultation, which took about two years, was finished, each sister completed a written response in a computerized form, indicating agreement, disagreement, or concern regarding each paragraph. Sisters were given the opportunity to elaborate on their concerns and even offer a reconstruction of the paragraph. Over 80 percent of the sisters responded to the drafts with many notes, 1,600 computer forms, and 8,000 index cards on the first drafts. After carefully reading and recording all responses, the committee returned its analysis to the Congregation.

During the summer of 1983, Sister Agnes Marie Gunn created one document from the four revised sections, blending the theological, juridical, and inspirational elements. Results from the two-day March 1984 CCR affirmed the document as a whole and identified areas of contention or confusion, such as the meaning of preference for the poor, pre-entrance, the missioning process, and the authority of regional superiors. Once again, the committee reworked the materials and a thoroughly revised second draft was ready for the opening of 1984 Chapter.

1984 Chapter

Although the numbers of delegates was smaller than in 1979 (85 as opposed to 109), there were more observers and members of the House of Intercessory Prayer. Since the previously closed pre-Chapter input sessions were now opened to the entire Congregation, nearly 800 sisters gathered to hear Pierre Wolff SJ, challenge them to embrace the creativity, inventiveness, and boldness of their heritage. Another speaker, Ladislus Orsy SJ, provided current information on canon law. Each sister then received her own copy of the General Council's report (a first!) and was invited to a question-and-answer session with the Council during the 1984 Chapter in June.

On June 28, 1984, Sister Dorothea Newell convened the 1984 Chapter and in her opening address issued the biblical challenge to choose life, raising crucial questions about Sisters of Saint Joseph identity, unity, the price of diversity, and other challenges facing the Sisters of Saint Joseph as an apostolic religious Congregation. She concluded her address by invoking the image of Christ in the desert, at the beginning of his public life:

> Like Jesus, who struggled in the desert, who learned obedience through what he suffered we can come to know the Will of God in the concrete circumstances of our lives. We can even come to know it together.

Meticulously critiquing the second draft of the *Constitutions* was the major work of the Chapter delegates. Governance, in particular, became a crucial issue. The Government Structures Committee surveyed delegates and observers regarding two proposed models; each included a six- to eight-member General Council with expanded responsibilities and a middle management staff with delegated authority. Although not significantly different from the proposed models, a transitional form of government was ultimately approved by the delegates, but only after considerable debate. Essentially, the five-person General Council would remain in place, with the understanding that this group would seek opportunities for exchange with the sisters and foster collaboration within the Church. The regional superiors were renamed area delegates to empathize that they exercise only delegated authority and had no actual decision-making power. The committee also altered the role of the education coordinators, designating them coordinators of ministries. The delegates, in an attempt to clarify the roles and responsibilities of these positions, enacted an ongoing review of congregational policies and procedures.

Unlike the proposed adaptions in congregational governance, the changes in local community life and structures as expressed in the *Constitutions* were more definitive, with an emphasis on each sister's responsibility for the quality of communal life. Valuing unity over uniformity, the sisters would commit to affirming the blessedness of diversity while striving to address with love and courage issues that hindered their unity. Structures and processes for the facilitation of shared decision making would be formulated to enhance communal life. For local leadership, the *Constitutions* renamed and redefined the role of local superior; she was now titled local coordinator. In her role, the local coordinator was to be at the center, not above, the sisters in the local community. In place of pursuit of perfection, sisters would strive to support and accept one another:

> We accept, reverence, and love ourselves and one another in our weaknesses, as well as in our strengths. Thus we endeavor to be realistic in our expectations as pilgrims on the way.

The Chapter of Election, facilitated by Robert Faricy SJ, took place July 19–21. Sister Dorothea Newell was re-elected Superior General, and the four Councillors were Sisters Eugenie Madeline, Margaret Fleming, Gerald Vincent McDevitt, and Kathleen Kean. Since three members of the General Council had been re-elected to their positions and changes in mid-level governance structures had been minor, the remaining years of the 1980s were characterized by stability and sustained efforts by the Administration to expand opportunities for presence, relationships, and consultation with the sisters. For example, in 1985 and 1987, there were special area meetings with the General Council. Local group gatherings or clusters were also initiated to deepen communication among local houses in particular geographic locales. In order to maintain a continuous focus on the Chapter enactments and new *Constitutions*, the Administration authorized a network of standing committees and ad hoc task forces to facilitate the implementation process.

After the close of 1984 Chapter, the third and final draft of the *Constitutions* was sent to Rome for approval. On October 15, 1987, Founders' Day, the new *Constitutions* was granted approval by Rome. On May 1, 1988, nearly 1,200 Sisters of Saint Joseph and SSJ Associates in Mission gathered at the Motherhouse, Chestnut Hill College, and Saint Joseph Villa to ritualize the receiving of the *Constitutions*. Sister Dorothea Newell declared the *Constitutions* to be a living document and commended the sisters for reclaiming their identity as apostolic women religious.

Congregational and Local Finances

While rewriting the *Constitutions* and its subsequent acceptance by Rome energized the entire Congregation, the Administration in their report to the 1984 Chapter set the stage to engage the sisters about their looming financial crisis. The decreasing number of sisters employed full-time caused a significant reduction in annual income, while the aging population at Saint Joseph Villa utilized nearly 35 percent of the annual income. Fortunately, the Sisters of Saint Joseph had bought into the Social Security program, from which 25 percent of the Congregation's revenues came. To add to the challenges, there were differences across diocesan lines concerning stipend packages for the sisters. Most dioceses contributed a small amount to health care, but few contributed to sisters' retirement. The highest stipend package was $7,580, and most ranged between $5,000 and $5,500. All of these troubling statistics were shared with the membership when the General Council made its report to the 1984 Chapter body.

Utilizing this data, the Council articulated a plan to build up the future support fund so that younger members might not be unduly burdened by monetary worries and retired sisters would be adequately provided for. In order to keep the mission as the central focus, the Administration concentrated on responding to the needs of the People of God, not merely on raising money. All financial planning would ultimately be for the good of the people served and the well-being of the sisters themselves.

The financial crisis facing the Sisters of Saint Joseph of Philadelphia was threatening most other congregations of women religious in the United States. A *Wall Street Journal* article (May 19, 1986) on the situation first alerted the general public to the plight of the sisters. "Sisters in Need: U.S. Nuns Face Crisis as More Grow Older with Meager Benefits" summarized the results of a study completed by the National Conference of Bishops that showed a gap of almost $2 billion between available retirement funds and monies need to meet financial and medical needs. In light of this troubling reality, the Tri-Conference Retirement Project, a joint effort by organizations of major superiors and the American bishops, worked to adjust diocesan compensation packages; they could only recommend and cajole! In November 1987, the bishops approved a 10-year national appeal and the first collections were taken up in December 1988. The first appeal grossed $25 million and benefitted 490 congregations.

In order to secure the Congregation's financial future, the first Development Office was established on September 28, 1988. Headed by Sister Madeline Franze, this initiative focused on building relationships with parishes, organizations, and individuals who shared a passion for the mission. It would help sustain the good works of the Congregation as well as cultivating donors and sponsoring major fundraising projects.

Even as the sisters worked to grasp the enormity and complexity of their finances on the edge of the 1990s, the foundational message came home in the voice of Sister Eugenie Madeline Gaddi, as she responded to questions about the 1989 Council Chapter report. Known for her reserve, Sister Eugenie with deep emotion, even tears, she asked the sisters to "take the facts seriously." With straightforward candor she told them, "It's not panic time; it's choice time." But it was her final sentence that would echo for many. She stressed that if the Congregation were to weather this, then, as sisters together, it was time to "change our hearts." She meant—and the sisters understood—that this financial crisis was about more than money. It was about consciously choosing both personally and collectively to authentically live their mission with Gospel simplicity.

1989 Chapter: The End of the Decade

Unlike previous Chapters, the one that ended the 1980s was not so much focused on content as on determining the direction the Congregation would take regarding the mission over the next five years. The General Council tried to help sisters become better acquainted with one another in order to facilitate the election of Chapter delegates. When the March 1988 CCRs took place, the attendees selected their center's representatives for the follow-up session with Administration. Over 90 sisters represented the 21 centers, and an additional 200 sisters attended as observers. Election of Chapter delegates began the next day. Though no formal assessment tool traced the impact of this change, there were new faces among the 1989 Chapter delegates.

Greater flexibility and inclusion also expanded involvement. Given the option to commit for a single day rather than a week, an average of 125 sisters came daily as participant observers. As nondelegates, they could address the Chapter body at the facilitator's discretion. Regular observers, about 70 per day, included SSJ Associates in Mission, coworkers, friends, family members, laity, and clergy. Thus, with a Chapter body of 95 delegates, approximately 300 persons participated in pre-Chapter weekends and regular Chapter sessions. Another 36 Sisters of Saint Joseph attended the House of Intercessory Prayer. All delegates, observers, and guests were welcome to the pre-Chapter enrichment sessions.

In addition to the strategy employed to diversify the delegate pool, another innovation proposed by the Council was the formation of a Chapter Planning Committee, selected from among the elected delegates. This measure effectively removed the responsibility for organizing the Chapter agenda from the Council itself. After considerable discussion, the delegates affirmed the proposal and recommendations for the committee to the Council. The appointees were Sisters Harriet Corrigan (Saint Pierre), Mary Dacey (Michael Francine), Mary Ellen Ford (Therese Immaculee), Mary Kieran McElroy, and Adele Solari (Anita David). Sister Kathleen Kean, Councillor, was the facilitator of the planning committee and liaison with the General Council. The delegates also officially affirmed the proposed outside facilitator, Sister Catherine Harmer MM, who worked with the nondelegate cofacilitators, Sisters Diane Driscoll (Joel Marie) and Merilyn Ryan (Teresa Miriam).

Based on the input from the March CCR, the Chapter Planning Committee developed a schema for the 1989 Chapter, affirmed by the delegates at their September 1988 pre-Chapter weekend, which established the centrality of the Mission for all Chapter work and espoused total membership collaboration. Three themes derived from the issues raised by the sisters were identified:

- *Collaboration for Mission*: Ministry Planning and Shared Decision-Making
- *Creativity for Mission*: Community Living and Use of Resources
- *Conversion for Mission*: Mission of Unity and Preferential Option for the Poor

During the next nine months (October 1988 to June 1989), the entire Congregation worked on the directional papers and directional proposals and engaged in a process of prayer, reflection, dialogue, and collaboration. In October and November, the 95 delegates participated in 50 gatherings of sisters at 41 different locations, while the General Council disseminated current data and analysis on *Membership as Related to Ministry* for local community dialogue. The delegates drafted and distributed three directional papers on the Chapter themes (January 1989) that included the past history of the issue, the current situation, and the direction recommended to the Congregation. Delegates used the sisters' critique of the first versions to create the second drafts for March 1989. By May 1989, over 88 percent of the Congregation had affirmed the elements, if not the exact wording, of the three directional papers.

Increased co-responsibility also came with the sisters' first opportunity to participate in the election process of congregational leadership. For nearly 20 years, sisters had suggested persons for local and mid-level leadership positions such as local coordinator, principal, and area delegate. However, only Chapter delegates nominated or elected sisters for the General Council. At the 1989 Chapter, the delegates affirmed a two-part process for soliciting input for choosing leadership from the entire Congregation. Consultation to establish criteria for these leadership roles and the creation of a nonbinding list of potential candidates was solicited from the sisters.

This process was as much educative as it was consultative. Preliminary to the March 1989 CCR, sisters reflected and dialogued on appropriate citations from the *Constitutions* accompanied by three articles dealing with leadership in the Church and religious life. At the CCR, leadership qualities were identified that supplemented those listed in the *Constitutions*. At the end of March, a list of 33 leadership qualities was formulated and disseminated. Each sister was invited to submit up to five names and to identify as many as five qualities about each person. In early May 1989, a list of 30 sisters who had been recommended for consideration was issued. While the sisters understood that, according to canon law, the delegates were not bound to vote only for those listed, they exercised coresponsibility by participating in the new process of generating a potential leadership pool.

On June 21, 1989, the Sisters of Saint Joseph celebrated the opening of the 1989 Chapter, fully ritualizing the breadth and depth of their transformation during the 1980s and their call to new hope for the future. Gathering in the five-story rotunda of Chestnut Hill College, approximately 1,110 sisters, SSJ Associates in Mission, and friends engaged in a festive spectacle woven around the Chapter directions of Conversion, Collaboration, and Creativity for Mission. Written, directed, and produced by Sisters Mary Ann Mulzet (Rosathea) and Rita Woehlcke (George Ellen), it presented highlights from the Congregation's past, present, and future in song, dance, readings, exhortation, and prayer. The following day, Sister Dorothea Newell, as Superior General, echoed the meaning of the celebration and decade in her opening Chapter address"

> We are gathered by the Spirit to see how we can move together in deeper fidelity to our mission at this point in our history, to the "more." Do not fear to hope! . . . Many of us would have preferred another set of realities. . . . (yet) let

us begin the work we have been given to do today. Chapter'89 has begun. In God's name and for the sake of God's people, let us go forth together.

Portrait of Sister Dorothea Newell

That outburst of affirmation probably surprised Sister Dorothea Newell much as her election as Superior General did in 1979. Shocked personally by the delegates' choice of her, Sister Dorothea had responded simply with the words of Moses, "Here I am. Who am I?" This response seemed prophetic, for she led the Congregation through what many saw as the desert experience of transformation in the 1980s.

Known to family, friends, and the Congregation as "Dottie," Sister Dorothea brought a breadth of congregational experience to her leadership. Originally from a family of nine in West Philadelphia, Dottie was the third of her siblings to be a Sister of Saint Joseph; another sister chose the Sister Servants of the Immaculate Heart of Mary, and a brother joined the Jesuits. Entering the Sisters of Saint Joseph in 1952, she taught elementary school for one year before becoming an English teacher for 11 years at Holy Family Academy in Bayonne, New Jersey. After three years on the novitiate staff in the late 1960s, Dottie was elementary school principal and superior at St. Kevin Springfield, Pennsylvania, and then vice principal and superior at the John Carroll School in Bel Air, Maryland. A founding member of the SSJ Center of Spirituality, she was appointed a regional superior in 1976, a role she held until her election.

As leader, Sister Dorothea recognized fully the "soul-sized" challenges and choices facing the Congregation. In Dottie, sisters saw a woman of great integrity as they experienced her deliberate approach to leadership, her attention to thorough and detailed communications, and her capacity to identity movements of the heart. With her Councillors, she continued and expanded the presence of the Administration among the sisters and with the broader Church. Impelled by her deep spirituality, her commitment to social justice, and her passion for the SSJ Mission, Dottie consistently called the sisters to embrace the graces for new life latent in their personnel and financial diminishment. With Sister Dorothea Newell's leadership, the Sisters of Saint Joseph embraced the reality of transformation and chose a new dance with their God, that of resurrection.

During the course of the Chapter, delegates also debated several controversial issues. Among these were sabbaticals, sisters living alone, and adopting a feminist perspective. Concerning sabbaticals, the delegates compromised and requested the Administration to investigate opportunities for a more extended period of spiritual or professional renewal. The issue of living alone ignited concerns about noncommunal housing, diverse ministries, and financial feasibility. The final resolution was to explore questions around housing from the perspectives of *ministry, finances, and community living*. The suggestion to adopt a feminist perspective in ministry planning arose from about 100 sisters and triggered vigorous discussion. Perceiving the term *feminist* as divisive for some and recognizing the need for education not only on feminism but on sexism, male chauvinism, and modes of collaboration, the delegates advised the Congregation to "continue to examine the Christian feminist perspective as we collaborate for mission."

Overall the 1989 Chapter officially produced just 11 enactments clustered around three themes. *Conversion for Mission* challenged the sisters to internalize their mission making it a touchstone for personal and communal choices. *Creativity for Mission* required comprehensive guidelines for personnel, a corporate approach to finances, and revitalization of community life centered on the Mission rather than a common work. *Collaboration for Mission* highlighted apostolic planning rooted in ministry as presence and each sister's coresponsibility for life together in mission and for personnel placement.

During the Chapter of Election, nominees for the position of superior general formally addressed the delegates providing a personal profile. This was a significant development for the Sisters of Saint Joseph, who traditionally had avoided even the appearance of politicking. On the last afternoon during the June 29–30, 1989, reflection days preceding the election, delegates formally nominated candidates for superior general. Each nominee responded to her nomination during a closed session. Adhering to a predetermined format, each sister spoke for three minutes or less, sharing her strengths, limitations, and expectations in the light of the direction articulated by the Chapter. When the delegates voted the next day, the live balloting was shown to a large crowd of observers via closed-circuit TV in the Saint Joseph Villa auditorium. Sister Margaret Fleming, Councillor for the previous 10 years, was elected Superior General. The other members of the Council were Sisters Patricia Kelly (Patrick Maureen), Helen Patrick Clifton, Dorothy Apprich (Rose William), and Annemarie Roche. The four Councillors were new; the first three had served as Area Delegates and the fourth as Coordinator for Continuing Formation.

Conclusion

With their 1989 Chapter, the SSJs witnessed, both to each other and to those they served, their transformation as apostolic women religious. During these last 10 years, they shed definitions and distinctions in their spirituality, ministry, and government that no longer fit. Called to embrace their contemporary situation, they had wrestled with God and each other to find hope and new life. Having completed their journey from interior renewal (1970s) through the fire of transformation (1980s), they now set forth with creativity, collaboration, and conversion for mission toward refoundation through deepening in the 1990s.

PUBLISHED SOURCES

Kashuba, Mary Helen, SSJ. *Tradition and Risk*. Virginia Beach, VA: The Donning Company, 1999.

ARCHIVAL SOURCES

Mount Saint Joseph Convent, Philadelphia, Pennsylvania
Primitive documents, records of General Chapters, personal papers, focus groups, and other records.

Chapter Six

Deepening Our Vision

1989–1999

Emerging from a decade of deep transformation, the Sisters of Saint Joseph of the 1990s found themselves situated in a country adopting a new worldview and a Church wrestling with controversy. Many Americans had their first experiences in globalization. Following George H. W. Bush, Bill Clinton's presidency ushered in an era of economic interdependence with multinational companies, women more a part of the social and political landscape, a new debate on immigration (diversity versus melting pot), and global recognition of climate change (the Kyoto Treaty). Internally the advantages of low unemployment, welfare reform, the American with Disabilities Act, and AmeriCorps (1993) contrasted with the terrorist attack on the World Trade Center (1993), the bombing in Oklahoma City (1995) and the killings at Columbine High School (1999). As the major power, the U.S. often combined diplomacy and economic pressures with military force as part of United Nations or NATO forces for crises in Kuwait (Operation Desert Storm), Somalia, the Balkans, and Haiti. New initiatives influenced by the United States helped procure peace in the Middle East and Northern Ireland while South Africa elected Nelson Mandela president, who then chose reconciliation over revenge. The Internet with the World Wide Web (1991) transcended barriers, providing new potential for global interaction, while images beamed from the Hubble Space Telescope (1990) shed light on great mysteries of the universe and Earth.

Within the Church, American Catholics seemed to be searching for unity while becoming strained by differences. Many sought a deeper spirituality and appreciated the diversity of traditions and ethnic influences in prayer, liturgy, and devotions. Others, in a new *restorationist movement* preferred the pre-Vatican Church of order and uniformity. Many Catholics tended to choose among Church teachings rather than adhere to the full body, while a growing number contested the legacy of Vatican II, seeing the Church as unraveling rather than renewing. National events sometimes crystalized the complexities. At the 1993 Denver World Youth Conference, John Paul II affirmed the importance of young people in the Church. In the same year, evidence of clergy sexual abuse was made public. Parish life, however, expanded with new emphasis on youth ministry and adult faith formation. Parish staffs grew and leadership styles changed. By 1999, there were almost 30,000 lay and religious working as paid parish ministers, most of whom were trained in theology, religious studies, or pastoral counseling. In a fourth of the nearly 2,000 parishes without a resident priest, laity and religious became administrators, performing virtually every function except saying Mass and administering the sacraments. Even while grappling with tensions within the Church, American Catholics in the 1990s still had a religious identity in the United States. Beyond their differences, they shared a faith rooted in a loving God, the sacraments, community, and commitment to the care of their neighbor.

In this context, the Sisters of Saint Joseph entered their own era of refoundation. During the 1989 Chapter, they had identified the centrality of their Mission as "touchstone." Using the Chapter enactments, the sisters worked during the last decade of the 20th century to interpret what this meant for them corporately and individually. In government, they pursued new styles of relationship locally and congregationally and designed a corporate approach to finances. In ministry, they considered apostolic planning models and personnel placement that rooted them in "presence" to those they served. In spirituality, they nurtured the concept of mission as core to their identity as apostolic women religious. In all of this they reclaimed for the new millennium their unique corporate identity as Sisters of Saint Joseph of Philadelphia.

MINISTRY

During the 1990s, the Sisters of Saint Joseph continued to grow in their understanding of ministry as integrally connected to the mission. Consequently, ministry planning for the 1990s led the Congregation to extend its vision beyond the limits of Project Withdrawal/Recommitment (PWR), which focused primarily on parish elementary schools, and examine both corporate and individual ministries in areas of service. In order to accomplish this task, the Congregation employed a method outlined in the 1989 Chapter enactments: apostolic planning conversations. As the name implied, these conversations depended on collaborative efforts and fostered both individual and communal responsibility. This approach was utilized not only within the Congregation but also by the General Council in its dealings with dioceses and parishes. The effect of diminishment in terms of aging and decreasing numbers was a key factor in the Congregation's ministry planning, and apostolic conversations created the opportunity for dialogue prior to any commitment of resources.

End of PWR and Corporate Commitments

In the first round of its apostolic planning conversations (1989–1992), the Congregation essentially ended its corporate commitments to parish elementary schools, including some in which sisters had served since the 1840s. In the process of PWR, the recommitment phase had only been temporary; so by the early 1990s, decisions had to be made on a large number of schools. The General Council hoped that the apostolic conversation process would lead to more creative, collaborative solutions to the problem of maintaining a presence to the people despite the Congregation's diminishing personnel. Since no long-term commitments could be made, a year-to-year evaluation seemed more feasible. Another important element in these conversations was the need for stipended ministries, and this posed difficulties for all constituents involved. In most cases, pastors and parish councils were open to this more fluid commitment to presence; as a result, only three of the 93 conversations resulted in the withdrawal of sisters. At one site in New Jersey, the sisters remained in parish ministry, even though the school was closed by the Newark Archdiocese.

The 1989 Chapter document *Congregational Guidelines for Decision-Making in Apostolic Planning* also delineated criteria to guide the discernment process involved in apostolic planning, ensuring that the mission of unity and reconciliation would always be the focal point. In addition, preference for the poor, community life, ministry, and resources were other factors considered in all future planning.

During the 1990s, ministry planning increasingly reflected the interplay of congregational efforts, diocesan and parish planning, and sisters' initiatives. When the parish decided to use the convent as the parish center at Our Lady of Good Counsel in Vienna, Virginia, the sisters continued serving there but moved to a new residence in nearby McLean. In June 1996, the Congregation posted three new ministry sites with housing in New Jersey. Sometimes sisters lived singly or in intercongregational settings in more distant locales. The Congregation also tried to maintain its presence in schools where the Sisters of Saint Joseph had a long history of service. When there were no principals for eight such schools in July 1997, sisters continued to minister in some capacity in all but one school located in Pottsville, Pennsylvania, where the Congregation had ministered since 1848.

The Missioning Process

Recognizing the scope and sensitivity of personnel placement, the General Council actively engaged sisters in creating a new missioning process. In January 1990, a task force for missioning was established. By January 1991, the task force presented its recommendations in three documents with an outline for a *Ministry Resource Book*. From January through March 1991, the sisters, in local communities and in forums on missioning, critiqued the drafts. In June 1991, based on the membership's affirmation of the documents, the Council approved them, responded to questions and concerns, and commissioned their implementation, which included finalizing the draft for the *Ministry Resource Book*.

The missioning process was now a continuous one and was no longer based on the traditional school calendar model of preceding decades. The last comprehensive change list was issued in May 1992. After that date, local houses received *Missioning Updates* of sisters' assignments, perhaps a dozen a year. In December 1995, the Congregation began publishing *Ministry Opening Booklets*, which identified ministry opportunities in congregational internal services, congregationally owned institutions, diocesan schools, health care, parishes, social service, and diocesan offices. The October 15, 1996, booklet also included a ministry sharing website, *Ministry Connect—Employment Opportunities in Service to Others*, sponsored by the New Jersey Ministry Resource Center for Women Religious.

New Perception of Ministry

Throughout the 1990s, within the context of the apostolic planning conversations and an evolving missioning process, the Congregation endeavored to deepen, both personally and corporately, the concept of ministry as a means of furthering the Mission. During the Ministry Day sessions in September 1991, nearly 900 sisters gathered to hear Sister Janet Mock CSJ, President of the U.S. Federation of the Sisters of Saint Joseph, speak on the centrality of mission: "Ministry is the way we enflesh our mission, so that wherever we are, whatever we do, however we serve, we speak to people [by our presence] of unity and reconciliation."

The sisters' responses to the *SSJ Survey '91* (November 1991) also revealed their grasp of this sense of mission and an increased appreciation for diversity in ministry. At the spring 1992 CCR, Sister Mary Beth Beres OP, identified changing paradigms as indicative of the signs of the time and observed that the post-immigrant US society required new forms of presence.

By the 1994 Chapter, most sisters had a clear understanding of the primacy of mission and understood that their personal presence was the common denominator in ministry. Statistics from the Chapter reports further demonstrated that the Congregation was becoming more diverse in the number and types of ministries, even as personnel diminished and the median age rose to 61. By 1994, sisters in active ministry decreased by 200 sisters to 1,303. Of these, 56.4 percent (734) were serving in education, compared with 65 percent in 1989; 43.6 percent (596) were now in varied ministries.

The 1994 Chapter was actually the first Chapter since the 1968 Chapter in which the issue of ministry was not debated. This seemed to validate the sisters' acceptance of presence as integral to ministry. To foster the Chapter's Vision Statement, the General Council provided opportunities for education and life planning and policies governing retirement. From January through March 1996, ministry clusters, conducted by the coordinators of ministry along with Sister Anna Louise Schuck (Councillor), discussed the importance of generating new ministries and housing opportunities. Life planning required every sister to assess her effectiveness in her current ministry and to prepare for the future.

The life planning endeavor, which evolved from the early 1990s ministry planning conversations, led to the establishment of a Life Planning Committee in 1995, which tried to assist sisters transitioning into a new phase of life. The committee provided a resource list to local convents to help sisters serving as caregivers to family members. It co-sponsored, with the SSJ Center for Spirituality, mid-life/later life workshops and life planning workshops that many sisters found valuable. The committee also urged sisters in transition to avail themselves of technology workshops offered by Chestnut Hill College, so they could gain more marketable skills in a new digital age.

The Life Planning Committee also worked with the Office of Apostolic Works and the General Council to develop new retirement guidelines that provided benchmarks for individual and corporate planning. At age 60, a sister was invited to consider her overall well-being and her plan for retirement. She was encouraged to decide if her health and well-being necessitated a transition into part-time ministry when she was 65 years old. Once a sister reached 70, she no longer needed to maintain a stipended position, although she was encouraged to volunteer her services. If a sister was still able to minister in a partially stipended service, she was free to pursue that position. These guidelines not only fostered a climate in which a sister would assess her own readiness for a transition from full-time ministry but also assisted the Congregation in its long-range planning.

By the late 1990s, sisters had become at ease with the practice of individualized ministries and valued the quality of presence that one sister could bring to those she served. For years, sisters who worked as Directors of Religious Education, social workers, or pastoral associates had experienced the solitariness of ministry. Now, sisters who ministered as teachers and principals might be the only Sister of Saint Joseph present in that school. It was now apparent that where even one Sister of Saint Joseph ministered, the entire Congregation was represented and its mission embodied in that particular sister.

The Role of Sponsored Works in Apostolic Planning

By the late 1990s, the Congregation owned and operated 14 institutions. Chestnut Hill College, Mount Saint Joseph Academy, Holy Family Academy, Cecilian Academy, Norwood-Fontbonne Academy, and Saint Joseph Academy Pre-School were educational facilities. There were three subsidized senior housing projects—Bethlehem Village, Academy Village, and Saint Joseph Village—as well as two spirituality facilities: The SSJ Center for Spirituality and Saint Mary by-the-Sea Retreat House. Two relatively new projects were The Dream Catcher (1996), an adult literacy program in North Philadelphia, and The Little Design Shoppe (1997), a store that sold hand-crafted articles made by the sisters. Saint Joseph Villa, the Congregation's own health care facility and retirement residence, was the final institution counted among those so-called sponsored works. In all of these entities, the Congregation invested both personnel and financial resources and supported planning endeavors. Thus, in 1999, as personnel resources continued to dwindle, the General Council maintained the presence of sisters, particularly in leadership roles, in these congregational works, committing 147 (16 percent) of 914 available sisters to either full- or part-time ministry in these institutions and projects.

Corresponding to the investment of sisters in these sponsored works was the expanded partnership with lay leadership in several of these works. While Chestnut Hill College had had lay persons as members of the board of directors since 1972, Saint Joseph Villa, added laity to its previously all-sister advisory board by creating subcommittees on ethics, finances, personnel, and property. New advisory groups were also established at Mount Saint Joseph Academy (1991), Bethlehem Village (1993), the SSJ Center for Spirituality (1997), and Norwood-Fontbonne Academy (1998). Instead of an advisory board, Cecilian Academy focused on parent partnership by initiating its first parent association.

Within the context of the apostolic planning, most congregational works engaged in some form of long-term planning. Mount Saint Joseph Academy and Chestnut Hill College both completed comprehensive planning and capital campaigns. Twice recognized as a National Blue Ribbon School (1992–1993; 1997–1998), the Mount's $5,000,000 capital campaign financed a new academic wing and funding for endowment, faculty development, and student financial aid. Chestnut Hill College's long-range plan included major curriculum developments like the introduction of new majors, a doctoral program in psychology, and a master space and marketing studies. Its $14,000,000 capital campaign paid for the first construction of new college buildings since 1962: physics and environmental science labs and a three-story state-of-the art convocation/communication building that housed an athletic center, high-tech classrooms, new offices, and conference/seminar rooms. Holy Family Academy, following a facilities study and Middle States Accreditation, implemented a Strategic Plan for Development (2000), and Norwood-Fontbonne Academy and Cecilian Academy developed their first strategic plans. Renovations at McSherrystown provided extended space for more child-centered services at the Saint Joseph Academy Pre-School. Saint Joseph Villa became a Medicaid provider (1996) and the first long-term health care facility in Pennsylvania to be certified by the Joint Commission for the Accreditation of Healthcare Organizations. Its major gift campaign raised over $1,200,000 as part of its 25th anniversary celebration (1993).

Financial planning for each institution aimed to reduce the congregational subsidy and to provide sisters with market value salaries rather than religious stipends. Mount Saint Joseph Academy and Norwood-Fontbonne Academy completed the transition to market value compensation for the sisters in 1996. Academy Village had used market value salary since its beginning in 1982, and Saint Joseph Village attained it for the fiscal year 1999–2000.

Beyond these multiple efforts to sustain congregational works, the General Council recognized the need to articulate the unique corporate role of these works in relation to the mission. In the late 1990s, following an internal study that included dialogue with the sisters engaged in the congregational works, the General Council established an umbrella designation for all 14: they were titled *sponsored works*. The General Council then clarified that

> The relationship that exists between the Congregation and its institutions/works is that of sponsorship. As a sponsor, the Congregation publicly identifies with, exerts appropriate influence on, and provides support for programs, projects, and institutions which further the mission of Jesus as expressed in the Mission of the Sisters of Saint Joseph.

The statement also eliminated previous distinctions among the 14 works. Rather than differentiating them as congregationally owned institutions, properties, or internal works, all were now viewed as sponsored works. In addition, the General Council created the new role of Director of Mission Effectiveness to facilitate the integration of the SSJ Mission with the unique purpose of each sponsored work. This director, a member of the Office of Apostolic Works, was to be a resource for planning, coordinating, and directing programs related to the mission, identity, and heritage of the Congregation.

The diversity among the sponsored works clearly reflected the scope of ministries identified in the *Constitutions*. They encompassed "the works of mercy . . . finding expression in all levels of education, in various human services, and in diverse forms of spiritual and pastoral ministry." Through all these works, the Congregation committed itself to espousing a unique form of corporate presence that made Christ visible to the world.

SPIRITUALITY

Understanding and Living the Mission

During the 1990s, the Sisters of Saint Joseph focused on the Mission as central to their apostolic spirituality. This emphasis reflected, in particular, the direction of the 1989 Chapter, which had identified the Congregation's need to internalize its mission. Father John Grindel CM, and Sister Sean Peters CSJ, researchers for the Lilly Endowment, clarified the primacy of mission and charism. Toward the end of the 1990s, Sister Sandra Schneiders IHM, theologian and writer on religious life, identified reclaiming the spirit of the Congregation as a centrifugal force for the Congregation's sense of being, claiming that "within this lies the potential, not for a restoration of pre-conciliar uniformity of doctrine and practice, but for a self-renewing reclaiming of the tradition in very new, perhaps even startlingly new, forms." Schneiders echoed the 1989 Chapter enactment to "engage one another and others in varied prayerful and informed ways, to share our understanding of what it means to live" the Sisters of Saint Joseph Mission.

In the five years following the 1989 Chapter, sisters were steeped in formative experiences to help them interiorize their mission of unity and reconciliation with a special preference for the poor. At the spring 1990 CCRs, sisters considered, through prayer, imagery, conversation, storytelling, and reflection, how they lived their mission, how they resisted it, and how they needed to change. Following the CCRs, a mosaic design, a prayer card, a resource booklet (August 1990), and a set of Lenten reflection leaflets (January 1991) utilized themes and stories of the sisters to help them sustain their fervor for the SSJ Mission.

Other resources that fostered a deeper understanding of the mission were "refoundation summers" and programs sponsored by the SSJ Center for Spirituality, the Federation, and the Valley Forge Event. During the summers (1991–1993) about 20 sisters participated in a week-long renewal program adapted from an international Federation event entitled Refounding for the Twenty-First Century, in which sisters explored the spirit of the first Sisters of Saint Joseph, the vows, and signs of the times. The Valley Forge Event (October 1992), sponsored by the SSJ Development Office, served as a significant vehicle for deepening awareness of the mission. Sisters who attended the formation team's charism workshop at the SSJ Center for Spirituality (1993) claimed they had seen, as if for the first time, the depth of the Congregation's early documents and the roots of the mission for unity, kindling their desire to deepen their own response to living the mission.

Continuing Work of the Commission for Justice

The 1989 directional paper on *Conversion for Mission* affirmed the growing social justice consciousness of the sisters. In the *SSJ Survey '91,* a large majority (85 percent) recognized working for justice as an essential part of the Mission. During the early 1990s, the Commission for Justice, led by its first full-time coordinator, Sister Mary Elizabeth Clark (John Victoria), focused the Commission's efforts on developing a greater sense of global stewardship and an appreciation of various cultures. The Commission for Justice also turned its attention to the role of women from the perspective of Christian feminism.

Living the Vision

This 1994 Chapter Vision Statement reads as follows:

> Rooted in a contemplative life stance and challenged by our broken world, we claim our prophetic voice as women to stand with marginalized persons and to treasure and care for the Earth.

This statement grew from the Congregation's efforts to internalize the SSJ Mission. In identifying brokenness within the Congregation, as well as in the world, the sisters acknowledged the challenge inherent in working for unity and reconciliation. In the first two years after the 1994 Chapter, the General Council focused on how to live this vision. Through the CCRs, sisters learned to use the Vision Statement as a tool for social analysis. They reflected on how to claim one's *prophetic voice,* and many discovered in their personal stories the ways they were already a voice for inclusion, mutuality, interdependence, and collaboration. In recalling the stories of past generations of Sisters of Saint Joseph, the sisters also found evidence of the living out of the Vision Statement in the past. For example, during the American Civil War, the sister-nurses ministered to both sides involved in the conflict, attempting through compassionate care to affect a spirit of reconciliation.

Another aspect of living the SSJ vision centered on becoming more cognizant of the heritage of the Congregation. To this end, a new heritage area was opened in the renovated vestibule and connecting parlors of the Motherhouse, displaying a full wall mural and many artifacts relating to the history of the Sisters of Saint Joseph in Philadelphia. Sisters Roberta Archibald (Robert Andrew) and Mary Rita Boyle (Alverna) provided information on the origins of the Congregation through articles published in the *Congregational Newsletter* and the Little Design seminars, using *The Sisters of Saint*

Joseph of Father Médaille in the 17th and 18th Centuries by Sister Therese Vacher CSJ, a French Sister of Saint Joseph. To stimulate discussion, Sister Roberta and Sister Mary Rita attempted to demonstrate that the vision statement generated by the 1994 Chapter had its roots in the founder's vision for his "little design."

In 1997, the anniversary of the 150th year of the Sisters of Saint Joseph's presence in Philadelphia, the theme of the celebration was Embracing the Mission. Through six public celebrations, the sisters expressed renewed dedication for the SSJ Mission. Two of these events were sponsored by the Development Office. One was a special dinner welcoming donors to liturgy and dinner at the Motherhouse (March 1997), and the other was an evening titled "The History of Sisters of Saint Joseph in Song" at the Philadelphia Academy of Music (October 1997). The latter event, with more than 1,500 sisters in attendance as well as prelates, clergy, Associates, and friends, marked 150 years to the day of the original Sisters of Saint Joseph arriving in Philadelphia. Mass was celebrated in Philadelphia's Cathedral of Saints Peter and Paul followed by a reception at the Wyndham Franklin Plaza Hotel. In his homily, Archbishop Francis B. Schulte of New Orleans and former student of Norwood Academy said:

> Today is far more than nostalgia . . . we give thanks and remember. And the more that we remember, the more we are impelled to an ever broader and deeper proclamation of thanksgiving . . . We must go on to other things. We need to look to religious life in the next century.

As part of the jubilee celebration, the Congregation decided to use gift money ($150,000) received from the Connelly Foundation, a major Catholic philanthropic foundation, to fund several projects integrally connected to the Vision Statement of the 1994 Chapter. First, "to treasure and care for Earth," 150 trees were planted on 13 sites in Philadelphia, McSherrystown, Cape May Point, and Bayonne. Second, to honor the sisters' commitment to "stand with marginalized persons and support the prophetic voice of women," a portion funded the Dreamcatcher, the new SSJ Literacy Project. Third, to respond to the challenges of a broken world, $100,000 became seed money for a new Fund for the Materially Poor. This newly established fund was created to supplement ministries that served poor and marginalized persons and was augmented yearly by the interest from the Congregation's working capital. Beginning in February 1999, 20 grants were awarded to both religious and nonprofit organizations.

The 150th anniversary year developed into a year of refoundation for the Congregation. For many, the intentional focus of prayer, reflection, study, action, and celebration on the living legacy of the Mission and Vision affirmed their identity as Sisters of Saint Joseph and filled them with hope. In addition, with so many involved in planning, participating, and enjoying the events, the sisters became energized with a new sense of corporateness. They told of rediscovering their unity, one not dependent on common dress or works but rather rooted in their common history and mission.

While every anniversary experience was special, the picnic celebration with former members where Sister Margaret Fleming (William Marguerite), Superior General, asked for their forgiveness was considered by many as the most salient moment. On June 22, 1997, in a tent on the Motherhouse ground, over 800 gathered for Eucharist during which Sister Margaret addressed the 300 former members present with unprecedented and heartfelt candor. She spoke directly to the pain:

> Without a word of good-bye, a postulant, novice, or professed sister would be gone from our midst . . . we whispered to one another . . . It was hard for us who remained not to be able to say good-bye . . . How hard it must have been for you, especially not knowing that we cared about you and we missed you.

Recalling a little known portion of the Philadelphia SSJ story, Sister Margaret Fleming affirmed the importance of the former members: "Did you know that Sister Elizabeth Kincaid and Sister Mary Joseph Clark, two of the four founding members, returned to Carondelet and left the Congregation? Where would we be if they had not ventured with Mother Saint John and Sister Magdalen Weber to begin this Philadelphia foundation?" She plainly asked for reconciliation: "During this jubilee year we, Sisters of Saint Joseph, ask others to forgive us our trespasses as we forgive those who trespass against us." Then Sister Margaret Fleming proclaimed a new unity for all sisters and former members: "We remember all of the sisters and former members who are not able to be with us today because of death or distance. It is every single one of them and all of us who by the grace of God created the 150 year history that we celebrate this year."

Well after the picnic, sisters cited the poignancy and power of Sister Margaret's words, which evoked tears of joy and healing. Her apology did much to assuage long-held feelings of loss, anger, and separation experienced by both those who stayed and those who left. Often sisters remembered the experience of the picnic with former members within the context of the many aspects of the anniversary year. They resonated with the General Council's analysis of the year:

> This year afforded all of us the opportunity to proclaim our belief in the surety of God's love for us, to seek and receive forgiveness, to celebrate God's fidelity to us in our mission and vision, and to recognize the gifts, talents, and zeal not only of the sisters who went before us but also of our Congregation at the present time.

Another issue associated with the Vision Statement was that of inclusive language. The 1994 Chapter recommended exploring the prospect of revising the *Constitutions* and *Directory* to accommodate inclusive language. The General Council, however, understood that changing the language of the Congregation's documents presented challenges that could provoke controversy. Local communities discussed an article about changing images of God, and about 600 sisters attended a talk by Monika Hellwig, theologian and author, that challenged them to keep their images of God fresh and counseled against taking any model or image of God literally. Sisters were invited to contemplate the images of God revered by other cultures as well.

For the fall 1988 CCR, the General Council disseminated, via print and video, a draft of both the *Constitutions* and *Directory* with proposed language changes and consulted the sisters about their willingness to use the draft. Over 900 supported this proposal, but nearly 300 expressed concerns. Some wanted to hear broader theological and scriptural views; others asked for the Church's position on such changes. Based on these responses, the General Council recommended in March 1999 that at least two more years of education, prayer, reflection, faith sharing, and possible revisions of the working draft. This decision supported those who desired a more radical shift in language paradigms while demonstrating sensitivity to those who still had reservations about the use of inclusive language.

Although the Sisters of Saint Joseph had already used the process of a Corporate Stand to denounce the evils of Apartheid, they decided to use the process of the Corporate Stand again with regard to the elimination of the death penalty. Since the early 1980s, the Commission for Justice had engaged sisters in facing the realities of discrimination and racism. The link between racism and the use of capital punishment was demonstrated convincingly by Sister Helen Prejean CSJ, activist and author of *Dead Man Walking: An Eyewitness Account of the Death Penalty in the United States*, which was also made into a movie. In April 1995, the Commission for Justice hosted a session with Sister Helen and in spring 1998 initiated remote preparation for the formal discernment process required for the corporate stand. The Commission for Justice realized that this formal action against the death penalty presented challenges and concerns not experienced during the corporate stand against Apartheid in 1988. Consequently, while following the basic procedure from 1988, the Commission arranged the components of the process with sensitivity to the sisters' struggles. For example, they initiated the process during Holy Week 1998, intentionally identifying with the execution of Jesus as a common criminal but focusing on the Paschal Mystery of Resurrection and Ascension.

During phase two (May to September 1998), the videotaped testimony of Sister Leonissa O'Brien, whose brother had been murdered in 1993, became the turning point for sisters:

> Before this I never believed in the death penalty but I always used to say I would wonder how I would feel if it happened to my family. Well, I soon found out and still don't believe in this for him (my brother's murderer). On Good Friday—5 years later, I was able to say his name aloud and to pray for him by name. I look at myself in 1994 and look at myself in 1998 and see God's grace working in me.

Other sisters whose families also experienced the intense suffering caused by this violence shared their stories, making many sisters realize how challenging it was to remain consistent in one's commitment to life despite overwhelming personal pain.

At the fall 1998 CCR, the sisters voted to take a corporate stand against the death penalty, and the Congregation formally promulgated this on December 10, 1998, the 50th anniversary of the United Nations Declaration of Universal Human Rights. In this proclamation, the Congregation expressed support for the families of victims and affirmed the dignity of all human life. Letters of declaration were sent to the media and to civic and Church leaders, including Pope John Paul II, President Bill Clinton, congressional committees, and bishops of all the dioceses where Sisters of Saint Joseph served. Sister Kathleen Coll (Peter Chanel) coordinated the implementation of this second Corporate Stand, including monthly alerts on impending executions, prayer vigils at the Motherhouse, and participation in on-site rallies and vigils. The *Congregational Newsletter* kept sisters apprised of these and other efforts. The overwhelming endorsement of this action against the death penalty unified the sisters in their commitment to live their Mission and Vision in a public way, to be leaven in the world.

The Centrality of Prayer

Throughout the 1990s, the Congregation reaffirmed the centrality of prayer as part of its mission to be "rooted in a contemplative life stance." Many sisters welcomed opportunities to integrate new learning about their heritage, images of God, connection with Earth, and their feminine voice into personal prayer. Sisters' retreat choices reflected this widening spectrum of interest. Some retreats accessed the spirituality of other cultures, like that of Native Americans, or blended Christian and Zen practice. Other retreats were based on the Vision Statement, such as one entitled "Contemplative Stance in a Busy World." For extended renewal, some preferred the new option for a 30-day Ignatian retreat at Cape May Point (1991). One sister chose a month-long summer sabbatical in House Springs, Missouri, where she learned to integrate spirituality into everyday living, especially with the feminist perspective. Reflecting on the breadth of diversity, one sister summed up what seemed a shared experience: "We have been able to work through differences and at the same time deepen our sense of charism and prayer life."

By the early 1990s, due to diverse ministry responsibilities, scheduling communal prayer times had become increasingly difficult. However, an even larger question loomed about what constituted communal prayer. In response to the Congregation's concerns about appropriate types of communal prayer, the General Council chose not to mandate but rather to call the sisters to co-responsibility for their prayer together. They asked Sister Mary Ann Mulzet (Rosathea), congregational liturgist, to engage sisters on the issues. For two years (1991–1993), she provided models of prayer and ritual, education, and invited discussion in two-hour sessions, attended by 20 percent of the Congregation. Rooting her input in the *Constitutions* and Church documents, Sister Mary Ann focused on God's presence in any gathering when sisters bonded through communal prayer. Most grasped what was essential, and in their local communities they recognized the need to reverence one another's values, expectations, and desires regarding communal prayer. While changes continued, most local communities worked at accommodating diversity and minimizing tension concerning prayer styles and language.

Vows, Formation, and Membership

In October 1996, the Congregation embarked on a study of the vows based on the Church's 1994 assessment of religious life *The Consecrated Life and Its Role in the Church and the World Today*. Issued by the worldwide synod of bishops, this document was the first broad-based reflection on religious life since Vatican II. The Congregation engaged three experts on the vows, Sisters Sandra Schneiders IHM, Judith Merkle SNDdeN, and Amata Miller IHM, to provide content for prayer, education, reflection, and discussion. Sister Sandra Schneiders presented the vowed life in the context of prophetic vision, while Sister Amata Miller, an economist, shared insights on poverty. Obedience was interpreted as active participation in both personal and corporate decisions, with an emphasis on responsibility and accountability. Chastity, with its roots in right relationships, was seen as a total giving of self, without reservations based on prejudices of any kind. This attempt to keep the vows central to the apostolic life allowed for greater freedom to live the mission and vision.

During the 1990s, the Congregation maintained its commitment to developing formation programs and supplying personnel, despite the steady decline in applicants to the Congregation. Just before the 1989 Chapter, there were 33 women in formation; by the mid-1990s, there were nine and by the end of the decade, five. This represented an 84 percent decrease in 10 years. Although the numbers were fewer, a three-person vocation/formation team (one full-time, two part-time) shared the responsibility for candidacy, prenovitiate, novitiate, and temporary profession.

Women of the 1990s

The applicants to the Congregation during this decade represented a variety of perspectives. Several had participated in some formal, extended volunteer program, such as the Vincentian Service Corps or Good Works sponsored by the SSJ Associates in Mission. The experiences these new members had with a global or multicultural society provided a new dimension to the initial formation program within the context of a community.

In the 1990s, the Congregation encouraged fuller support from all sisters for welcoming and mentoring new members. In vocation ministry, to welcome young women meant becoming an "inviter." Sister Geraldine Muller (George Kathleen) (1987–1995) and her successor Sister Kathleen Pales (1995–2001), assisted by local community contact sisters and the 12-member vocation ministry advisory team, educated sisters on national trends about young adults and their vocation choices. Sisters learned that the primary reason why some young adults had not considered a religious vocation was that they had not been invited to do so. One candidate confirmed this: "I had been impressed by the sisters for a long time, but it wasn't until one sister actually asked me, that I began to see it as a possibility for myself."

Two projects—Opt for the City, and Good Works—offered young adults an experience of religious life through service, simple lifestyle, and community living. In Opt for the City, designed by vocation directors in the Philadelphia area, participants ministered for a week in inner-city Philadelphia and lived in neighboring convents such as St. Anne, Visitation, St. Michael, and St. Hugh. Good Works, begun in 1989 as a joint effort of the SSJ Vocation Office, SSJ Associates, and Chestnut Hill College, engaged volunteers in living the SSJ Mission with the sisters. By 1999, three Good Works programs had evolved: Good Works Kentucky, a three-week program in the Appalachian region of eastern Kentucky; Good Works Camden (New Jersey), a week in inner-city Camden, New Jersey; and Good Weekend Works, also in Camden. While only a few sisters were directly involved in these projects, which had between nine and 20 volunteers at any one time, the *Congregational Newsletter* highlighted these programs as avenues of invitation.

By the 1990s there was no longer a designated site for the initial formation program; the young women (candidates and postulants), lived in different geographic settings where they had a supportive local community experience They were able to hold salaried positions with flexible hours that allowed them to attend classes with their director, participate in formation weekends, and attend congregational events and the intercongregational formation program for young men and women called InSearch. In this model, every sister in a local community had the responsibility of assisting the young woman as she attempted to live the SSJ Mission and way of life. The formation director worked with the local community, and in each situation, one sister in the local house served as the formal mentor for the candidate.

During the 1990s, the Congregation experimented with two different novitiate arrangements to further develop the local community aspect of the canonical year. For three years (1992–1995), the novice director and the one novice participated in the local community of Nazareth House, a small home on the edge of the Saint Joseph Villa grounds; but regular classes were conducted at the Motherhouse. By the mid-1990s, Nazareth House became too small, and anticipating the possibility of more than one novice, the General Council transferred the program back to the Motherhouse. In August 1996, two novices and their director helped establish Resurrection Community, a local community of seven sisters located in a renovated area of the Motherhouse.

Situating all stages of initial formation within a local community reinforced the fuller aspect of formation and acknowledged the women's desire for community life. InSearch and the CSSJ Federation programs of the 1990s provided opportunities for bonding with peers that individual formation programs could no longer offer. Previously, CSSJ Federation programs supplemented those of a particular congregation, but now the CSSJ Federation programs for novices and temporary professed sisters became more comprehensive. In 1995, the Sisters of Saint Joseph of Philadelphia hosted the Collaborative Novitiate Program, which had become the pivotal ongoing formation experience in the Federation. Although this event was conducted in part by Sister Sheila Holly (Ann Sheila), Director of Novices, there were no Philadelphia novices in attendance. In addition to Chestnut Hill, Cape May Point also served as a venue for retreats and other Federation programs. At a time when most congregations of women religious were grappling with the problem of declining numbers, the CSSJ Federation initiatives in formation offered not only a solution but a valuable resource both for those who participated and for the Congregation itself. In particular, these experiences provided the all-important peer connections that no single Congregation was able to offer due to fewer new members.

Although their experience of religious life in the formation stages was not the same as that of women entering in the 1990s, those who entered the Congregation from the mid-1970s through the 1980s had been part of the changes in formation resulting from Vatican II. These sisters also were members of considerably smaller parties than those of the 1950s or 1960s, and so peer relationship was an aspect of personal growth that required special attention. In fall 1997, Sister Sheila Kennedy, who entered the Congregation in 1976, initiated a "Newer Members Cluster" for those who had entered since 1975. Of the 63 potential attendees, about 20 formed a core group. Though smaller than anticipated, the core members met monthly during the next two years, aiming to build relationships among themselves and to develop a shared sense of responsibility for the Congregation. For those who participated, the cluster seemed to create a stronger social network.

The associate relationship continued to thrive. With the Associate Advisory Board members, Sister Roberta Archibald and Margot Zuccarello, co-directors (1990–1995), collaborated with their regional and CSSJ Federation counterparts and developed materials for an orientation process. The SSJ Associates in Mission hosted annual gatherings that featured nationally recognized speakers in the areas of spirituality and justice. They participated in North American Conferences for CSSJ Associates and, with the Brentwood Congregation, hosted the 1995 North American Conference at Chestnut Hill College.

GOVERNANCE

Local Community and Congregational Governance Models and Issues

Since 1979, local houses had been given the option of electing their own superiors instead of having them appointed. However during the 1980s, only 20 percent of the 139 houses took advantage of this option. By the late 1980s the Administration more actively encouraged local communities to exercise this form of co-responsibility in leadership, and by 1992, nearly 60 percent of the local houses held such elections.

As the number of elected local coordinators increased, some groups creatively adapted the role itself. In one house a sister agreed to take the role for a three-year term only on the proviso that everyone in the local community would share the role, and they agreed. Another house proposed electing their local coordinator annually instead of for a three-year term. In other situations, practically all of the coordinator's responsibilities were distributed among the sisters themselves. The coordinator's main duties ranged from house liaison with the area delegate to picking up the package of materials distributed each August to the local houses. In a few instances, one sister was listed as coordinator, but she mainly acted as a liaison for all general communications.

Created to implement the 1989 Chapter suggestion for a three-year focus on renewal for community living, the Community Life Committee was formed and its work was fundamentally educative. The committee offered workshops on communal prayer, trained facilitators and mediators to serve local communities, and developed initial house meeting materials to foster a common vision. They also helped create the option for a sister to have a conversation with a potential local community about its lifestyle within the context of the *Constitutions* as part of the missioning process.

In all local houses, a modification of goal setting—intentionality—was adopted in fall 1993 to help sisters in each house to identify and clarify their values, hopes, and desires for communal living. In doing this, local communities began to converse at a much deeper level about their shared vision regarding communal life at the local level. Following the 1994 Chapter, the General Council developed a formal process to guide these discussions called the Statement of Intent. At the initial house meeting, the local community began the process of identifying and articulating shared values and at the conclusion formulated a written statement that each sister signed; a copy of the statement was sent to the Council.

With regard to congregational Administration, the Superior General and Council tried to create a more visible presence among the membership by enhancing existing vehicles of communication and by actually visiting the local communities. The consolidation of several publications into the *Congregational Newsletter* in spring 1992 not only guaranteed a more uniform dissemination of information but also led to an increased knowledge of the collaboration, creativity, and conversion that characterized the congregational network of relationships.

To actually be more present to a greater number of sisters, and to be a sign of unity in the Congregation, Sister Margaret Fleming made visiting local communities a priority during her first term. From January 1990 through June 1994, she traveled to over 140 local communities, sharing meals and prayer and soliciting responses to the most fundamental question: How we can sustain and strengthen our unity and diversity as we affirm the gifts of the Holy Spirit in each other as individuals and as a body?

In October 1991, the General Council disseminated a questionnaire which 89 percent of the Congregation (1,425 sisters) completed. The survey, entitled *Probe the Heart—Celebrate the Future,* was designed to provide a corporate profile of the sisters' values, attitudes, and feelings. Results showed that most sisters had a high tolerance for diversity in local community and ministry yet disagreed on how to handle the conflicts that sometimes ensued. According to the data, half tended to use active conflict management styles such as collaboration and assertiveness, while the other 50 percent favored passive styles such as accommodation and avoidance. Most sisters felt a strong corporate sense of responsibility for the Congregation and desired to be involved in decision making. Although two-thirds of the responses viewed authority as collegial, the remaining third saw it as hierarchical. The evidence from the survey clearly suggested that a sister's view of authority and handing of conflict were related to her expectations of leadership, approach to community life, and perceptions of ministry and Church. With approximately two-thirds of the responders signaling a desire for increased collegiality in governance, there was reason to believe that this might result in the congregational leadership's willingness to expand opportunities for sisters' participation in decision making. In fact, in preparing for the 1994 Chapter, the General Council solicited the names of those they thought could serve on the Chapter Planning Committee from the sisters and used this input as part of their discernment.

1994 Chapter: Content and Processes

The 1994 Chapter was referred to as a Visioning Chapter because its outcome was intended to be a corporate statement that would characterize the Congregation's vision for living out the mission during the next five years. The sisters' desire for increased participation resulted in two types of delegates: deliberative (125) and consultative (154). The role of the latter included every aspect of the proceedings except the voting during the Chapter of Election. In addition to these delegates, there were at least 100 observers (sisters and associates). This was the largest group (380) that had ever attended Chapter proceedings. From the preparation for the Chapter to its conclusion, the impetus toward full congregational participation underscored all the events and proceedings.

Pre-Chapter education included optional gatherings with input by Sister Veronica O'Reilly CSJ, of Peterborough, Canada. More than 900 sisters gathered at 23 sites across the Congregation from July through September 1993. The traditional enrichment days continued with Diana Hayes lecturing on "Global Perspectives" (December 1993) and Janet Ruffing RSM, speaking on "Religious Life Now and into the Twenty-first Century" (January 1994). Minor modifications in the preliminary aspects of the leadership election process included members sending personal calls to leadership to an unlimited number of sisters, rather than submitting the names of only five sisters. During this same period, based on the sisters' focused reflections, the Congregation identified five elements to be included in the vision: claiming the centrality of prayer in our personal and communal lives, becoming more inclusive, addressing the injustices of our day, valuing community life as shared life, and claiming our power as women.

On June 24, 1994, Sister Margaret Fleming convened the 1994 Chapter and evoked Father Médaille's vision for the first sisters, by quoting Maurice Nepper SJ, a French scholar on SSJ origins. His portrait of a Sister of Saint Joseph described an ordinary woman ready to hear God's word and do God's work. The 1994 Chapter was to be an ordinary time of fidelity in which the sisters challenged each other to promote unity and love and to focus on the spirit and mission of the Congregation in the context of the "miseries" of the day.

During the five-day Chapter of Affairs, the shortest in the Congregation's history, the delegates affirmed the Vision Statement, four broad steps, and two action statements. On June 27, those in attendance applauded after hearing the fifth draft of the Vision Statement, and on June 28, the statement was unanimously approved. The statement itself was brief and concise, and every word had been carefully chosen:

> Rooted in a contemplative life stance and challenged by our broken world, we claim our prophetic voice as women to stand with marginalized persons and to treasure and care for the Earth.

Its very simplicity made it memorable, and its verbal economy seemed to reinforce the directness of its purpose and the clarity of its intent. To implement this vision, the delegates identified four broad steps that emphasized ownership, participation, and collaboration. In effect, these steps guaranteed the commitment of the Sisters of Saint Joseph to maintain a presence with poor, oppressed, and marginalized persons; work for the equality and empowerment of women; network for systemic change; and make explicit their interdependence with creation.

Two internal topics—governance and inclusive language—became Chapter actions, addressing issues that, according to data from the SSJ survey, indicated divergent opinions among the sisters. The delegates wanted ongoing study and experimentation on issues related to governance but scrupulously avoided using the latter term because of its implications. The final form of the action statement avoided ambiguity:

> That the Chapter empower the new leadership to engage the Congregation in examining our governance structures and in imagining new models in light of our mission and the vision of this Chapter and take the steps toward adjusting and experiencing emerging structures as needed.

The issue of inclusive language was fraught with considerable tension especially because it touched on culture and ideology as well as individual attitudes toward social justice and feminism. The first proposal, introduced by Sister Anne Myers (Patrick Christine), was straightforward: to edit the *Constitutions* and *Directory* to reflect inclusive language. When this proposed broad step was later withdrawn, there remained enough support to reintroduce the idea as a Chapter action. After lengthy discussion, the delegates crafted a more prudent approach, which allowed for possible potential action. Once again, the topic proved too sensitive and controversial to gain broad-based support for definitive action.

On the evening of July 29, 1994, the Chapter of Elections began. To establish the final leadership pool, all 273 deliberative and consultative delegates, rather than only the canonical electors, nominated 16 of the 37 sisters still available for possible election to leadership positions. During the pre-election reflection days, all Chapter participants, not just the electors, entered into a time of discernment. In a new process, the 16 nominees spent a day and a half in reflection at the Motherhouse facilitated by Sister Janet Mock CSJ. The remainder prayed about the graces needed for the membership to choose and support new leadership. On July 2, the day before the election, each nominee briefly addressed the delegates, sharing the gifts she would bring to leadership. On July 3, all delegates and sister-observers, SSJ Associates in Mission, and other friends of the Congregation assembled in the Chapter room where they witnessed the live voting of the deliberative delegates. Sister Margaret Fleming was re-elected Superior General, and Sisters Patricia Kelly (Patrick Maureen) and Annemarie Roche (Thomas Veronica) were again elected Councillors. The new Councillors were Sister Anna Louise and Sister Merilyn Ryan (Teresa Miriam).

As a result of the 1994 Chapter action on governance, the most significant and perhaps dramatic change in governance happened in local communities. For them, the General Council in October 1994 outlined a four-step process with a response form titled Statement of Intent. In the process, the sisters individually reflected on the *Constitutions'* passages about local governance, the 1994 Chapter Vision Statement, broad steps, and actions. Next they conversed about local structures to further the Mission and Vision, worked for consensus on which structures to adopt, and completed, for the General Council's acceptance, a Statement of Intent form signed by each sister. While not overtly connected to the 1980s movement for intentional communities, the Statement of Intent process led local communities to identify their shared vision.

On the local level, most houses chose a governance model that promoted co-responsibility, although the size of the group was a major factor in determining the structures to facilitate the sharing of responsibilities. Groups of six or fewer tended to assign areas of responsibility to an individual sister; larger groups seemed to form committees. In Bethlehem, Pennsylvania, two small local communities held meetings together, alternating sites. They also shared duties: one sister from one house was the social justice contact for both houses, while a sister from the other convent served as dual vocation contact. Two large local communities, one in Newark and one in Philadelphia, decided to create two smaller local communities within the same convent but with different organizational structures, intended outcomes, and evaluative criteria. Another large group chose a council of three sisters to guide them, while another house organized a network of committees that reported to a house council. Most frequently identified areas of responsibility were communication, finances, spirituality, housekeeping/maintenance, and community life. Some houses formed separate committees for celebrations and for care of the sick. In the diversity of new structures, there was one dramatic change common to practically all: most local communities no longer had a person designated as local coordinator. The few houses that retained a coordinator made the selection from among the group.

As local communities designed and lived their emerging structures, commonalties surfaced in their hopes and problems. Communities had to grapple with handling times of sickness or other emergencies because there was no one designated "to make a split second decision." In the midst of busy ministry schedules, sisters often struggled with amount of time needed for collaboration and consensus building. Local communities were often stretched to deeper levels of trust, respect, and understanding. Sometimes they succeeded; sometimes not.

Changes involving congregational structures were more modest. Since the 1970s, the general council's public leadership style, augmented by increased consultation and collaboration, had been the operative mode of governance. Modifications in the role of the ministry coordinators and in the work provided by congregational offices, commissions, and committees were generally supported by the membership. However, the Congregation continued to debate internally the role of the area delegate or even the need for this position. While the governance task force's first consultation on this role in March 1995 produced no clear insights, the General Council and the area delegates took an emerging process approach, making some changes. The locus for initiative shifted from the area delegate to the local community and the individual sister. The local community identified the timing for the area delegate's visit and the kind of interaction desired, such as a faith sharing and meal, or prayer and meeting. Some local houses opted for a cluster gathering with neighboring convents. Previously, the area delegate met individually with each sister during the annual visit, but now either the sister or the area delegate initiated the personal interview at least once in a three-year time frame. Although the role of area delegates was becoming more pastoral and less authoritative, they assisted with local governance questions, housing issues, and conflict management as needed. By 1999, however, even with these adaptations, there was a lack of clarity about the delegated authority of the role and the services required by the sisters. After many years and permutations of the role, there was still no consensus about the specific position itself as part of the Congregation's governance structure.

Finances in the 1990s: Implications for Governance

Resolutely focused on their Mission, the Sisters of Saint Joseph steadfastly implemented the 1989 Chapter enactment for developing a more corporate sense of finance to further responsible participation in community living, in ministry, and in congregational endeavors. During the 1990s, three major efforts were undertaken: increased monetary compensation for services, consolidation of finances through central banking, and the inauguration of the development program.

The booklet *Change Our Hearts* (1990) became a mainstay for communicating financial information. The publication covered practical points like the use of ATM machines, promulgated new policies such as the new personal spiritual enrichment fund, provided CCR preparation, reported on consultations, and gathered ideas for Financial Advisory Board cluster meeting agendas. In effect, this little booklet linked the practical to the ideal, focusing on the call to simplicity of life, the common good, and stewardship of resources.

During the 1990s, the Congregation, in its negotiations with the bishops and pastors of the 15 dioceses in which sisters served, stressed the need for an increase in the stipends, since this compensation was its chief financial support for current and future needs. The Congregation was in the middle of a 20-year window of opportunity (1987 to 2007) when the majority of the sisters would still be able to earn full compensation. Advocating for increased compensation was also directly aligned with the planning goals recommended by the Tri-Conference Retirement Office. The stipend package usually included medical coverage and other benefits, such as rent-free housing in a convent. As a result of negotiations, in 1994 the stipend ranged from $11,980 to $19,680, depending on the diocese. By 1999, the compensation had increased from a range from $14,700 to $27,500.

The Tri-Conference Retirement Office recommended in 1990 that the General Council transition to market value salaries for the sisters employed in congregationally owned institutions in 1990. This would achieve parity for both lay and religious employees. However, these packages would not include housing or transportation benefits. By 1999, two of the six congregationally owned educational institutions, Mount Saint Joseph Academy and Norwood-Fontbonne Academy, had attained market value for the 28 sister employees. In other Church-related work, there were 77 Sisters of Saint Joseph (about 7 percent) receiving market value compensation.

Another attempt on the part of the Congregation to secure its financial resources centered on health care options. By 1999, most sisters under 65 were enrolled in plans that used preferred provider organization networks (PPOs). Since the sisters ministered in multiple states and dioceses, using these plans extended their benefits through national networks. Building on their decision (1972) to buy into Social Security, the Congregation took full advantage of government services, so that by 1999 most sisters over 65 were on the federal Medicare program, and those in Pennsylvania and New Jersey were enrolled in the state-sponsored Medicare supplement.

In addition to stipends and health care, the issue of housing continued to be of paramount importance, since living in residences other than those provided by the parish or diocese could be an expensive venture that the Congregation could only afford in exceptional cases. During the 1990s, over 90 percent of the sisters lived in convent housing. About 56 percent lived in parish convents or diocesan faculty houses, and slightly more than 30 percent lived in the 12 congregationally owned residences, including Saint Joseph Villa (226 sisters). In the mid-1980s the Congregation began renting a few residences, usually recently vacated parish convents, for sisters whose ministry did not provide housing or for active senior houses. However, the number of sisters in these rented properties was only 66, or 5 percent of the Congregation.

In some cases, the sisters sought housing that would suit congregational guidelines. They would cut back on other areas of the budget to cover the rental cost. Some enterprising sisters found landlords who would accept the standard diocesan housing subsidy, while a few others applied for HUD subsidized residences. In 1999, another 6.1 percent of the Congregation (79) were living in these alternate housing arrangements.

Recommended for study and possible implementation by the 1989 Chapter, central banking became the second endeavor in a movement toward a more corporate sense of finance. Conceptually, all management of monies derived from income, disbursement of funds, and accounting would be handled at the congregational level. Practically, central banking eliminated the need for monthly assessments and created parity regarding the monthly budget sent to every local house. It also provided more capital for investments and allowed for greater flexibility in management of funds. The practice clearly reflected the ideal that all things be held in common.

In order to fully educate the sisters on the concept of central financing and its necessity, the Congregation used the financial bulletin *Change of Heart*, along with video/audio presentations, cluster meetings, and the Corporate Centers for Reflection (CCR). This process began in February 1990 and concluded with the November 1991 CCR. In the formal consultation at the November 1991 CCR, 79 percent supported the central financing model in which all monies were "pooled and administered centrally." The General Council affirmed the majority opinion and made the decision to adopt central financing.

From January 1992 through July 1995, the Congregation initiated the process that would transfer all monies from the local houses to the central account. By May 1, 1992, all savings had been centralized using two cash management systems. Religious Communities Trust (RCT), a part of the Christian Brothers Investment Group, managed savings accounts of smaller houses, and Merrill Lynch handled the larger houses. Each local house transferred its savings from local banks to a designated subaccount of the Congregation's master account where the funds formed one large interest-earning account. Four months later, the Congregation began to centralize all income, so that stipends and salary monies were sent directly to the congregational finance office, which then disbursed monies to each local house subaccount. By June 1993, centralized checking was in effect. Local checking accounts were closed and houses did all banking, both savings and checking, from one subaccount. Finally, in 1995, all local communities returned excess savings from their local house subaccounts to the congregational finance office and kept only what was needed for ordinary cash flow purposes.

While the house budgets seemed adequate and the benefits of central banking readily apparent, the issue of the sisters' personal budgets continued to be problematic. To try to accommodate the diverse needs of individuals, the Congregation proposed a budget range, between $600 and $1025 (1994–1995). In 1999, the Congregation provided monies for spiritual enrichment that sisters could access, and it adjusted the personal budgets to allow for annual cost of living increases.

In the succeeding years, the Congregation used its corporate voice for the mission with the capital generated by central financing. Annual financial reports highlighted the positive return from central financing on investment income especially in the strong 1990s economy. In 1995, the first year of full implementation, the transfer of $1,097,203 from local accounts to the central congregational account was a significant factor in the 39.3 percent increase in investment income compared with that in 1992. Chapter reports and the *Congregational Newsletter* detailed the continuous diversification of the Congregation's investment portfolio since the mid-1980s. The sisters were corporate shareholders and had the enhanced capacity to use this power for socially responsible action. Using the research from the Interfaith Center on Corporate Responsibility (ICCR), a New York-based national organization of about 250 religious investor groups that held $50 billion in investments, the Sisters of Saint Joseph regularly voted their proxies and sponsored resolutions to influence a corporation. At the 1995 annual meeting of Coca-Cola shareholders, Sister Mary Elizabeth Clark, Justice Coordinator, received resounding applause for her commendation of the CEO for his cooperation with the South African Council of Churches in preparing a Code of Conduct for Business in South Africa. In 1996, the Congregation challenged Wal-Mart on equality issues in the workplace in a shareholder resolution. Such actions were proof that central financing offered a much greater impact for Sisters of Saint Joseph to live their mission of unity and stand with the marginalized and disenfranchised.

Development: Projects and Campaigns

Following a pre-campaign year (1989–1990) in which the Congregation realized $1.4 million from fund-raising efforts already in place, the Sisters of Saint Joseph embarked on a 10-year comprehensive campaign to raise $25 million. The SSJ Development Office envisioned a three-phase plan with increased sub goals as the project gained momentum: $5,000,000 in 1990–1993, $8,000,000 in 1994–1996, and $12,000,000 in 1997–2000. By December 31, 1998, a total of $25,912,632 had been collected! Three factors contributed to this achievement: the strong leadership of the General Council, the comprehensive plan, and the sisters' commitment to participate with the laity.

The need to provide for the sisters' retirement was the driving force behind most of the fund-raising efforts of the Development Office. The year-long silver anniversary celebration of Saint Joseph Villa (June 26, 1993, to March 19, 1994) was the Congregation's first attempt at major gift solicitation, resulting in contributions totaling $1,200,000. In the 1997 annual report the Development Office cited over 2,000 memorial gifts, 31 grants, 35 bequests, and matching funds from 20 companies. At the same time, the National Religious Retirement Office awarded the Sisters of Saint Joseph three supplemental grants totaling $600,000.

Special events were another aspect of the comprehensive development plan, and the Development Advisory Board used these to create heightened awareness of the SSJ Mission. From spring 1991 through fall 1999, the six major dinner events, three anniversary celebrations, three concerts, two golf tournaments, and two cruises "to nowhere" were designed to broaden our circle of friends, thereby increasing contributions to the SSJ Support Fund and to identify possible major benefactors. One such event, held at the Valley Forge Music Fair in October 1992, showcased the combined talents of 254 sisters, associates, and friends. Titled Sisters of Saint Joseph: Celebrating God's Design, and co-produced by Sisters Mary Ann Mulzet and Madeline Franze (Teresa Joseph), the performance connected the past history of the Sisters of Saint Joseph with the present. Nearly 3,000 persons attended the show, which netted over $80,000.

1999 CHAPTER:
DEEPENING THE COMMITMENT TO THE MISSION

The last Chapter of the twentieth century was to be a Deepening Chapter. Instead of exploring new territory, the delegates would re-evaluate existing commitments and strive to deepen them over the next five years. The Chapter Planning Committee, guided by facilitator Sister Janet Roesener CSJ, identified a key phrase from the *Constitutions* that became the theme of the Chapter Event: "How Great Is the Love to Which We Are Called, How Deep the Responsibility." The theme was set to music by Sister Regina Gormley (Joseph Regina) and artistically rendered in a logo by Sister Carole Pollock (Laura Edward). This simple phrase became the heartbeat of the Chapter body.

One major change that preceded the 1999 Chapter deliberations was an alteration to the process of electing delegates. In order to increase both active participation and co-responsibility, the General Council formulated a new policy that made it possible for any sister to be a canonically elected delegate. It required that a sister receive 10 percent of the votes. There were no limitations on the number of votes a sister could cast. At the 1999 Chapter, 374 sisters (28 percent of those eligible) were voting delegates, along with the five ex officio members of the General Council.

The 1999 Chapter was officially convened the weekend of February 13–14, 1999, a Valentine weekend, a fitting occasion to ponder the implications of the theme. The basic question generated by the Chapter deliberations was: How is God inviting us to deepen our identity as Sisters of Saint Joseph and our commitment to our Mission and Vision?

At the first meeting of the June Chapter session, Sister Margaret Fleming forthrightly summarized the fundamental choice threading the Chapter's work. Recalling the hardships suffered and love offered by their founder and foundresses in the past 350 years, she reiterated the Chapter's purpose: "The people of God in our Church and in our world need the members of this Chapter Body to deepen the mission and vision of the Sisters of Saint Joseph, to take on the responsibility of refounding our congregation to meet the challenges of a new millennium." Rooting the Congregation's corporate response in the heart of each sister, she challenged, "Are you willing to be a foundress?" "For what am I willing to suffer, to make sacrifices, to disturb myself, so that our mission and vision can deepen within me and address the miseries that are crushing my dear neighbor?"

During the summer sessions, four responses emerged. The sisters would examine and evaluate their identity (Who We Are), community living (How We Are Together), service to the "dear neighbor" (How We Are for the Dear Neighbor), and approach to new membership (Extending Our Mission into the Future). From these four, the delegates generated 36 concrete subtopics that were narrowed to 14. A committee of 14 volunteer writers then drafted a Chapter document integrating the subtopics with the four main themes, using as a framework the Chapter mantra of great love and call for deepening. After review, the delegates offered some points for revision but affirmed the total draft.

When critiquing the subtopics under membership, the Chapter body directly faced a particular challenge: the Congregation's openness to women of other cultures. Delegates asked, "What can we as a Congregation do to be more aware of and more welcoming toward women of other cultures?" In a special forum, four sisters responded to the question about being a woman from a particular culture in the Congregation. Sister Janice McGrane, with her life experience of dealing with crippling arthritis, explained that she was "different" because she was a Sister of Saint Joseph with a disability, claiming that persons with disabilities are often considered persons of another culture. She encouraged the Congregation to broaden its perceptive on whom might be invited. Sister Dorismarie Gonzalez (Jose Marie), who spoke of herself as "an assimilated Puerto Rican with an Hispanic last name," offered this perspective: "When *I* think of *other* cultures I think of all of *you!*" Sister Clarisa Vazquez described how being in the Congregation had helped her grow in her identity "as a Latina," and she expressed gratitude for sisters who had chosen to minister bilingually and biculturally. Sister Patricia Ralph asked, "What do you see right now? A young woman who is a Sister of Saint Joseph or a black woman who happens to be a Sister of Saint Joseph?" She recommended that sisters go into others' culture without patronizing, but with an open mind, open heart. The reflections of these sisters challenged their listeners to see the potential for personal conversion in embracing the Chapter's commitment to invite, welcome, and support new members of all cultures, backgrounds, and ages.

On July 1, the Chapter body unanimously approved the final draft of the Chapter 1999 document, which in a single page articulated the reaffirmation of the Mission and Vision. As one, the sisters pledged to deepen their understanding of their charism, proclaim their shared mission, and be reconcilers and risk takers who challenge injustices and foster right relationships. Cherishing the "dear neighbor," they would support the Congregation's sponsored works as creative expressions of their mission and recommit to maintaining their presence with marginalized people and advocating for women. Believing in their future, as Sisters of Saint Joseph, they claimed responsibility for inviting and supporting new members and associates, and establishing new forms of connectedness that would also enhance the visibility of the Congregation.

Portrait of Sister Margaret Fleming

Sisters hearing Sister Margaret Fleming's words during the 1999 Chapter realized that they echoed the core spirit of her leadership in the 1990s. Over and over, Sister Margaret Fleming—"Peg," as she was known to the sisters—led them with disarming simplicity and astute vision. A native of Orange, New Jersey, Peg entered the Congregation in 1956 after her graduation from Chestnut Hill College. Elected to the General Council in 1979, Peg had been a young delegate at the 1968 Chapter and then dean of students at the College for 11 years, including the years of turbulence in the 1970s. As a councillor in the 1980s, Peg suffered deeply with sisters the pain of their transformation. In the 1990s, she recognized that she was leading the sisters toward regrouping and refounding after the storm. From her love of sports and experience as a basketball player, Peg called the Congregation to a sense of team. The sisters needed to be cheering each other on, caring for each other as co-players, being co-responsible, speaking truth to each other for the good of all, and being corporate in new ways.

In her approach, Peg often characterized herself as an ordinary person moving among extraordinary persons, the sisters of the past and present. She regularly laced her letters, talks, and conversations with references to the first sisters, offering her listeners ways to find new meaning in the SSJ origins. Many saw in Peg what she described about Mother Saint John Fournier, "a woman of deep faith and humility and having great zeal and a spirit of adventure" who was by "nature reticent about her own accomplishments." Tall in stature and heart, Peg passionately worked to empower the Sisters of Saint Joseph to live out their mission and vision by always espousing how great was the love to which they were called and how deep their responsibility for each other, the "dear neighbor," and the planet.

1999 Chapter of Election

The Chapter of Election (July 2–4) was co-facilitated by Sisters Janet Mock CSJ, and Janet Roesener CSJ. After reflecting on the scope of public and internal responsibilities required of congregational leaders entering a new millennium, the Chapter body nominated 19 sisters from the group of 38 available for leadership. All delegates then engaged in discernment: the nominees at Chestnut Hill and electors at Holy Family College. Following the period of discernment, Sister Janet Roesener facilitated interaction between nominees and electors. Instead of the nominees addressing the Chapter body individually, they formed two panels and fielded questions about their life experiences and leadership qualities. Another new aspect of the process, called "leanings," allowed electors to indicate their preferences among the nominees. These leanings were shared with the nominees. On July 4, in the presence of more than 700 Sisters of Saint Joseph, associates, and friends, the electors chose Sister Patricia Kelly as Superior General. Sister Merilyn Ryan and Sister Anna Louise Schuck were re-elected as Councillors. The newly elected new Councillors were Sister Anne Myers and Sister Mary Barrar.

FACING THE FUTURE

The last General Chapter of the decade was also the last of the twentieth century for the Sisters of Saint Joseph. Having forged their identity from their founding in 1650 through the close of World War II, they had, in the past 55 years, reclaimed it. Graced by members and leaders passionate about their Mission of Unity, the sisters had struggled together cautiously, and at times hesitantly, to be reshaped into God's design for them. They had embraced renewal, wrestled through transformation, and chosen to be refounded in their spirituality, ministry, and governance. As they stepped into the new millennium celebrating the 72-Hour Peace Vigil at Chestnut Hill, the sisters did not fear to hope. They were ready anew for any and every good work.

The Jubilee Year 2000 marked the 350th anniversary of their foundation in LePuy, France, when six young women came together to form the Congregation of the Great Love of God. Their spirit can still be discerned today in this Congregation of the Sisters of Saint Joseph of Chestnut Hill, Philadelphia, who have dared to proclaim: *How Great Is the Love to Which We Are Called, How Deep the Responsibility* for the life of the world.

PUBLISHED SOURCES

Grindel, John A., CM, and Sean Peters, CSJ. Religious Life Issues in a Time of Transition. *Review for Religious* 51, no. 2 (March/April 1992).

Kashuba, Mary Helen, SSJ. *Tradition and Risk.* Virginia Beach, VA: The Donning Company, 1999.

Sandra M Schneiders, IHM. Congregational Leadership and Spirituality in the Postmodern Era. *Review for Religious* 57, no. 1 (January/February 1998).

ARCHIVAL SOURCES

Mount Saint Joseph Convent, Philadelphia, Pennsylvania

Primitive documents, records of General Chapters, personal papers, focus groups, and other records.

Timeline

1944–1999

1944: Special Chapter of Election
1946: Saint Mary by-the-Sea retreat house, Cape May, New Jersey, returned to Sisters of Saint Joseph by US Coast Guard
1947: Centennial of SSJ arrival in Philadelphia
1950: 1950 Chapter
1950s: Rapid expansion of SSJ educational ministries in many dioceses and archdioceses
1952: Participation in National Conference of Women Religious following the International Conference in Rome at invitation of Pope Pius XII
1955: Motherhouse Chapel renovated
1956: 1956 Chapter
1960: Fontbonne Postulate opened
1961: Erection of new Mount Saint Joseph Academy, Flourtown, Pennsylvania
1962: 1962 Chapter
1962: Second Vatican Council in Rome
1966: Retirement of Mother Marie Estelle Duggan, Mistress of Novices, after 34 years
1967: Congregational Regions created with Regional Superiors
1968: Opening of Saint Joseph Villa, Flourtown, Pennsylvania, for infirm and retired sisters
1968: 1968 Chapter: Renewal Chapter, Session I
1969: 1968 Chapter: Renewal Chapter, Session II; *Design for Excellence* produced

1972: Formation of SSJ Renewal Team, the Médaille Team
1974: 1974 Chapter: *Design for Excellence II* produced
1975: Opening of SSJ Center for Spirituality
1977: Introduction of CCRs for consultation about apostolic direction
1978: Expansion of SSJ ministries beyond school ministry
1979: 1979 Chapter: rewriting of SSJ *Constitutions*
1979: Implementation of Chapter mandate to restructure apostolic works and reallocation of personnel
1979: *Focus,* first congregational newsletter published
1980: Project Withdrawal/Recommitment initiated
1980: SSJ Commission for Justice inaugurated
1982: Academy Village, McSherrystown, Pennsylvania, subsidized senior housing opened
1983: 125th Anniversary of SSJ arrival in Chestnut Hill
1984: 1984 Chapter: *Constitutions* Chapter as mandated by Vatican II
1984: Coordinators of Ministry positions introduced
1984: Third World Missions initiated in three countries
1984: SSJ Associates in Mission established: partnership with laity
1984: Bethlehem Village, Flourtown, Pennsylvania, subsidized senior housing opened
1987: *SSJ Constitutions* approved by Rome
1987: Rural domestic ministries begun in Kentucky
1988: SSJ Corporate Stand against Apartheid adopted
1988: SSJ Development Office established
1989: 1989 Chapter: Creativity, Collaboration, and Conversion for Mission
1990: *Change Our Hearts,* financial newsletter introduced
1994: 1994 Chapter: Articulation of Vision Statement
1995: CSSJ Federation Event in Philadelphia; picnic celebration at Chestnut Hill
1996: Literacy project established
1997: 150th Anniversary of SSJ's arrival in Philadelphia
1998: SSJ Corporate Stand against the death penalty
1999: 1999 Chapter: Deepening the Commitment to Mission

General Councils

1944–1999

1944–1950

Mother Mary Thecla Brennan, Superior General
Mother Divine Shepherd Flaherty, Assistant
Mother Saint Pierre Byrne
Mother Philomena Kelly
Mother Teresa Vincent Harney

1950–1956

Mother Mary Thecla Brennan, Superior General
Mother Divine Shepherd Flaherty, Assistant
Mother Philomena Kelly
Mother Mary of Bethany McGuiness
Mother Teresa Vincent Harney

1956–1962

Mother Divine Shepherd Flaherty, Superior General
Mother Mary Thecla Brennan, Assistant
Mother Philomena Kelly
Mother Mary of Bethany McGuiness
Mother Saint Thomas McInerney

1962–1968

Mother Divine Shepherd Flaherty, Superior General
Mother Mary Thecla Brennan, Assistant
Mother Mary of Bethany McGuiness
Mother Letitia Maria Gleason
Mother Victorine Riehl

1968–1974

Mother Alice Anita Murphy, Superior General
Mother Divine Shepherd Flaherty, Assistant, died November 27, 1969
Mother Francis Ines Moloney, died January 9, 1971
Mother Lilian Teresa McClain, died September 2, 1971
Sister Consuelo Maria Aherne
Sister Loyola Marie Coffey, appointed January 17, 1970
Sister Mary Thomas Murphy, appointed February 10, 1971
Sister Clare Michael Keating, appointed November 2, 1971

1974–1979

Sister Alice Anita Murphy, Superior General
Sister Consuelo Maria Aherne, Assistant
Sister Agnes Marie Gunn (Agnes David)
Sister Clare Michael Keating
Sister Marie Ellen Hegarty
Sister Mary Thomas Murphy, Councilor-at-Large
Sister Saint Ursula Egan, Councilor-at-Large

1979–1984

Sister Dorothea Newell (Ignatius Loyola), Superior General
Sister Agnes Marie Gunn (Agnes David), Assistant
Sister Saint Ursula Egan
Sister Eugenie Madeleine Gaddi
Sister Margaret Fleming (William Marguerite)

1984–1989

Sister Dorothea Newell, Superior General
Sister Eugenie Madeleine Gaddi, Assistant

Sister Margaret Fleming
Sister Kathleen Keane (Helen Therese)
Sister Gerald Vincent McDevitt

1989–1994

Sister Margaret Fleming, Superior General
Sister Patricia Kelly (Patrick Maureen), Assistant
Sister Helen P. Clifton
Sister Dorothy Apprich (Rose William)
Sister Annemarie Roche (Thomas Veronica)

1994–1999

Sister Margaret Fleming, Superior General
Sister Patricia Kelly, Assistant
Sister Annemarie Roche
Sister Anna Louise Schuck
Sister Merilyn Ryan (Teresa Miriam)

1999–2004

Sister Patricia Kelly, Superior General
Sister Merilyn Ryan, Assistant
Sister Anne Myers (Patrick Christine)
Sister Anna Louise Schuck
Sister Mary Barrar (George Mary)

For most of our history, only the superior general and the first councillor (assistant) were full-time members of the general council and lived at Mount Saint Joseph Convent. Other councillors, usually designated the second, third, and fourth councillor, in order of election, had regular ministries as well as their council responsibilities.

The 1974 Chapter of Election enacted a number of changes affecting the general council. Everyone, including the superior general and assistant, would now be called "Sister." The membership of the general council expanded to include the superior general and six councillors. The first three councillors elected would be full-time and required to live at the Motherhouse. Two new part-time positions, councillors-at-large, were created. These sisters also had other concurrent ministries and lived where they worked. The councillors-at-large experiment did not last long.

In 1979, the composition of the general council was restructured to include the superior general with four full-time councillors.

Index

Administration Committee, of Chapter of Affairs: Session I 1968, 71–72
African Americans, 31; in Catholic schools, 119–120; Cecilian Academy for, 121; school integration challenges with, 34–35; schools for, 7
Aherne, Sister Consuelo Maria, 43, 75, 103, 108, 109–110
annual retreats, 15–16; in 1980s, 139–140; attendance at, 47–48; extended options for, 1990s, 173; innovations in, 1970s, 85–86; living arrangement renovations for, 140; Murphy's reforms for, 85–86; recreation at, 48; at Saint Mary by-the-Sea, 26–27, 47, 140; schedule of, 47; spirituality and, 47–48
antipoverty programs, 89
apartheid, 144–145
apostolic planning conversations, 162–163, 164, 166–168
Archbishop Ryan Memorial School for the Deaf, 20
associate relationship, 147–148
attire: alterations to, 66; *Decrees* on, 24, 28, 50; mandates for, 92; original, 2; of Sisters of Saint Joseph of Philadelphia, 8; Sisters of Saint Joseph of St. Louis and, 6; veil and, 3, 91–92, 93. *See also* habit

Baney, Sister Margaret Isabel, 32–33

baptismal name, vows and, 87–88
Bennis, Sister Ann Edward, 71
Bernardin, Cardinal Joseph, 129
Bethlehem Village, 135, 138
Black Daughters. *See* Sisters of a Happy Death
blind and deaf schools, 37
boarding schools, 4, 9, 40
Brennan, Mother Thecla, 32, 59, 61–62
Brown, Sister Margaret Rose, 37
Burdier, Mother Jeanne, 2
Burke, Mother Josephine Rosarii, 67

Callahan, Sister Helen de Chantal, 54
canonical year, 52, 97, 176
CARA Survey. *See* Center for Applied Research in the Apostolate Survey
Carter, Jimmy, 81
Catechism of the Vows (Cotel), 53
Catholic Girls' High School, 17–18
Catholic Home for Girls, 121
The Catholic Hour, 29
Catholics: 1950s expansion of, 31–32; African Americans in Catholic schools, 119–120; changing trends in schools, 1970s, 118–119; Council of Trent's reforms and restrictions for, 1; economic optimism pre-World War I of, 16; modernization and, 28; restorationist movement of, 1990s, 161–162; Vatican II changes for, 65,

66; women's colleges for, 18; women's rights and, 16
Catholic University of America, 19
CC. *See* Corporate Collaborative
CCR. *See* Centers for Corporate Reflection
Cecilian Academy: for African American women, 121; closing, 133; curriculum expansion of, 40; facility expansion of, 39
CECP. *See* Corporate Ecclesial Commitment to People
Center for Applied Research in the Apostolate Survey (CARA Survey), 91–92, 106
Centers for Corporate Reflection (CCR), 90, 105, 107, 125, 184; challenges and outcomes of, 111; purpose and process of, 111
central banking, 184–185
change list, 32, 88
Change of Apostolate Policy, 136–137
Change Our Hearts, 183
The Chapter, 113
Chapter of Affairs: 1974, 106; 1994, 179–180; Session II 1968, 77–78
Chapter of Affairs: Session I 1968, 69–74; Administration Committee of, 71–72; attendance of non-delegate superiors at, 74; Community Life Committee of, 72–73; conclusion of, 74; confidentiality and communication in, 73–74; Flaherty addressing, 69; habit debates in, 73; Prayer Life Committee of, 70–71, 83
Chapter of Election: 1974, 107; 1984, 153–154; 1994, 180–181; 1999, 189; Session I 1968, 74–75
Chapter of Faults, 12
Chapter Planning Committee, 156
chastity, 50–51, 87–88, 142
Chestnut Hill College, 18, 20, 36, 115–116, 117; autonomous functioning of, 132; expansion of facilities at, 39–40, 60; financial concerns of, 133; new directions of, 1970s, 122–123; planning and capital campaigns of, 1990s, 166–167
Christian Family Movement, 31
civil disobedience, 143–144

civil rights movement, 89
Civil War, 10
Cleary, Sister Demetria, 148
CMSW. *See* Conference of Major Superiors of Women
Code of Canon Law (1917), 22–23; revision of, 24; spirituality impact of, 45
Code of Canon Law (1983), 129, 146
Collaborative Novitiate Program, 176
colleges: financial burden of, 19; living arrangements for sisters' education at, 116; sisters' education at, 19–20; Sisters of Saint Joseph of Philadelphia opening, 18. *See also specific institutions*
commercial schools, 38
Commitment to People (CP), 126
Commitment to Works (CW), 126
Committee for the Future, 92
communal prayer: concerns about, 1990s, 174; creativity in, 86; resources for, 139–141. *See also* prayer
Communion, Sisters of Saint Joseph of Philadelphia encouraging, 29
Communities Responding to Overcome Poverty (CROP), 90
community collaboration, 3
Community Life Committee: of Chapter of Affairs: Session I 1968, 72–73; of General Chapter of 1979, 149–150; of General Chapter of 1989, 177
Concilium, 65
Conference of Major Superiors of Women (CMSW), 59, 68, 100
Congregational Guidelines for Decision-Making in Apostolic Planning, 163
congregational liturgist, 141
Congregational Newsletter, 173, 175, 178
Conlin, Sister Francis Loretto, 34, 35–36
Connelly Foundation, 170
Consortium Perfectae Caritatis (CPC), 100, 114
Constitutions, 49, 52, 172; General Chapter of 1984 on revisions of, 153–154; lay sisters in, 3; redistribution of original, 76; rewriting, 1980s, 151–152; Rome approving new draft of, 1984, 154; vows in new, 1980s,

141–142
Constitutions Coordinating Committee, 151–152
convents: living arrangements in, 44–45; Mount Saint Joseph Convent, 14, 20; opening new, 32; upkeep of, 25
Conversion for Mission, 169
Conway, Sister George Edward, 115
Cooke, Mother John Eudes, 66
Coordinating Committee for renewal, 102
Corporate Collaborative (CC), 126
Corporate Ecclesial Commitment to People (CECP), 114, 126, 130
corporate renewal work, of Médaille Team, 105
Corporate Stand, 144–145, 172
Corporation of Sisters of Saint Joseph, 14
Cotel, Peter, 53
Council of Trent (1563), 1
CP. *See* Commitment to People
CPC. *See* Consortium Perfectae Caritatis
CROP. *See* Communities Responding to Overcome Poverty
CSSJ Federation programs, 176
CW. *See* Commitment to Works

Dead Man Walking: An Eyewitness Account of the Death Penalty in the United States (Prejean), 172
death penalty, 172–173
Decrees: on attire, 24, 28, 50; exceptions to, 24; General Chapters enactments and customs in, 23; lasting impact of, 23–24; on obedience, 49–50; poverty and, 25; on *Rule* interpretation and fidelity, 22; updating, 49
Dei Verbum, 65
Delone Catholic High School, 122
Deluol, Louis, Rev., 8
Denver World Youth Conference, 162
Design for Excellence, 102, 106
Design II, 108
Detroit Method of Reading, 36
Director of Mission Effectiveness, 167
Directors of Religious Education (DREs), 124, 131
Directory, 52, 172, 180
Donohue, Mother Miriam Gertrude, 66

Dougherty, Cardinal Dennis, 21, 24–25, 58–59
Doyle, Sister Salvator, 33
The Dream Catcher, 166
DREs. *See* Directors of Religious Education
driving restrictions, 65, 87
Dubay, Father Thomas, SM, 95; as director for spiritual renewal, 82, 102; seminars of, 82–83, 103; survey and analysis of, 102–103
Duggan, Mother Marie Estelle, 27, 53–54, 55, 104

education: Catholic schools changing trends in, 1970s, 118–119; financial burden of, 19; impact of, 21; individualization trends in, 120; initiatives in, 1970s, 120; ministry and, 4; Murphy on expansion projects in, 123; new models in, 1970s, 120–121; personnel ratios in, 1970s, 121; religious studies in, 117–118, 124; relocations and personnel assignments for, 43–44; sexuality understanding through, 87; Sisters of Saint Joseph of Philadelphia focusing on, 9, 10–11, 29; staffing problems for, 33, 124–125, 131, 132–133; teacher rating system for, 11. *See also* schools; sisters' education
Egan, Sister Saint Ursula, 107, 108, 114
elections: General Chapter of 1979 modifications to, 112–113; General Chapter of 1989 process of, 157, 159; General Chapters and, 23; governance and, 13, 22; of Newell, 158; *Rule* on, 74. *See also* Chapter of Election
Ember Week, 23
Emmaus Community, 147
The Eucharistic Letter (Médaille), 2
Evangeli Nuntiandi, 113
examen, 26
executions, 4

FAB. *See* Financial Advisory Board
faith communities, schools as, 120
faith sharing, 86, 140–141

Federation of the Sisters of Saint Joseph, 59

finances: in 1990s, 182–185; Aherne's obligations with, 108, 109–110; central banking and, 184–185; Chestnut Hill College's concerns with, 133; crisis with, 1980s, 154–155; educational and college burden of, 19; General Chapter of 1974 on, 109–110; General Chapter of 1984 on, 154; governance and, 60, 182–185; institutional planning for, 167; living arrangements and, 1990s, 183–184; sisters' education and, 19, 115; Sisters of Saint Joseph of St. Louis struggles with, 7; stipend packages and, 183

Financial Advisory Board (FAB), 91, 151

Financial Advisory Committee, 109–110

Fitzmaurice, Sister Mary Alacoque, 38

Flaherty, Mother Divine Shepherd, 33, 33–34, 48, 59; Chapter of Affairs: Session I 1968 address of, 69; habit alterations of, 66, 73; horarium changes of, 65; leadership portrait of, 61–62

Flaherty, Mother Maria Concepta, 27

Fleming, Sister Margaret, 114, 179; on heritage, 171; portrait of, 188–189

FOCUS, 149

Fontbonne, Jeanne, 4, 5

Fontbonne Academy, 40

Ford, Gerald, 81

formation, 51; changes in, 1980s, 146–147; decline in candidates and, 146; in early 1970s, 93–95; geographic flexibility for, 175; juniorate stage of, 53, 95, 98; in mid- to late 1970s, 95–98; mistress of juniors for, 55; mistress of novices and assistants for, 53–54; mistress of postulants and novices for, 55; novitiate stage of, 52–53, 94–95, 96–97, 147; personalization of, 94; postulancy stage of, 51–52, 96–97, 146–147; pre-entrance stage of, 96; programs for, 1990s, 174; teacher training and, 97; temporary profession stage of, 147; Vatican II changes for, 93–94

Formulary, 46, 65

Fournier, Mother Saint John, 8, 12, 13, 14

France, 1, 14

French Revolution (1789-1794), 4

Gaddi, Sister Eugenie Madeline, 155

Gaudium et Spes., 65

General Chapter, 49; *Decrees* on enactments and customs of, 23; elections and, 23; governance and, 58–59; occurrence and purpose of, 13; procedures of, 58; Sisters of Saint Joseph of Philadelphia establishing, 13

General Chapter of 1968, 67–68; ambiguity of, 106; Chapter of Affairs: Session II of, 77–78; Chapter of Affairs Session I of, 69–74; Chapter of Election: Session I of, 74–75; as Chapter of Renewal, 67; committees for, 67, 68; conclusion of, 78; delegate selection at, 68; habit controversy of, 77, 78; legacy of, 79; new identity forged by, 79; between sessions of, 75–77. *See also* Chapter of Affairs: Session I 1968

General Chapter of 1974, 84; Chapter of Affairs of, 106; Chapter of Election of, 107; enactments of, 106–107; finances and, 109–110; implementing, 108–109; obedience and, 88; Poverty Committee of, 89–90; on principalship, 117; results of, 89–90; SSJ Center for Spirituality mandate of, 84–85; vocation programs of, 95; weekend-clearout problem addressed at, 106–107

General Chapter of 1979, 88; Community Life Committee of, 149–150; election modifications of, 112–113; habit enactments of, 93; preparations for, 112–113; proceedings of, 113–114; results of, 90–91

General Chapter of 1984: Chapter of Election of, 153–154; *Constitutions* revisions and, 153–154; on finances, 154; governance and, 152–154; Newell addressing, 152–153; PWR and, 131–132

General Chapter of 1989, 159–160; Chapter Planning Committee of, 156; Community Life Committee of, 177; direction chosen by, 155–156; election process at, 157, 159; enactments of,

159; Newell addressing, 157–158
General Chapter of 1994, 165; Chapter of Affairs of, 179–180; Chapter of Election of, 180–181; content and processes of, 179–182; governance and, 180, 181–182; inclusive language and, 180; preparation for, 179; as Visioning Chapter, 179
General Chapter of 1999, 186–188, 189
General Council: governance of, 108, 148–149; local presence of, 1990s, 178; of Newell, 148–149; superior general and, 56–57
Getz, Paul, 42
GI Bill, 31
Gonzalez, Sister Dorismarie, 187–188
Good Works, 175
Gorbachev, Mikhail, 129
governance: from 1650-1700, 3; from 1700-1799, 4; from 1847-1900, 11–14; from 1900-1944, 21–25; from 1944-1965, 56–62; from 1969-1979, 98–114; from 1980-1989, 148–159; from 1989-1999, 177–186; bishops' regulations and, 24–25; compensation and, 25; congregational renewal and, 1969 to 1979, 102–104; with congregational themes, 150; constituents of effective, 114; diminishing membership, 1969-1979, 98–99; discipline and behavior in, 23; elections and, 13, 22; finances and, 60, 182–185; formalization of, 21–22; General Chapter and, 58–59; General Chapter of 1984 and, 152–154; General Chapter of 1994 and, 180, 181–182; of General Council, 108, 148–149; of local community life, 149–151; local superior and, 57–58; national conferences of women religious and, 59; of Sisters of Saint Joseph of St. Louis separating from Lyon, 7; structural changes in, 1965-1969, 66–67; superior general and General Council in, 56–57; titles and, 22–23
Grelis, Sister Winifred, 70, 83, 84
Gunn, Sister Agnes Marie, 37, 114, 116, 152

habit: alterations to, 28; changes in, 1969-1979, 91–93; Chapter of Affairs: Session I 1968 debates on, 73; Flaherty's alterations to, 66, 73; General Chapter of 1968 controversy over, 77, 78; General Chapter of 1979 enactments on, 93; Murphy on guidelines for, 91; new models of, 1980s, 145–146; pride in wearing, 5, 28; restrictions on, 28, 49–50; simplicity of life and, 91; sisters' valuing, 93; in spirituality context, 145; on vacation, 92; Vatican II on, 67
health care, 41–42, 123, 133–134, 183
Hegarty, Sister Marie Ellen, 86
high schools, 38
Hogan, Sister Loretta, 108, 135
Holistic Living days, 142
Holtz, Sister Jean, 83
Holy Family Academy, 39, 122, 133, 167
HOPE. *See* House of Prayer Experience
horarium, 26, 44; adaptations to, 46–47, 140; Flaherty's changes to, 65
House of Prayer Experience (HOPE), 84; locations and styles of, 83; models of, 83; success of, 83–84
housing. *See* living arrangements

IC. *See* Individual Choice
ICCR. *See* Interfaith Center on Corporate Responsibility
Individual Choice (IC), 126
Individually Prescribed Instruction (ISI), 120
Initial Teaching Alphabet (*ITA*), 36
InSearch, 175, 176
insignia design, 146
intentional community, 150
Interfaith Center on Corporate Responsibility (ICCR), 144, 185
Interim Assembly of 1977, 88, 96–97, 112
Internet, 161
ISI. *See* Individually Prescribed Instruction
ITA. *See* Initial Teaching Alphabet

John Paul II (pope), 129, 162
John W. Hallahan school, 17–18
juniorate stage, of formation, 53, 95, 98. *See also* temporary profession stage, of

formation
Kean, Sister Kathleen, 84, 86, 108, 110
Kenrick, Bishop Francis Patrick, 8
Kieran, Mother Mary John, 10, 12, 13, 14, 15
kindergartens, 36–37
Kirby, Sister Mary Xavier, 122
Knobbs, Sister Catherine, 135

lace and ribbon making, 2, 4
Lannen, Mother Mary Clement, 13, 14, 15, 21, 23
Latinos, 31, 35
lay sisters, 3; compensation of, 25; in *Constitutions*, 3; decreasing numbers of, 21; household duties of, 12, 20–21; rank given to, 21, 25, 58–59
lay teachers, 21; acceptance of, 34; ratios of, 1970s, 121, 125; schools hiring, 33–34
LCD. *See* Local Community Development
Leadership Conference of Women Religious (LCWR), 59, 100, 114
Life Planning Committee, 165
The Little Design Shoppe, 166
living arrangements: annual retreat renovations for, 140; in convents, 44–45; debates over, 72–73; finances and, 1990s, 183–184; in orphanages and shared homes, 2–3, 4; in rented dwellings, 4; school closures impact on, 131; in schools, 44–45; for sisters' education at college, 116; of Sisters of Saint Joseph of Philadelphia, 11–12
Local Community Development (LCD), 105; renewal through, 110; resistance to, 110
local community governance, 149–151
local superior, 57–58, 72
Loughery, Sister Bernard Francis, 34–35, 36
Lumen Gentium, 65, 86–87

MacDonald, Sister Matthew Anita, 133
Madeleine, Sister Eugenie, 114
Mandela, Nelson, 161
Martin, Sister Felicitas, 36
Mayhew, Sister Helen Anthony, 89

McCloskey, Sister Nicolita, 54
McCormick, Mother Mary Andrew, 55
McElroy, Sister Mary Kieran, 42
McEvoy, Sister Assisium, 10–11, 19, 27; on practical application of church teachings, 28; on sisters' education needs, 20; spirituality instructions of, 14–15
McGlone, Sister Rosalia, 19
McGrane, Sister Janice, 187
McGraw, Mother Gertrude Helene, 66–67
McLaughlin, Sister Martin Joseph, 54
McPeak, Sister Francis Xavier, 57
McSherrystown Academy, 12–13
Médaille, Jean-Pierre, 2, 3, 14, 29
Médaille Team, 1972-1975: corporate renewal work of, 105; formation of, 103–104; leadership development of, 105; training of, 104
Meditations for Special Occasions, 46
mental health, 87
Mexicans, 31
ministry: from 1650-1700, 2–3; from 1700-1799, 4; from 1847-1900, 8–11; from 1900-1944, 17–18; from 1944-1965, 32–45; from 1969-1979, 114–126; from 1980-1989, 130–139; from 1989-1999, 162–168; *change list* and, 32, 88; Change of Apostolate Policy and, 136–137; data gathering on, 1980s, 130; demographic changes in, 1980s, 137–138; education and, 4; end of corporate commitments for, 163; expanding, 37, 123–124; individualized, 165–166; to Latinos, 35; missioning process revised, 1990s, 164; new perception of, 1990s, 164–166; nontraditional, 136–137; personnel assignments and missioning process of, 1980s, 138–139; relocations and personnel assignments for, 43–44; restructuring of, 1980s, 130–131; staffing problems for, 33, 124–125, 131, 132–133; summer, 136; Third World, 136. *See also* education
Ministry Opening Booklets, 164
Ministry Resource Book, 164
the Mission, 140, 154; apostolic planning furthering, 164; centrality of, 156, 159;

jubilee celebration and, 169–170; refoundation summers and, 168; social justice and, 169; understanding and living, 168–169
Missioning Updates, 164
mission year, 52–53, 97, 147
mistress of juniors, for formation, 55
mistress of novices and assistants, for formation, 53–54
mistress of postulants and novices, for formation, 55
Mock, Sister Janet, CSJ, 164
Montgomery, Sister Catherine Marie, 54
Morton, Mother Saint Gervase, 18–19, 33, 36
Motherhouse Infirmary, 41–42, 56, 96
Mount Saint Joseph Academy, 9, 11, 122, 133, 167; new facility for, in 1961, 39; planning and capital campaigns of, 1990s, 166
Mount Saint Joseph College, 18, 20
Mount Saint Joseph Convent, 14, 20
Mount Saint Joseph Normal School, 19–20
Muller, Sister Geraldine, 175
Munafo, Sister Antoinette, 117–118, 135
Murphy, Mother Alice Anita, 74, 75, 77, 78, 82, 110; annual retreats reforms of, 85–86; background of, 99–101; CMSW and LCWR role of, 100; CPC role of, 100; on education expansion projects, 123; on habit guidelines, 91; national stature of, 100; personality of, 99; political labels dismissed by, 99; as superior general, 101

National Congress of Major Superiors, 59
National Sisters' Survey, 68, 72, 73
Nazareth House, 176
Neno, Father Pacificus, 15
Nepper, Marius, 2
Neumann, Saint John, 14
The New Companion to the Breviary, 140
Newell, Sister Dorothea, 114, 130, 139; election of, 158; General Chapter of 1984 address of, 152–153; General Chapter of 1989 address of, 157–158; General Council of, 148–149; leadership team of, 148; portrait of, 158–159

"Newer Members Cluster", 176
NFA. *See* Norwood-Fontbonne Academy
Nixon, Richard, 81
Norwood-Fontbonne Academy (NFA), 121–122, 133, 167
novitiate stage, of formation, 52–53, 94–95, 96–97, 147

OAW. *See* Office of Apostolic Works
obedience, 65; *Decrees* on, 49–50; General Chapter of 1974 and, 88; interpretations of, 1980s, 142
O'Brien, Sister Leonissa, 172–173
Office for Religious Education, 117–118
Office of Apostolic Works (OAW), 135, 165
Office of Personnel Services, 114
Office of the Blessed Virgin, 26
Office of the Holy Ghost, 26
O'Halloran, Sister Clare Joseph, 42
O'Hara, Cardinal John, 33
Opt for the City, 175
orphanages: living arrangements in, 2–3, 4; in post-World War II years, 41; Sisters of Saint Joseph of Philadelphia opening, 8–9, 41. *See also specific institutions*

Pales, Sister Kathleen, 175
papal approbation, of *Rule*, 21–22
Paradise School for orphan boys, 20, 121
Paul VI (pope), 88–89, 113
Perfectae Caritatis, 65, 87, 88
personnel assignments, 43–44, 88, 138–139
Pino, Sister Grace, 141
Poor People Campaign, 1968, 89
postulancy stage, of formation, 51–52, 96–97, 146–147
poverty: antipoverty programs, 89; CROP and, 90; *Decrees* and, 25; interpretations of, 1980s, 142; movement against, 89; Paul VI on, 88–89; spirituality and, 25, 50
Poverty and Simplicity: A Holistic Approach (Rivello), 90
Poverty Committee, of General Chapter of 1974, 89–90

prayer: centrality of, 1990s, 173–174; communal resources for, 139–141; concepts and types of, 1940s to 1960s, 45–46; creativity in communal, 86; in English compared to Latin, 26; *Formulary* for, 46; horarium adaptations and, 46–47; personal experience in, 27, 139–141; re-examining, 70–71; renewal and re-evaluation of, 1970s, 82–84; *Rule* regulating, 27; schedule of, 15, 23, 26; shared, 86, 140–141; SSJ Center for Spirituality programs for, 139; Triduums and, 26. *See also* House of Prayer Experience

Prayer Life Committee, of Chapter of Affairs: Session I 1968, 70–71, 83

pre-entrance stage, of formation, 96

Prejean, Sister Helen, CSJ, 172

private academies, of Sisters of Saint Joseph of Philadelphia, 18

Probe the Heart—Celebrate the Future survey, 178

procuratrix, 57

Project: Withdrawal/Recommitment (PWR): challenges of, 131; end of, 163; General Chapter of 1984 and, 131–132; limits of, 162; process of, 130–131

prophetic voice, 169

Puerto Ricans, 31, 35

PWR. *See* Project: Withdrawal/Recommitment

Quakers, 8

racism, 89

Ralph, Sister Patricia, 188

Rawle, Sister Celestia, 54

RCT. *See* Religious Communities Trust

Reagan, Ronald, 129

Reception Day, 52, 66

refoundation summers, 168

Refounding for the Twenty-First Century, 168

Religious Communities Trust (RCT), 184

religious studies, 117–118, 124

relocations, education missions and, 43–44

Renewal Chapter 1968. *See* General Chapter of 1968

renovation, spirituality and, 48–49

Renovationis Causam, 93, 95

Renovation program, 86

retirement, 123, 165, 183

retreats. *See* annual retreats

Rivello, Sister J. Roberta, 90

Rogers, Mother Mary James, 24

Ronollo, Sister Arleen, 113

Rosati, Bishop Joseph, 6

Rudegeair, Sister Marie, 134

Rule, 2, 3; *Decrees* on interpretation and fidelity of, 22; on elections, 74; papal approbation of, 21–22; poverty and, 25; prayer regulated by, 27; Sisters of Saint Joseph of Philadelphia implementing, 15

Sacred Heart Hall, 82

Sacrifice Drive 1959, 60–61

Saint Ann's Widows' Home/Villa Laboure, 40

Saint Joseph Academy, 39

Saint Joseph Housing Corporation, 135

Saint Joseph Villa, Cheltenham, 41–42

Saint Joseph Villa, Flourtown, 123, 133–134, 166

Saint Mary by-the-Sea, 26–27, 47, 140

Saint Rose High School, 38

Scanlon, Mother Mary, 39, 121

Schneiders, Sister Sandra, IHM, 168

schools: accreditation of, 19, 40, 122, 167; African American integration challenges facing, 34–35; for African Americans, 7; African Americans in Catholic, 119–120; for blind and deaf, 37; boarding, 4, 9, 40; changing trends in, 1970s, 118–119; closing, 122, 133; colleges, 18; commercial, 38; expansion and renovation of, 39–40, 60; as faith communities, 120; fundraising for, 39; high schools, 38; impact of, 21; kindergartens, 36–37; lay teachers hired by, 33–34; living arrangements and closures of, 131; living arrangements in, 44–45; overcrowding problems facing, 33; personal lives impacted by expansion of, 32–33; private academies, 18; religious studies in, 117–118, 124;

reputation of, 21; senior centres, 17; Sisters of Saint Joseph of Lyon opening, 5; Sisters of Saint Joseph of Philadelphia opening, 9, 10, 11, 12, 17–18, 32–33, 39–40; Sisters of Saint Joseph of St. Louis opening, 6–7; staffing problems for, 33, 124–125, 131, 132–133; urban enrollment in, 1970s, 119–120. *See also* education
school supervisors: curriculum and texts developed by, 36–37; purpose of, 35–36; training by, 36
Schuck, Sister Anna Louise, 94, 95–96
Schulte, Archbishop Francis B., 170
senior centres, of Sisters of Saint Joseph of Philadelphia, 17
senior housing facilities, 134–135, 166
sexuality, 94; chastity and, 50–51; education for understanding, 87
Shanahan, Bishop John W., 24
shared prayer, 86, 140–141
Sharing the State of the House, 141
Sheen, Bishop Fulton J., 29, 31–32
Shield, Sister San Jose, 37
sin, spirituality and, 26
sisters' compensation, 25
sisters' education: 1950s and 1960s expansion of, 42–43; challenges of, 42–43; at colleges, 19–20; financial hardships and, 19, 115; Gunn on importance of, 116; living arrangements at college for, 116; master's degrees pursued in, 116; McEvoy on needs for, 20; professional competence of, 1970s, 114–117; for Sisters of Saint Joseph of Philadelphia, 18–21; standards of, 43; state requirements for, 19–20; success stories of, 43
Sisters of a Happy Death (Black Daughters), 5
Sisters of Saint Joseph: from 1650-1700, 1–3; from 1700-1799, 3–4; from 1800-1899, 5–16; from 1900-1944, 16–29; Americanization of, 29; education efforts of, 5; executions and, 4; foundation of, 2; French Revolution and, 4; occupations of, 2–3; post-revolutionary growth of, 5; refoundation of (1808-1836), 5–6. *See also specific topics*
Sisters of Saint Joseph Inter-Congregational Bulletin, 59
Sisters of Saint Joseph of Harrisburg, 12–13
Sisters of Saint Joseph of Lyon, 5–6, 6, 7
Sisters of Saint Joseph of Philadelphia: applicant numbers declining for, 1970s, 98, 98–99; associate relationship and, 147–148; attire of, 8; business skills and, 14; Civil War and, 10; colleges founded by, 18; Communion encouraged by, 29; congregational leadership of, 1969-1979, 99; education focus of, 9, 10–11, 29; future of, 189–190; General Chapter established by, 13; growth of, 14, 17; Harrisburg splitting and rejoining with, 12–13; heritage and jubilee celebration of, 169–170; immigrant backgrounds of, 8, 17; insignia design for, 146; living arrangements of, 11–12; modernization and, 17, 28; Neumann counseling, 14; orphanages opened by, 8–9, 41; private academies opened by, 18; restoration and expansion projects of, 60–61; *Rule* implemented by, 15; schools opened by, 9, 10, 11, 17–18, 32–33, 39–40; senior centres established by, 17; sisters' education and, 18–21; teacher rating system of, 11; traditional values of, 32; women's rights tensions within, 16. *See also specific topics*
Sisters of Saint Joseph of St. Louis: attire and, 6; financial struggles of, 7; Lyon governance separation of, 7; origin of, 6; schools opened by, 6–7
Smither, Mother Marie Emily, 72
Social Action Committee, 90
social justice initiatives, 142–145, 169
social justice movement, 89
South Africa, 144–145
spirituality: from 1847-1900, 14–16; from 1900-1940, 26–29; from 1944-1965, 45–51; from 1969-1979, 82–98; from 1980-1989, 139–148; from 1989-1999, 168–177; annual retreats and, 47–48; chastity and, 50–51; *Code of Canon Law* (1917) impact on, 45; French

traditions of, 14; habit in context of, 145; horarium adaptations and, 46–47; McEvoy's instructions for, 14–15; poverty and, 25, 50; Renovation program and, 86; renovation programs for, 48–49; "separation from the world" and, 27–28; from 1700-1799, 3; sin and, 26; SSJ Center for Spirituality, 84–85; vision and, 169–173; vow interpretations and, 49. *See also* House of Prayer Experience; prayer

sponsored works, in apostolic planning, 166–168

SSJ Center for Spirituality, 84–85; apartheid and, 144–145; prayer programs of, 139

SSJ Commission for Justice: civil disobedience policy of, 143–144; Corporate Stand and, 144–145, 172; inauguration of, 142–143; public commitment of, 143; subcommittees of, 143

SSJ Development Office, fundraising campaigns and, 185–186

SSJ Religious Education Information Sheet, 118

Stinson, Mother Bonaventure, 19

stipend packages, 183

St. Joseph Academy, 122

summer ministry, 136

superior general, 22–24, 56–57, 72; local presence of, 1990s, 178; Murphy as, 101

supervisors. *See* school supervisors

Swift, Father Thomas, SJ, 103–104

To Teach as Jesus Did, 118, 120

temporary profession stage, of formation, 147. *See also* juniorate stage, of formation

Third Plenary Council of Baltimore (1884), 10, 21

Third Sunday Program, 96

Third World ministry, 136

Thomas, Sister Mary, 37

titles, governance and, 22–23

Tressler, Mr. Terry C., 134

Triduums, 26

Tucker, Sister Leona, 37

United Farm Workers (UFW), 90

University of Pennsylvania, 19

urban schools, 1970s enrollment in, 119–120

Vacher, Marguerite, 2

Vatican II, 43; Catholic Church changes of, 65, 66; formation changes of, 93–94; on habit, 67; renewal and, 67, 76, 81–82, 86–89; vows and, 86–89

Vazquez, Sister Clarisa, 188

veil, 3, 91–92, 93

Vietnam War, 81, 94, 102

Villanova University, 20, 117

Vision Statement, 1994, 169, 170, 172, 179–180

vocation programs, 95–96

vows: baptismal name and, 87–88; guidelines for, 87; in new *Constitutions*, 1980s, 141–142; spirituality and interpretation of, 49; study of, 1990s, 174; Vatican II and, 86–89. *See also* chastity; obedience; poverty

Weber, Mother Magdalen, 12

weekend-clearout problem, 106–107

widows' homes, 40

Women of Hope, 138

women's rights, 31, 94; in 1970s, 81; in 1990s, 161; Catholics and, 16; Sisters of Saint Joseph of Philadelphia tensions over, 16; to vote, 16

Wood, Archbishop James, 12

Zalot, Sister Charlotte, 141